I0322223

www.ingramcontent.com/pod-product-compliance
Lightning Source LLC
Chambersburg PA
CBHW081218230426
43666CB00015B/2788

TEACHER'S EDITION

ELLEN J. RANK

Additional digital techniques:
Sunny Yudkoff

**Techniques for students
with special learning needs:**
Lisa Friedman

Editorial consultant:
Dina Maiben

Book and Cover Design: Itzhack Shelomi
Project Editor: Terry S. Kaye

Copyright © 2009 Behrman House, Inc.
Springfield, New Jersey
www.behrmanhouse.com
ISBN: 978-0-87441-822-4
Manufactured in the United States of America

CONTENTS

INTENT AND PURPOSE OF THE KOL YISRAEL SERIES	3
USING THE TEACHER'S EDITION	4
Structure of the Teacher's Edition	4
Pacing	5
Family Education	5
Reinforcing Prayer Awareness	5
Using the Chalkboard, Whiteboard, or SMART Board™	5
Alef–Bet Review	5
USING THE DIGITAL APPLICATION	6
CONTENTS OF DIGITAL APPLICATION	7
WORD CARDS	9
WORD CARD TECHNIQUES AND GAMES	11
CLASSROOM GAMES	11
TIME MANAGEMENT	13
ASSESSMENT	14
PRAYER MASTERY ASSESSMENT CHART	15
TECHNIQUES FOR STUDENTS WITH SPECIAL LEARNING NEEDS	16
TEACHING TECHNIQUES	
Chapter 1: Modeh/Modah Ani	17
Chapter 2: Brachot	25
Chapter 3: Brachot Shel Mitzvah	37
Chapter 4: Brachot Shel Shabbat	47
Chapter 5: Kiddush	61
Chapter 6: Havdalah	69
Chapter 7: Brachot Shel Yom Tov	79
Chapter 8: Mah Nishtanah	93
Chapter 9: Birkat Hamazon	101
Chapter 10: Sh'ma	111
Wrap It Up! Fun Prayer Activities	121

INTENT AND PURPOSE OF THE *KOL YISRAEL* SERIES

Welcome to *Kol Yisrael*—a multimedia Jewish educational experience!

The *Kol Yisrael* series is the first Hebrew program to combine the best of Jewish education with the best of today's technology, integrating text-based lessons with digital learning. This approach helps you motivate your students as you guide them in an exploration of the rich traditions of Jewish life. And it works wherever they may be—in the classroom, at home, or in front of a computer! By sending students from the printed page to computer-based reinforcement activities and then back to the text again, *Kol Yisrael* helps you keep today's tech-savvy students engaged in the material and on track in their learning.

Kol Yisrael 1, the first in this three-volume series, introduces students to a selection of prayers that help students feel comfortable performing Jewish home rituals, such as reciting Shabbat and holiday blessings, and singing the Mah Nishtanah. The ten lessons invite students to learn the meaning of each prayer, its background, and how it helps us live according to Jewish principles. Both the text and digital application reinforce the message that prayers can help us increase *sh'lom bayit*—peace in the home.

Kol Yisrael leads students into this world of Jewish learning and values with the help of Batya and Ben—twin characters the same age as the students, around nine or ten years old. Batya and Ben's constant questioning and funny conversations help make the prayers relevant to the students' lives. With the twins' help and encouragement, and whimsical interjections from Doug, their pet fish, students practice their Hebrew decoding skills, explore Torah teachings, link prayer words to modern Hebrew, and learn vocabulary they can use every day!

Batya and Ben grow alongside students as they make their way through *Kol Yisrael 1*, *2*, and *3*. Just like the students, the twins develop from beginning Jewish learners into young Jewish community members about to celebrate their bar or bat mitzvah. Just like the students, Batya and Ben explore critical issues of what it means to come of age as a Jewish adult. Just like the students, Batya and Ben explore what it means to connect with Israel, what it means to play a role in the Jewish community, and, most importantly, what it means to be a member of the Jewish family—to be a member of *Kol Yisrael*!

Why Use *Kol Yisrael*?

While the goals of *Kol Yisrael* are similar to the goals of other prayer series—fluent prayer reading with comprehension and familiarity with the worship service—the innovations of *Kol Yisrael's* structure and methods set it apart.

The *Kol Yisrael* series:

- Uses kid-friendly language to explore the meaning of and reasons behind prayer—so students understand the words they are saying and why we pray.
- Draws life lessons from the prayers (saying thank you helps you get along with others; being kind to our siblings can help contribute to a peaceful family life)—so students understand how prayers can help each of us act like a mensch.
- Places prayers in the context of a story about a boy and a girl just like your students—so students remain engaged with the text and see *kids just like them* praying.
- Uses the computer to add audio-visual components and a gaming approach to reading and comprehension exercises—so students work through the lessons in ways that entertain *and* educate.

The integrated learning model in *Kol Yisrael* draws on both traditional (*pencil-to-paper*) and innovative (*mouse-to-screen*) techniques. The computer-based aspects of *Kol Yisrael*:

- Extend Jewish learning from the classroom into the home.
- Allow students of varying learning styles and capabilities to progress at their own pace.
- Challenge students to solve puzzles, play games, and complete activities that reinforce classroom learning.
- Include assessment materials after lessons 3, 6, and 10 that let you and your students check their progress.
- Recognize the tech-savvy lifestyles and skills of today's students.
- Depend on the *Kol Yisrael* text! The *Kol Yisrael* texts present the prayers, Hebrew words, and Jewish lessons that the digital applications practice and

reinforce. Each *Kol Yisrael* chapter also includes the section, "Clue to Cyberspace," which presents an activity or puzzle that will help students succeed in the digital application, such as a clue to earn bonus points in a game.

The *Kol Yisrael* text and digital application are partners. They complement each other, enrich each other, and under your guidance they work together to excite students and engage them in modern Jewish learning.

USING THE TEACHER'S EDITION

This Teacher's Edition contains the entire text of *Kol Yisrael 1*, reproduced in reduced size. The pages are annotated with suggested activities, teaching methods, and other information to assist you in planning and executing your lessons. Every element in the textbook is covered, including the introduction of new vocabulary, the reading of each prayer or blessing, the review and reinforcement of all material, as well as ways to integrate the digital application into classroom lessons.

Before assigning the computer activities, familiarize yourself with the digital application in its entirety. This will allow you to pick and choose the activities you feel will best address the needs of your students and your lesson goals.

Keep in mind that students learn in different ways, and any student's primary learning mode may be aural, visual, or tactile. Similarly, teachers teach in different ways. Don't feel obligated to use a method that does not feel comfortable with your teaching style. By the same token, remember that since students learn in different ways, you should vary your teaching methods accordingly. Feel free to repeat an activity or method that worked especially well for you and your students.

The information and suggestions in this Teacher's Edition are intended to assist you in developing your own teaching plan. You do not need to follow every suggestion on every page; rather, the guide provides you with many different options from which to choose. Only you know what works best for your class and with your teaching style.

Structure of the Teacher's Edition

Each section of the Teacher's Edition indicates the corresponding page number in the student text. In addition, each chapter in the Teacher's Edition contains the following features:

ABOUT THE PRAYER A brief description of the prayer or blessings presented in the chapter. The history or source of the liturgy is often included.

LEARNING OBJECTIVES Specific learning goals for each chapter.

WORDS AND PHRASES Comprehensive list of new Prayer and Related words.

INSTRUCTIONAL MATERIALS A listing of text pages, relevant word cards, and the level in the digital application.

WHERE WE ARE A brief synopsis of what the characters Batya and Ben are doing, and where in the house we are meeting them.

INTRODUCING THE LESSON A set induction to introduce students to the central ideas of the chapter's prayer or blessings.

INTO THE TEXT A discussion or activity connected to the first page of each chapter. This first page serves to introduce a main idea of the prayer or blessing before students see the actual text.

DIGITAL APPLICATION Prompt for students to use the digital application—either at home or in school—as well as ideas for introducing digital activities or reinforcing their lessons during class.

ASSESSMENT Techniques for assessing reading fluency and knowledge of prayer content. Includes online assessment at www.behrmanhouse.com.

WHAT'S NEXT? A discussion introducing students to the prayer or blessings of the upcoming chapter.

Each chapter in this Teacher's Edition also contains many of the following enrichment ideas, supplementary information, and activities:

 Reading and Reciting—Ideas and techniques to help students improve their reading fluency.

 Prayer Vocabulary—Ideas and activities to help students learn and retain new vocabulary.

 Digital Application—Directions about when students should reinforce activities in the book on their computers.

Understanding Prayer—Enrichment activities and discussions to help your students understand the core meaning of prayers and blessings.

 Game Box—Review exercises and activities to enhance the lesson's learning experience.

 Repeating Roots—Discussions and exercises to illustrate the relationship between words that share the same root letters.

 Photo Op—Ideas for using the book's photos and captions as teaching tools.

 Our Tradition—Stories and excerpts from classical Jewish texts that reflect core Jewish values.

 Sh'lom Bayit—Activities and discussions that focus on the value of *sh'lom bayit*.

Pacing

Students differ in ability. Teachers differ in style. Schools differ in the number of class sessions scheduled each week. Ultimately, you must decide how to pace your class through the text.

The ten chapters in *Kol Yisrael 1* vary in length from six to twelve pages. Some may take two or three class sessions to cover, while others may take four or more. Remember that the digital application is an ideal way to extend classroom instruction time into the home. Almost every digital activity is addressed separately in the Teacher's Edition. However, feel free to assign students the entire chapter's digital activities for one at-home learning session. Each chapter has five to eight digital exercises. For more information about pacing and timing, see "Time Management" on page 13.

Family Education

A partnership between home and school can help your students reach their greatest potential, and every effort should be made to facilitate this partnership. The digital application for *Kol Yisrael 1* is the perfect solution to home review and practice. Students will enjoy the interactive games while reviewing and practicing the prayers and blessings they studied in class. The digital application can provide students with additional contact, repetition, and reinforcement of material they have already learned in class. It extends your classroom time and is a terrific way to involve parents in their children's studies.

You may wish to e-mail or send home a letter after the first day of class telling parents about *Kol Yisrael 1* and introducing them to the digital application. Explain that you will be able to assesss students' progress online. (See Using the Digital Application, page 6, and Assessment, page 14) You can find a sample letter online at www.behrmanhouse.com. The letter contains steps for using the digital application, including sign-on instructions, and a link to a demo site for parents to try out the digital application themselves.

Reinforcing Prayer Awareness

Begin each class with a short (two- to five-minute) recap of the prayers and blessings students have learned to date. Ask individual students to take turns as leaders. You may choose to end the service by having the class recite the blessing for engaging in study: לַעֲסוֹק בְּדִבְרֵי תוֹרָה, found on page 24 in the pupil edition.

Using the Chalkboard, Whiteboard, or SMART Board™

Use the chalkboard or whiteboard to introduce new words and prayers, to answer questions, to play games, and to present assignments. Vary the way in which you use the board. You might, for example, write in letters of different colors and sizes. Draw, or have students draw, illustrations related to prayer vocabulary and to rituals. Invite students to come to the board to practice vocabulary.

If you have a computer projector or a SMART Board™ in your school, use it to introduce students to the *Kol Yisrael* digital application. Demonstrate the sign-on procedure and the home page. Allow students to practice their reading interactively and to play a few digital games in front of the class. Remember that with a SMART Board™ a student acts as a live, digital "mouse."

Alef–Bet Review

Begin the year with a thorough review of the letters and vowels in the Hebrew alphabet. Use an *alef-bet* poster, *alef-bet* flashcards, or the Word Cards for the students' primer from the previous year. You can also use a transitional reading text such as the *Back-to-School Hebrew Reading Refresher* to review and drill Hebrew decoding before students begin *Kol Yisrael 1*.

USING THE DIGITAL APPLICATION

Your students will delight in playing the games and activities in *Kol Yisrael 1* digital application. These exercises reinforce the prayer concepts and vocabulary introduced in the textbook.

Introducing the Digital Application

When introducing students to the *Kol Yisrael 1* text, point to one of the computer mouse icons that appear throughout the chapters. The mouse icon indicates that there is a corresponding activity, such as a reading exercise or a matching game, in the digital application. (The Teacher's Edition also will remind you when to prompt students to use the digital application.)

Students are also motivated to solve riddles and puzzles in the text ("Clue to Cyberspace") that provide clues to score bonus points in the digital application.

Before assigning activities for the first time in *Kol Yisrael 1* digital application, make sure students note the class serial number. Every student in the class uses the same serial number to become a member of the *Kol Yisrael 1* digital database. You too will use the serial number to assess your class's progress online. After entering the class's serial number in their computer, students will be asked to register with a unique user name and password. The students will then be members and the database will begin to track and store their results on the activities.

You may also wish to record students' user names so you have a master list in case students forget the name they used to become a new member. You may wish to send the class's serial number and the student's user name home to his or her parents. Students can keep their passwords private.

Tracking Students' Digital Activities

There are three ways to assess students' progress in the digital application:

1. Log on to www.behrmanhouse.com and click the blue "Assessment" button at the bottom left of the screen. Click on *Kol Yisrael* and select the picture of *Kol Yisrael 1*. Put in your class's serial number. Review your students' results.

2. Students can print out a lesson summary when they have completed all the activities in a lesson and bring it in to class.

3. Students can e-mail the lesson summary directly to you. You may wish to set up a separate e-mail account to receive this information.

Inform your students how often you intend to assess their progress online. You may wish to check their progress each time you assign an activity, or you may prefer to do so after they complete a chapter in the book.

The following chart outlines the games and activities included in the digital application for *Kol Yisrael 1*:

 Indicates that students use a clue from the textbook.

CONTENTS OF DIGITAL APPLICATION

Blessing/Prayer and Room in Digital House	Game/Activity	Purpose
Lesson 1 Ben's room — מוֹדֶה/מוֹדָה אֲנִי	Reading מוֹדֶה/מוֹדָה אֲנִי	Practice reading the prayer.
	Arrange Your Books Matching	Review new vocabulary.
	Feed the Fish Matching	Review new vocabulary.
	Clean Your Closet	Learn Hebrew words for clothing.
	Fish Tales Game	Play the game and review vocabulary.
Lesson 2 Kitchen — בְּרָכוֹת	Reading בְּרָכוֹת	Practice blessings for various foods.
	Unpack the Groceries	Match foods and blessings.
	Concentration	Review new vocabulary.
	Ben's Skateboarding Game	Review new vocabulary.
Lesson 3 Study — בְּרָכוֹת שֶׁל מִצְוָה	Reading בְּרָכוֹת שֶׁל מִצְוָה	Practice reading blessings of mitzvah.
	Arrange Your Books	Review new vocabulary.
	Tic Tac Toe	Review new vocabulary.
	Ping Pong	Play the game and review vocabulary.
Lesson 4 Dining room — בְּרָכוֹת שֶׁל שַׁבָּת	Reading בְּרָכוֹת שֶׁל שַׁבָּת	Practice reading Shabbat blessings.
	Candle Lighting	Practice reading candle lighting blessings.
	Set the Table Matching	Practice new vocabulary.
	Hamotzi	Place the words of Hamotzi in order.
	Batya's Vert Skate Game	Play game and review vocabulary.
Lesson 5 Dining room — קִדּוּשׁ	Reading קִדּוּשׁ	Practice reading the blessing.
	Kiddush Matching	Review new vocabulary.
	Kiddush Sling Game	Review meaning of new vocabulary.
Lesson 6 Patio — הַבְדָּלָה	Reading הַבְדָּלָה	Practice reading the Havdalah blessings.
	Reading אֵלִיָּהוּ הַנָּבִיא	Practice reading the words of the song.
	Havdalah Puzzle Matching	Match word parts to form complete words.
	Tic Tac Toe	Review the new vocabulary.
	Ping Pong Havdalah	Play game and review vocabulary.

Blessing/Prayer and Room in Digital House	Game/Activity	Purpose
Lesson 7 בִּרְכוֹת שֶׁל יוֹם טוֹב Family Room	Reading רֹאשׁ הַשָּׁנָה	Practice reading the blessings over apples and honey and before blowing the shofar.
	Reading סֻכּוֹת	Practice reading the blessings over lulav and etrog and sitting in the sukkah.
	Reading חֲנֻכָּה	Practice reading the Hanukkah blessings.
	Reading פֶּסַח	Practice reading the seder blessings.
	Reading פּוּרִים	Practice reading the blessing recited before reading the megillah.
	Holiday Word Search	Review the holiday vocabulary words.
	Holiday Match	Review holiday blessing vocabulary.
	Holiday Sling Game 👍	Review the objects used on holidays.
Lesson 8 מַה נִּשְׁתַּנָּה Dining Room	Reading מַה נִּשְׁתַּנָּה	Practice reading the Four Questions.
	Seder plate	Review the items on the seder plate.
	Four Children Matching	Review the Hebrew for the four children.
	Batya's Vert Skate Game 👍	Play game and review vocabulary.
Lesson 9 בִּרְכַּת הַמָּזוֹן Kitchen	Reading בִּרְכַּת הַמָּזוֹן	Practice reading.
	Holiday Bread Matching	Review when matzah and hallah are eaten.
	Food List Matching	Learn the Hebrew names of foods.
	Ping Pong Birkat Hamazon 👍	Play game and review vocabulary.
Lesson 10 שְׁמַע Batya's room	Reading שְׁמַע	Practice reading.
	Hebrew Word Search	Review new vocabulary.
	Feed the Fish Matching	Review new vocabulary.
	Batya's Vert Skate Game 👍	Play game and review vocabulary.
Review 1		Review vocabulary and prayer concepts in Lessons 1–3.
Review 2		Review vocabulary and prayer concepts in Lessons 4–6.
Review 3		Review vocabulary and prayer concepts in Lessons 7–10.

THE PRAYERS OF OUR PEOPLE I • כָּל יִשְׂרָאֵל

WORD CARDS

The following is a list of words included in *Kol Yisrael 1*. All Prayer Words are identified by the 📖 icon.

1. מוֹדֶה 📖 — thank, give thanks (boy/man)
2. מוֹדָה 📖 — thank, give thanks (girl/woman)
3. אֲנִי 📖 — I
4. מֶלֶךְ 📖 — ruler, king
5. חַי 📖 — live, living
6. בְּבַקָשָׁה — please
7. תּוֹדָה — thank you
8. בָּרוּךְ 📖 — blessed, praised
9. אַתָּה 📖 — you (boy/man)
10. הָעוֹלָם 📖 — the world
11. לֶחֶם 📖 — bread
12. אֲדָמָה 📖 — earth
13. פְּרִי, פֵּרוֹת 📖 — fruit(s)
14. עֵץ — tree
15. בְּרָכָה, בְּרָכוֹת — blessing(s)
16. יְיָ — Adonai
17. אֱלֹהֵינוּ — our God
18. אָמֵן — Amen
19. קִדְּשָׁנוּ 📖 — makes us holy
20. בְּמִצְוֹתָיו 📖 — with God's commandments
21. וְצִוָּנוּ 📖 — and commands us
22. לַעֲסוֹק 📖 — to engage
23. בְּדִבְרֵי 📖 — in the words of
24. תּוֹרָה — Torah
25. לִקְבֹּעַ — to affix
26. מְזוּזָה 📖 — mezuzah
27. מִצְוָה, מִצְוֹת — commandment(s)
28. בְּרָכָה, בְּרָכוֹת שֶׁל מִצְוָה — blessing(s) over the commandments
29. אֲשֶׁר — who, that
30. נֵר 📖 — candle
31. בּוֹרֵא 📖 — who creates
32. הַגֶּפֶן 📖 — the vine
33. הַמּוֹצִיא 📖 — who brings forth
34. חָתָן — bridegroom
35. כַּלָּה — bride
36. צְדָקָה — tzedakah
37. נֵר תָּמִיד — eternal light
38. זָכוֹר — remember
39. שָׁמוֹר — observe
40. שַׁבַּת שָׁלוֹם — a peaceful Shabbat
41. שָׁלוֹם — peace, hello, good-bye
42. שְׁלוֹם בַּיִת — peace in the home
43. קָדוֹשׁ 📖 — holiness
44. זִכָּרוֹן 📖 — memory
45. זֵכֶר 📖 — memory
46. (לְ)מַעֲשֵׂה בְרֵאשִׁית 📖 — (of the) work of creation
47. (לְ)יְצִיאַת מִצְרַיִם 📖 — (of the) going out from Egypt
48. (בְּ)אַהֲבָה 📖 — (in/with) love
49. (וּבְ)רָצוֹן 📖 — (and in/with) favor
50. יוֹם הַזִּכָּרוֹן — the Day of Remembrance
51. יוֹם הָעַצְמָאוּת — Israel's Independence Day
52. מַזְכִּיר, מַזְכִּירָה — secretary (man/woman)
53. בְּשָׂמִים 📖 — spices
54. אֵשׁ 📖 — fire
55. הַמַּבְדִּיל 📖 — who separates

56.	קֹדֶשׁ	holy
57.	חוֹל	everyday
58.	הַבְדָּלָה	separation
59.	שָׁבוּעַ טוֹב	a good week
60.	שָׁבוּעַ	week
61.	אֵלִיָּהוּ הַנָּבִיא	Elijah the Prophet
62.	לִשְׁמֹעַ	to hear
63.	קוֹל	sound, voice
64.	שׁוֹפָר	shofar
65.	בַּסֻּכָּה	in the sukkah
66.	לוּלָב	lulav
67.	אֶתְרוֹג	etrog
68.	חֲנֻכָּה	Hanukkah
69.	נִסִּים	miracles
70.	בַּזְּמַן הַזֶּה	at this time
71.	הָאֲדָמָה	the earth
72.	אֲכִילַת	eating (of)
73.	מַצָּה	matzah
74.	מָרוֹר	maror/bitter herbs
75.	שָׁנָה טוֹבָה וּמְתוּקָה	a good and sweet New Year
76.	שְׁמַע	hear
77.	סֻכָּה, סֻכּוֹת	booth(s), hut(s)
78.	בְּרוּכִים הַבָּאִים	Welcome!
79.	חֲנֻכִּיָּה	Hanukkah menorah
80.	נֵס גָּדוֹל הָיָה שָׁם	a great miracle happened there
81.	סֵדֶר	order, Passover seder
82.	יוֹם טוֹב	a good day, Jewish holiday
83.	חַג	holiday
84.	חַג שָׂמֵחַ	happy holiday
85.	הַלַּיְלָה	the night
86.	הַזֶּה	this
87.	מַה נִּשְׁתַּנָּה	the Four Questions
88.	הַ-	the
89.	לַיְלָה	night
90.	הַזָּן	who feeds
91.	טוּבוֹ	(God's) goodness
92.	(בְּ)חֶסֶד	(with) kindness
93.	מָזוֹן	food
94.	בִּרְכַּת הַמָּזוֹן	the blessing after a meal, Grace after Meals
95.	טוֹב	good
96.	הַכְנָסַת אוֹרְחִים	welcoming guests
97.	כֹּל/כָּל	all
98.	יִשְׂרָאֵל	Israel
99.	אֶחָד	one
100.	כַּוָּנָה	deep concentration
101.	שַׁדַּי	God
102.	בְּנֵי יִשְׂרָאֵל	Children of Israel
103.	מְדִינַת יִשְׂרָאֵל	State of Israel
104.	עַם יִשְׂרָאֵל	Nation (People) of Israel
105.	אֶרֶץ יִשְׂרָאֵל	Land of Israel
106.	אֵל	God
107.	שֵׁם	name
108.	מַה שִּׁמְךָ?	What is your name? (to a boy or man)
109.	מַה שְּׁמֵךְ?	What is your name? (to a girl or woman)
110.	שְׁמִי	My name is…

כָּל יִשְׂרָאֵל · THE PRAYERS OF OUR PEOPLE I

WORD CARD TECHNIQUES AND GAMES

There are 110 Word Cards for *Kol Yisrael 1*. They include (a) the words listed in the section called "Prayer Words" in each chapter, and (b) other related key words and phrases in each chapter. The Teacher's Edition offers specific suggestions for presenting the Prayer Words. Word Cards for other related words and phrases can be presented as they are introduced in the student edition. These words may be used along with the Prayer Words for games and review activities.

1. Display a number of Word Cards on the board. Provide a clue about one of the words and ask students to find and read the correct word. For example: What is the second word in the blessing formula? (אַתָּה)

2. Distribute several Word Cards to the class. Have students look only at the Hebrew words or phrases on the cards. Call out, one at a time, the English meanings of the Hebrew words or phrases. Ask the student with the corresponding Hebrew card to stand up, display the card, and read the word or phrase. Or switch, and call out the Hebrew words.

3. Post at least six words in a column on the board. Ask individuals or teams to take turns "climbing up the ladder" by reading, and translating, if you choose, the words in the column in ascending order. Score one point for each word translated correctly. Then play again by having students read the words in descending order to climb down the ladder.

4. Make a packet of ten Word Cards. Arrange the class in a circle and have the students pass the packet around the circle while playing music on a CD player. (Try to use Jewish or Israeli music.) When the music stops, the student holding the packet should read and/or translate the top card. Then, let the student place the card at the bottom of the pile and the game continues in the same fashion.

CLASSROOM GAMES

Games can add variety and energy to your classroom. They reinforce learning and capture students' attention through a fun, lively medium. As you plan to use the games below, or others you may develop or choose to use, keep the following considerations in mind:

1. Choose games that improve specific skills and reading fluency—games that have pedagogic value.

2. Use games that move quickly. Don't spend more time on a game than it deserves.

3. Stop when students' interest begins to wane.

4. Choose games appropriate to the age group.

5. Use games that are easy to follow and organize. Explain rules clearly. Avoid complicated directions. You want students' attention focused on the skills being reinforced, not on rules.

6. Maintain control of the class.

7. When playing a game with the entire class, make sure that all students are actively involved and can experience success.

The Secret Word

Invite two students to the front of the room to be the "contestants." Show everyone but the two contestants a Word Card (the secret word). Students raise their hands to volunteer one-word clues to help the contestants guess the word. Contestants take turns calling on students until one of the contestants correctly guesses the secret word. The contestant who guesses the secret word remains at the front of the class; the student who gave the final clue takes the place of the other contestant.

שֶׁקֶט, בְּבַקָּשָׁה!

Distribute Word Cards for words contained in a single prayer or blessing (you need not have all of the prayer or blessing words to do this activity). Students must arrange themselves in order of the appearance of the words in the prayer or blessing, without any talking or making any sound. Once students are standing in the correct sequence, invite the class to chorally recite the prayer or blessing.

אוֹי!

Materials: Small pieces of paper; shoe box or coffee can

Neatly write 10 to 15 Prayer Words or Related Words on pieces of paper. Write אוֹי! on three pieces of paper. Fold all pieces of paper in half and place them in the box or can. Divide the class into three or four teams. Teams take turns picking words. If they read and translate the word correctly they get to keep the word. If not, they must return the word to the box/can. If a teams draws an אוֹי!, they yell אוֹי! and then return all their words (except the אוֹי!) to the box/can.

When no more words remain in the box/can or you have reached a pre-set time limit, the team with the most words wins.

Odd Word Out

Write four words on the board. Three should be related, and one should be unrelated. Challenge students to circle the "Odd Word Out."
(example: תּוֹרָה - אֲדָמָה - לַעֲסוֹק - בְּדִבְרֵי)

Mishpaḥah Madness

Divide the class into two teams (two families–*mishpaḥot*). Assign, or have teams choose, a Hebrew family name, such as Ben-David, for their team. Invite the first student player from each team to come to the front of the room. Show the two students a Word Card. The students raise their hands if they know how to read and translate the word. Call on the first student who raises his or her hand. If that student correctly reads and translates the word, the team earns two points. If not, the other player tries to read and translate the same Word Card. If neither player gives the correct answer, their teammates can raise their hands and, after being called on, read and translate. One point is earned when a teammate, rather than a player, answers correctly. For variety, you may wish to challenge students to name a prayer or blessing in which the word appears or an occasion on which a phrase is said. The team with the most points after all Word Cards have been presented is the winning team.

מָצָאתִי—I Found It!

Have students locate a word or phrase on a given page, based on clues that you provide.

Sample clues may include:

- Find the words in the Kiddush with the root letters זכר.
- Find the words that mean, "(of the) work of creation."
- Find the first blessing in the Kiddush.

Have students call מָצָאתִי! ("I found it!") when they locate the word or phrase. The first student who calls מָצָאתִי! should read the word or phrase correctly. If successful, he or she receives a point. If not, the other students have an opportunity to call מָצָאתִי!, read the word or phrase, and score.

Hebrew Baseball

Using four chairs (one for each base), create a mock baseball diamond in your classroom. Divide the class into two teams and have them sit on opposite sides of the room. Choose a team to be at bat. That team will send one student at a time to home plate. That student chooses the difficulty level of the question that he or she will answer: a single, double, triple, or home run. The higher the chosen hit, the more difficult the question you will ask. You may wish to prepare questions for each level in advance.

Sample questions:

- For a single: What is the English translation of the word בְּדִבְרֵי? (*in the words of*)
- For a double: When do we recite הַמּוֹצִיא? (*Before eating any kind of bread*)
- For a triple: What blessing do we recite before eating fruit? (בּוֹרֵא פְּרִי הָעֵץ)
- For a home run: What are four names that include the name יִשְׂרָאֵל? (עַם יִשְׂרָאֵל; מְדִינַת יִשְׂרָאֵל; בְּנֵי יִשְׂרָאֵל; אֶרֶץ יִשְׂרָאֵל)

If the answer is correct, the student advances that number of bases (and anyone already on base advances the same number as well). If the student is incorrect, he or she is out. After three outs the other team comes to bat. Play as many innings as you'd like, but make sure the second team gets its final turn at bat.

Concentration

Create one set of 3" × 5" index cards with Hebrew words, and one set of cards with the English translations (or illustrations). You may wish to use the same words reviewed in the digital application's Prayer Word Concentration game. All cards should be blank on one side. Combine both sets and shuffle together.

Place all cards, word-side up, on the floor or a large table. Then turn the cards over so that the blank sides face up. Ask students individually (or in teams) to try to match the Hebrew and English word (or picture) pairs by turning any two cards over.

If they match, award the player the matched pair of cards. If they do not match, place the cards back in their original position, word side down, and ask another student (or the other team) to go. Continue the game until all cards have been removed. The player or team with the most matches wins.

Tic-Tac-Toe

Draw a Tic-Tac-Toe diagram on the board. Divide students into two teams, X and O. Show a Word Card or choose a word reviewed in that lesson's digital version of Tic-Tac-Toe, then call on a student from Team X to read the Hebrew word. If the student reads correctly, ask him or her to place an X in one of the squares. Then it is Team O's turn; show another Word Card, and call on a student from Team O to read it.

Variations:

- Students must read the word on the Word Card and the sentence (or line) in the prayer passage that contains the word before placing a mark in a square. (You can facilitate the game by telling the student which line contains the word.)
- Students must read the Hebrew and give the English meaning before placing an X or an O in a square.
- Students must answer questions about the prayer passage(s) in order to place an X or an O in a square.

מַה הַמִּילָה?—What's the Word?

Have a student choose a word from the chapter. The other students must guess what the word is, based on questions they ask. They can ask any question that will help them guess the word.

Suggested questions:
- Is the word masculine or feminine?
- Is the word a person, place, or thing?
- How many letters are there in the word?

The class may ask as many questions as they like, but each student may guess only once. The student who guesses correctly receives a point and chooses the next word. The student with the most points at the end of ten rounds is the winner.

Siddur Squares

This game can be played using the questions from one of the lessons, or as a review of several lessons. Before the game, prepare X and O signs by writing a large X on six sheets of construction paper and a large O on another six sheets of construction paper.

Select nine students to serve as the "siddur squares." You might place three chairs in a row. Direct three students to sit in the chairs, three to stand behind the chairs, and three to sit on the floor in front of the seated students. Divide the remaining students into two teams, X and O. You or a student can serve as moderator.

The first player on Team X will select one of the nine siddur squares, and the moderator will ask one of the prepared questions from the lesson being reviewed. The siddur square student should give an answer, and the Team X player must agree or disagree with the answer. If the Team X player is correct (that is, agrees with a correct answer or disagrees with an incorrect answer), then Team X should receive an X in that square. The siddur square student who answered that question will hold (and display) an X marker.

Continue in the same fashion with Team O. Continue, alternating teams, until one team has three squares in a row, diagonally, vertically, or horizontally.

TIME MANAGEMENT

Deciding how to spend your valuable class time is crucial when planning your lessons. Ideally, each class session should be divided into at least four distinct components:

1. An opening activity to review previous material or to set the tone for the new lesson
2. Introduction of new material
3. Reinforcement of new material
4. A closing activity to summarize and reinforce the lesson's content and prepare students for the next lesson

The amount of time spent on each component will depend on the overall amount of time available for Hebrew instruction and on what you wish to accomplish. Preparing a lesson plan in advance of every class session will help you to manage your time so that your goals can be met. Keep in mind that the digital application allows you to extend your class time with at-home learning sessions.

Your lesson plan should include (1) lesson goals, (2) instructional materials needed, (3) planned activities/time estimates, (4) homework, and (5) notes.

If You Meet Once a Week for Hebrew Instruction...

If your school meets 1 to 1½ hours per week for thirty weeks, you should allow approximately three classroom sessions per chapter. Keep in mind that some chapters introduce more than twenty new Hebrew words and phrases, while others introduce only a few. In addition, some chapters focus on blessings and prayers comprised of one or two verses, while others focus on longer blessings and prayers. Therefore, some chapters will require more than three classroom sessions, while other chapters may be covered in two class sessions.

If You Meet Twice a Week for Hebrew Instruction...

If your school meets 2 to 3 hours per week for thirty weeks, you should allow four to six classroom sessions per chapter. Use as many of the techniques described in this Teacher's Edition as possible to enrich the content of the text and digital application.

ASSESSMENT

Assessment enables both you and your students to gain a clear understanding of where each student is in the learning process and what the next steps should be. Assessment is primarily a process for helping students grow and learn. It can also help you to plan future lessons and to check how well you yourself are doing.

A variety of assessment tools are available for *Kol Yisrael 1*.

- **PRAYER MASTERY ASSESSMENT CHART**—Toward the end of each chapter, check each student's reading fluency and comprehension of the prayer, key words, and phrases. Photocopy the chart on the next page for each student. Keep a record of the student's progress by writing a comment and dating the chart after each assessment is complete. Keep the charts in a dedicated folder or binder.

- **REVIEW SHEETS**—You will find worksheets with answer keys online at www.kolyisrael.net. Use the worksheets to review key prayer concepts and vocabulary at the end of each chapter.

- **DIGITAL APPLICATION**—Assess students' progress at www.behrmanhouse.com. The digital application also includes Reviews after Lessons 3, 6, and 10. (Refer to page 6 for information about how to assess progress online.)

Doug the Fish Puppet

For fun, you may wish to create a puppet of Doug, Batya and Ben's pet fish. Use the drawing of Doug found on page 128. Whenever Doug is telling a story or talking to the students, you, or a student, can hold up the Doug puppet. Be sure to tell your students that they can call Doug "Doug *ha-dag*," meaning "Doug the fish." Explain that the English name Doug is a play on the Hebrew word for "fish."

PRAYER MASTERY ASSESSMENT CHART

Student Name: _____

Understands key words and phrases	Explains meaning of prayer	Reads prayer fluently	
			1. מוֹדֶה/מוֹדָה אֲנִי
			2. בְּרָכוֹת
			3. בְּרָכוֹת שֶׁל מִצְוָה
			4. בְּרָכוֹת שֶׁל שַׁבָּת
			5. קִדּוּשׁ
			6. הַבְדָּלָה
			7. בְּרָכוֹת שֶׁל יוֹם טוֹב
			8. מַה נִּשְׁתַּנָּה
			9. בִּרְכַּת הַמָּזוֹן
			10. שְׁמַע

TECHNIQUES FOR STUDENTS WITH SPECIAL LEARNING NEEDS

All children learn and develop differently, and no two students will acquire Hebrew skills in exactly the same way. Students with special learning needs bring additional challenges to the classroom; teachers can serve their students best by recognizing each child's individual strengths. *Kol Yisrael 1* provides a broad variety of activities, including traditional pencil-to-paper exercises as well as mouse-to-screen reinforcement activities, that can be modified for all kinds of learners. Consult with your religious school director to learn about each student's specific learning needs.

While these strategies are geared toward students with special learning needs, all students can benefit from the techniques and modifications listed below:

- **Form a bond with your students.** Reach out before school starts by sending home a letter or e-mail or by calling to introduce yourself to your students. Begin the year with a "get-to-know-you" game. Students who feel that their teacher takes a genuine interest in their lives outside of Hebrew school are more likely to stretch academically.

- **Start with an assessment.** Give students the opportunity to review their basic decoding skills. It is more effective to move gradually into the content than it is to remediate once a student has fallen behind. This will also help to prevent students from feeling as if they are failing at a task.

For students with:

- **Attention problems:** Seat the student close to you and minimize distractions, such as students tapping their pencils on their desks or noise in the hallway. Repeat directions. Privately establish a refocusing system with the student, such as a gentle tap on the shoulder or approaching his or her desk. Help students organize their papers and supplies. Provide an extra copy of texts for use at home. Ensure homework assignments are written down.

- **Auditory processing issues:** Minimize noise and distractions. Have the student repeat directions back to you to ensure understanding. Provide students with a written copy of verbal instructions.

- **Visual processing difficulty:** Read written directions aloud. For individual seatwork, allow the student to work with a madrich or madrichah or a buddy to read the information aloud. Have the student use an index card to track the line being read or cover the portion of the page not being worked on. Be willing to provide an alternative activity such as highlighting instead of circling key vocabulary.

- **Emotional concerns, such as shyness or lack of self-esteem:** Allow students to participate in choral reading, if they prefer, rather than reading out loud individually. Assess students one-on-one until they feel more confident. Provide positive reinforcement regularly to boost self-esteem.

- **Behavioral problems:** Set firm but reasonable expectations. Minimize transitions such as changing activities abruptly, and inform students of schedule changes. Maintain a positive relationship with parents, for example, by returning messages promptly. Find out what works for the student at home and in secular school to mirror in your own classroom where possible.

Remember, students may fall into more than one category and will benefit from a combination of strategies. Above all, embrace your students, knowing that each is created *b'tzelem Elohim* (in God's image).

מוֹדֶה/מוֹדָה אֲנִי

ABOUT THE PRAYER

The מוֹדֶה/מוֹדָה אֲנִי prayer, in which we thank God for allowing us to awaken to a new day, is traditionally recited at home immediately upon rising. It is believed to be based on Lamentations 3:23: *They are renewed each morning; great is Your faithfulness* (חֲדָשִׁים לַבְּקָרִים רַבָּה אֱמוּנָתֶךָ).

LEARNING OBJECTIVES

Students will be able to:

- Identify מוֹדֶה/מוֹדָה אֲנִי as the first prayer recited each morning.
- Read מוֹדֶה/מוֹדָה אֲנִי fluently.
- Define key words found in and related to מוֹדֶה/מוֹדָה אֲנִי.
- Describe what we are thanking God for in מוֹדֶה/מוֹדָה אֲנִי.
- Explain the importance of saying "Thank you."

NEW WORDS AND PHRASES

Prayer Words:

thank, give thanks (for a boy or man)	מוֹדֶה
thank, give thanks (for a girl or woman)	מוֹדָה
I	אֲנִי
ruler, king	מֶלֶךְ
live, living	חַי

Related Words:

please	בְּבַקָּשָׁה
thank you	תּוֹדָה

INSTRUCTIONAL MATERIALS

Text Pages 4–9
Word Cards 1–7

Digital Application: Lesson 1—in Ben's Room (see page 7 for a list of games and activities)

TITLE OF THE SERIES

Draw students' attention to the title of the series, כָּל יִשְׂרָאֵל.

Explain: One of the names for the Jewish people is Israel, יִשְׂרָאֵל. The Torah describes how God gave Abraham's grandson, Jacob, a new name: Israel, יִשְׂרָאֵל. The Torah tells us that יִשְׂרָאֵל had twelve sons from whom the Jewish people are descended. Since יִשְׂרָאֵל is considered to be the ancestor of all the Jewish people, we call ourselves בְּנֵי יִשְׂרָאֵל, Children of Israel, or simply יִשְׂרָאֵל. (Note: It may be helpful to draw the above information on the board as you present it to your students.)

Tell students that כָּל means "all." Challenge students to translate the phrase כָּל יִשְׂרָאֵל. (*"All of Israel" or "All of the Jewish people"*)

As a class, brainstorm a list of different things that "All of Israel" does. Invite students to create sentences that begin with כָּל יִשְׂרָאֵל. (*Sentences may include:* כָּל יִשְׂרָאֵל *prays with a siddur;* כָּל יִשְׂרָאֵל *gives tzedakah;* כָּל יִשְׂרָאֵל *studies Torah.*)

WHERE WE ARE

We meet Batya and Ben in their bedrooms as they are waking up in the morning, the time when מוֹדֶה/מוֹדָה אֲנִי is traditionally recited. The prayer serves as a daily reminder of the importance of saying "Thank you."

PEACE IN OUR HOME

Focus students on the phrase שְׁלוֹם בַּיִת. Call on a volunteer to explain the meaning of שְׁלוֹם בַּיִת.

Ask: Why is שְׁלוֹם בַּיִת important? (*Responses may include: so we get along better with brothers and sisters; so the family is happier; so our parents don't need to yell*) Remind students that in this program not only will they learn Hebrew prayers and many Hebrew words, but they will learn how to add to their family's שְׁלוֹם בַּיִת.

Explain that students will be able to practice Hebrew on their computer at home. For every chapter in the book there is a corresponding chapter in the digital application. They'll be able to play exciting games online such as skateboarding, ping-pong, and sling. Tell students that all of these activities take place in Batya and Ben's digital home. Remind students about the value of *sh'lom bayit*. Just like Batya and Ben, students can help bring peace into their homes.

INTRODUCING THE LESSON

Begin the lesson by thanking your students for being there and for participating in class.

Ask the following open-ended questions: How did you feel when I thanked you? When do *you* say thank you? Whom do you thank? Why is it important to say thank you?

Inform students that our tradition teaches that God, as well as people, deserves thanks. Invite students to suggest different things for which a person might express thanks to God. Explain that in Chapter 1 students will learn the very first prayer that is recited each morning: מוֹדֶה/מוֹדָה אֲנִי. The words of this prayer express thanks to God for allowing us to wake up to a new morning.

INTO THE TEXT

Write the words מוֹדֶה and מוֹדָה on the board. Explain that both words mean "thank," but girls and women say מוֹדָה while boys and men say מוֹדֶה. Ask all the girls in the class to say מוֹדָה and then have all the boys say מוֹדֶה. Inform students that in Hebrew all verbs have a female form and a male form. Often, as in the word מוֹדָה, the female form ends with ה ָ.

If your students are familiar with the words מוֹרֶה and מוֹרָה, ask them how these words are similar to מוֹדֶה and מוֹדָה. Have students guess if a מוֹרָה would say מוֹדֶה or מוֹדָה.

Invite students to open to page 4. As a class, read aloud the name of the prayer מוֹדֶה/מוֹדָה אֲנִי. Point to yourself as you say the word אֲנִי. Have students echo אֲנִי and point to themselves. Challenge students to say the English meaning of מוֹדֶה/מוֹדָה אֲנִי. Ask all the girls to say מוֹדָה אֲנִי and all the boys to say מוֹדֶה אֲנִי.

Call on volunteers to describe the illustrations of Batya and Ben. Remind students that מוֹדֶה/מוֹדָה אֲנִי is a prayer said upon waking up in the morning.

Direct students to read and complete page 4 with a partner. Call on volunteers to share their responses with the class.

Ask: What are some things for which you say thank you in the morning? (*Answers may include: thank parent for breakfast; thank sibling for getting out of the bathroom; thank bus driver for ride to school*) Inform students that Jews all over the world say thank you to God as they wake up to a brand-new day.

THE PRAYERS OF OUR PEOPLE I • כָּל יִשְׂרָאֵל

 **Reading Rounds**

As a class, chorally read the consonant-vowel combinations in "Reading Rounds."

Have students practice "Reading Rounds" with a partner.

Similar Sounds

Direct students to connect the letters with similar sounds and to check their answers with a partner.

Reading Skills

Begin by reading each word part aloud and having students echo that word part. Students then read word parts to a partner, taking turns as they read to one another. To further reinforce the reading, invite the class to read all the word parts chorally. Applaud your students for a job well done!

Ask students to identify specific sounds. For example, have students circle all word parts that contain the sound "eh" or underline all word parts containing the sound "m." Ask how many word parts they circled.

For fun, challenge students to sing the word parts to a familiar tune, such as "Yankee Doodle."

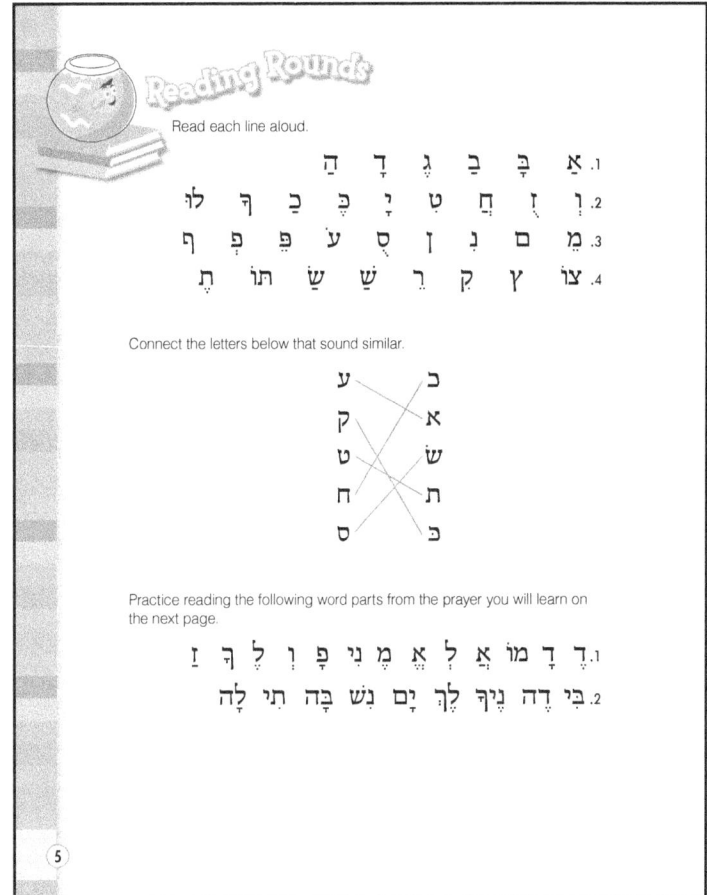

19 CHAPTER 1

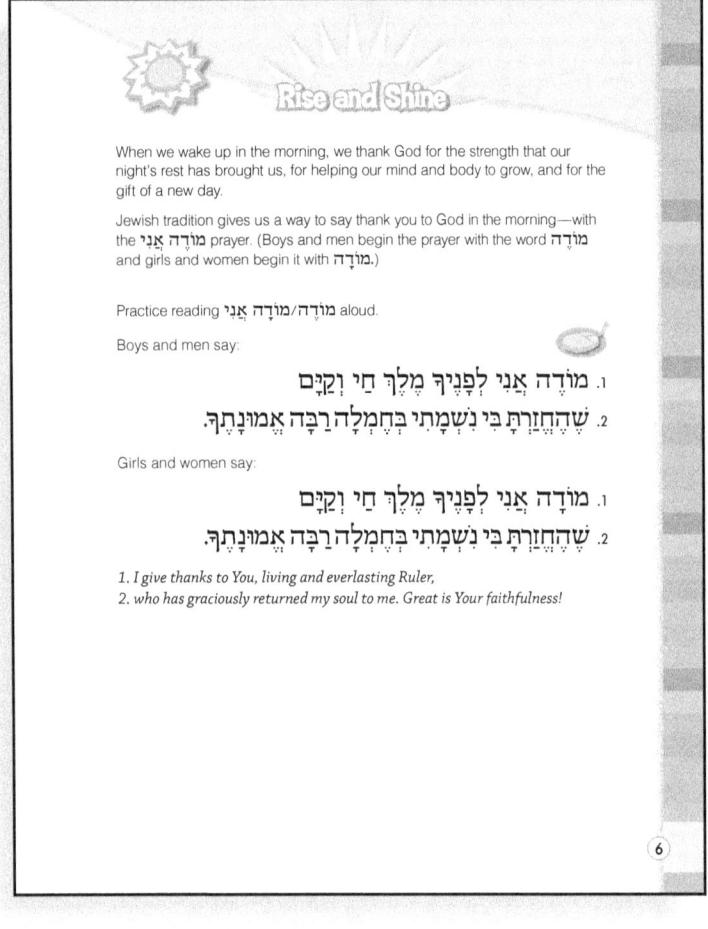

Rise and Shine

Have students silently read the description of the מוֹדֶה/מוֹדָה אֲנִי prayer on page 6. Review by asking questions such as: What are we thanking God for? (*Strength from a night's rest; helping our minds and bodies to grow; the gift of a new day*) How is the prayer different when recited by a girl from when it is recited by a boy? (*A girl says* מוֹדָה, *a boy says* מוֹדֶה)

Direct all the boys to say מוֹדֶה אֲנִי and all the girls to say מוֹדָה אֲנִי (line 1). Explain that all the other words in the prayer are the same for boys and for girls.

Recite the rest of line 1 and invite the class to echo the line. Read aloud the second line and, again, have students echo the line. Repeat all of line 1 beginning with מוֹדֶה and have all the boys echo the words. Do the same with line 1 beginning with מוֹדָה, having all the girls echo the words. Read line 2 aloud and invite all students to echo this line. Repeat this several times, having different groups of students echo the lines. When you feel they are ready, invite individual students to recite both lines together. Model the difficult words in line 2 and have students repeat them after you.

Invite students to sit in a circle. Go around the circle having each student read one word of the prayer. The first student says מוֹדֶה or מוֹדָה, the second says אֲנִי. Continue until all students have had several turns. Invite volunteers to read one or both lines of the prayer.

Digital Application

Tell students that at home, before the next class, they should click on מוֹדֶה/מוֹדָה אֲנִי and enter Ben's room in the digital application. Once in Ben's room, students can click on the graphic of the books to practice reading מוֹדֶה/מוֹדָה אֲנִי. Point out that the male and female readers of the prayer have different accents. In the next class, ask students why the male and female voice had different accents. (*Female is American; male is Israeli*) Ask if any students have family in Israel. How are their accents different?

Personalizing the Prayer

Direct students to the English translation of מוֹדֶה/מוֹדָה אֲנִי and read the translation together as a class. Ask the following questions: Who is giving thanks? (*Answers may include: individual people; we all are;* כָּל יִשְׂרָאֵל); Who is being thanked? (*God*); How is God described in this prayer? (*living and everlasting Ruler*); What does it mean to be an "everlasting Ruler"? (*the prayer says that God will rule over us for all time*); According to the prayer, what is God being thanked for? (*for returning our souls to us*). Guide students to understand that the words of מוֹדֶה/מוֹדָה אֲנִי express thanks to God for bringing us to a brand-new day. Invite students to describe events that have taken place in the last few days for which they are thankful.

Consider inviting the cantor or music teacher to teach your students to chant מוֹדֶה/מוֹדָה אֲנִי.

Digital Application

In Ben's room, students can click on "Arrange Your Books" to practice their new prayer vocabulary, including the words מוֹדֶה (give thanks), וְקַיָּם (and everlasting), חַי (living), and מֶלֶךְ (ruler). In the next class, ask students what it means to describe God as a "living ruler." What does it mean for a human to live? What might it mean for God to live?

Prayer Words

Present each word to the class. As a class, create hand motions for each of the words. For example, a student points to him- or herself when saying אֲנִי. Invite students to create their own hand motions as they chorally recite מוֹדֶה/מוֹדָה אֲנִי.

Explain to students that Hebrew letters also have numerical values. Present them with the numerical values for א to י (1 to 10). Challenge students to calculate the numerical value of חַי: (ח = 8) + (י = 10) =18. Explain that Jewish people often give $18 (or a multiple of $18) for a gift as a way of wishing someone a good, long life. Many people wear necklaces or earrings with a חַי design. You may wish to bring in a piece of jewelry to show students, or invite students to bring in their own jewelry that has a חַי design.

Display Word Cards #1–5. Ask students to read each word card aloud. Call on students to read:

- the two words related to the word תּוֹדָה.
- the word ending with a final form letter.
- the word meaning "I" for both a girl and a boy.
- the word that sometimes decorates a piece of jewelry.

Personal Prayer

Have each student write a personal thank you prayer and illustrate it on a sheet of construction paper. Create a prayer bulletin board displaying students' blessings.

Odd Word Out

Have students complete the "Odd Word Out" activity alone or with a partner. Direct students to read the ten words aloud as they identify the words that do not belong in מוֹדֶה/מוֹדָה אֲנִי (בַּיִת, יַיִן, and שַׁבָּת). Call on a volunteer to read the new word at the bottom of the page. (בַּיִת)

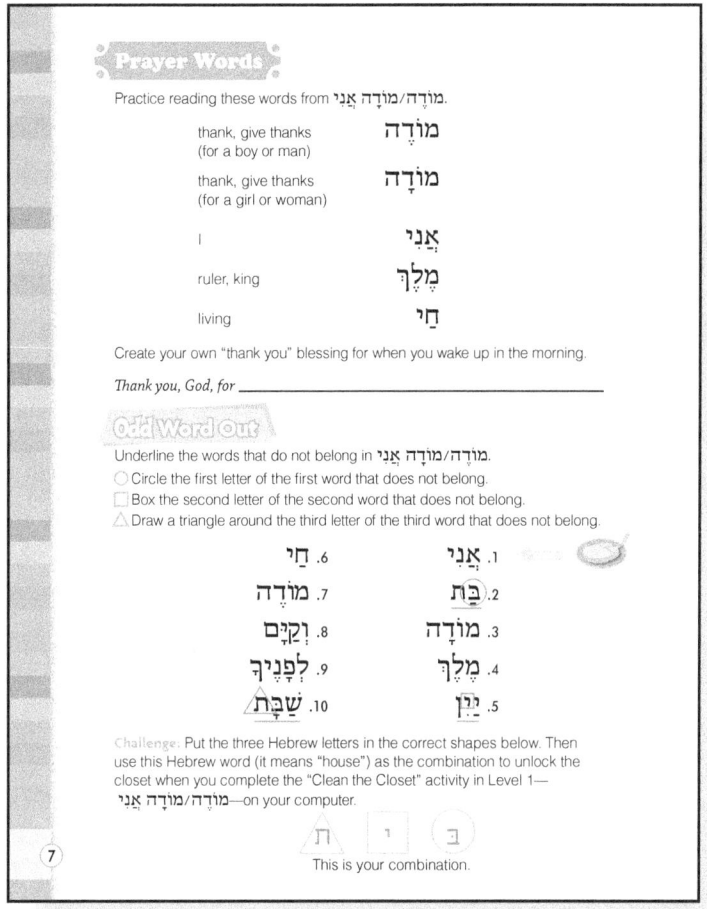

To help students remember the Hebrew word for house, encourage students to complete the following sentences: I say תּוֹדָה in my בַּיִת when… (Sample sentence: I say תּוֹדָה in my בַּיִת when my sister helps me with homework.)

Digital Application

In Ben's room, students can click on the "Clean Your Closet" activity to learn and review the Hebrew word בַּיִת (house, home) and the words for clothing, which include: כּוֹבַע (hat), חוּלְצָה (shirt), מִכְנָסַיִם (pants), גַּרְבַּיִם (socks), סְוֶדֶר (sweater), נַעֲלַיִם (shoes), and סַנְדָּלִים (sandals).

Remind students to use the Hebrew clue from their book to unlock the closet in this online activity. In the next class, challenge students to name the Hebrew words for the clothes they are wearing that day. What might they wear during the summer? Fall? Winter?

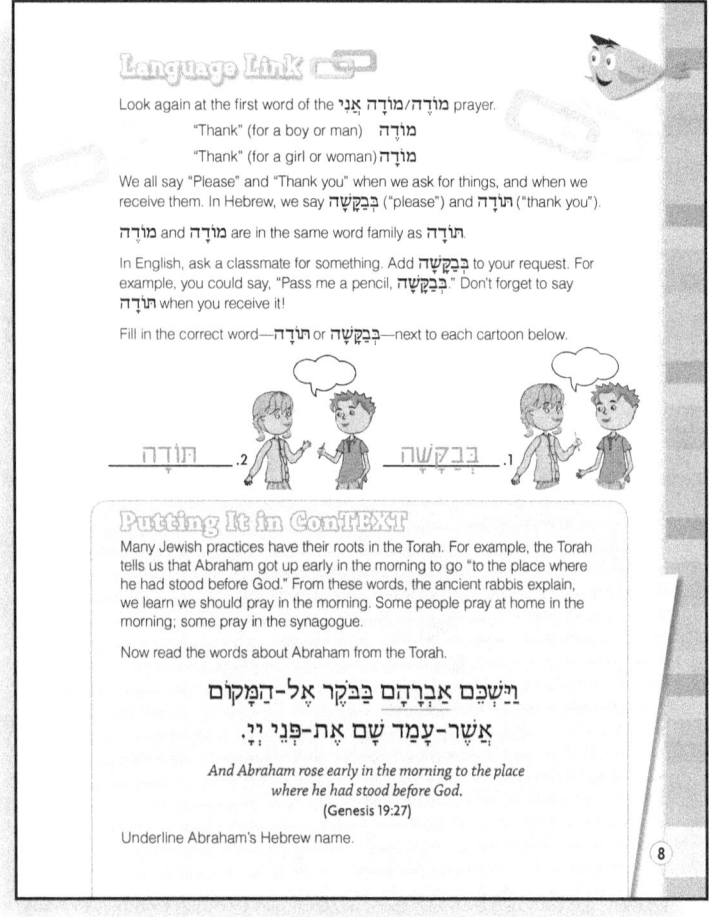

Language Link

Write the following questions on the board: How does a girl say "I thank" in Hebrew? How does a boy say "I thank" in Hebrew? What is a family? What do you think a "word family" is?

Direct students to read "Language Link" with a partner and to jot down answers for the questions that are written on the board.

Call on pairs to share their answers. Write students' definitions for *family* on the board. (*Suggestions may include: a group of people living together; a group of persons that have the same parents; a group of things related by common characteristics*) Guide students to understand that a family is made up of different persons or things that share similar characteristics or a similar history. Ask: What are some characteristics you share with other members of your family? (*Examples may include: we all like music; we all have brown hair; my sister and I both like cookie dough ice cream; my siblings have the same parents and grandparents.*)

Invite the class to chorally read the sixth line in the text with you. Focus students on the phrase "word family" and have students share their definitions for this phrase. (*Suggestions may include: words that have similar letters; words that have similar meanings*)

Encourage students to say בְּבַקָשָׁה and תּוֹדָה in place of "please" and "thank you" when the occasion arises. You may wish to tell your students that בְּבַקָשָׁה also means "You're welcome."

Putting It in ConTEXT

Divide the class into two groups. Direct one group to list occasions when prayers are said at home (*a seder; Friday evening Shabbat dinner; Ḥanukkah; in a sukkah*) and have the second group list times when prayers are recited in synagogue (*on Shabbat morning; during religious school worship services; at a wedding*). Have the groups share their answers with the class.

Ask students to read silently "Putting It in ConTEXT." As a class, chorally read Genesis 19:27 in Hebrew and in English. Have students underline the Hebrew name for Abraham and chorally repeat אַבְרָהָם. Ask students to circle the letters that represent Adonai. If students are not yet familiar with יְיָ explain that יְיָ is an abbreviation for Adonai—whenever we see יְיָ we say "Adonai." Have students put a rectangle around the time of day Abraham went to the place where he had stood before God (early in the morning). Explain that based on the actions of Abraham, our tradition teaches that it is especially praiseworthy to recite prayers and do other mitzvot early in the morning. That is why many people hold a brit milah (a bris) early, at breakfast time.

Digital Application

Ask students who has a pet fish. How often do they feed the fish? How do the fish react? Ask students to complete the "Feed Your Fish" matching activity, located in Ben's room in the digital application, to review new vocabulary, which includes: תּוֹדָה (thank you), מוֹדֶה (thank, for a boy), מוֹדָה (thank, for a girl), and בְּבַקָשָׁה (please).

Partner Talk

Direct students to read and discuss "Partner Talk" with a partner. Encourage students to share their thoughts with the class.

Hand the Doug puppet to a student and ask that student to read Doug's questions. Call on volunteers to respond to the questions. Invite students to describe something kind that a family member has recently done for them or another family member. Have students write a תּוֹדָה card to the family member. A student might, for example, write to an older brother: *Michael,* תּוֹדָה *for DVR'ing my show last night.*

Ask students to describe how they hope the person will feel when they receive the card and how they expect to feel after the person reads it.

Clue to Cyberspace

Have students work with a partner to read the words on the ladder and solve the riddle. (אֲנִי) Ask each student to point to אֲנִי. Each student should point to him or herself.

Digital Application

Challenge students to click on the "Fish Tales Game" in Ben's room to review the Hebrew words for various fruits, which include: תּוּת שָׂדֶה (strawberry), בָּנָנָה (banana), תַּפּוּחַ (apple), and תַּפּוּז (orange). Reinforce the vocabulary of the game during the next class. Hang pictures of the fruit around the classroom. Announce the Hebrew name for each fruit and ask students to stand next to or point to the picture of that fruit.

Questions, Questions

Divide the class into two or three teams. Have the teams take turns answering questions based on מוֹדֶה/מוֹדָה אֲנִי. Questions may include: How does a girl say "thank"? (מוֹדָה); Which ancestor prayed to God early in the morning? (*Abraham*) Where do people recite מוֹדֶה/מוֹדָה אֲנִי? (*at home; in synagogue*) What is the Hebrew word for "living"? (חַי) Each team receives a point for a correct answer. The team with the most points wins.

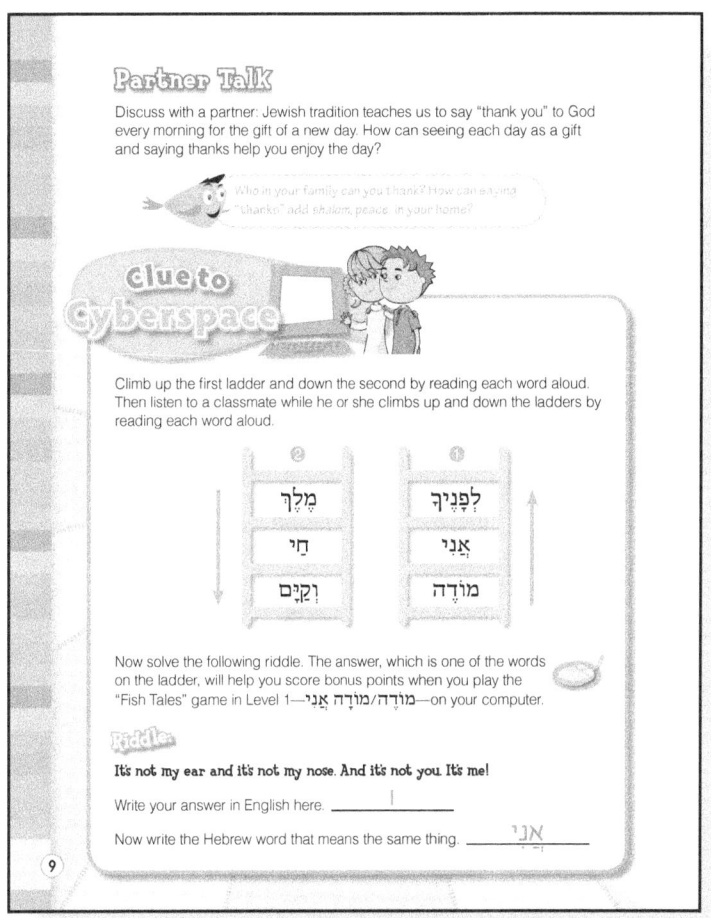

My Own Siddur

Consider having each student create his or her own siddur. Prepare the first page of the prayer book by copying the מוֹדֶה/מוֹדָה אֲנִי prayer onto the bottom of a white sheet of paper. Give each student a copy of this page and instruct the students to draw an illustration that represents this prayer or to write a few sentences that give the prayer personal meaning. As your students study each new prayer they may add a new page to their personal siddur. Keep the sheets in a folder or a narrow three-ring binder, and have students decorate a colorful label for their siddur.

23   CHAPTER 1

Assessment

As students are working on any of the above activities, meet individually with students to assess reading fluency and knowledge of prayer content. Use the Prayer Mastery Assessment Chart on page 15 of the Teacher's Edition to keep track of student progress. You can also assess students' progress online at www.behrmanhouse.com. Click on the blue "Assessment" button at the bottom of the screen, select *Kol Yisrael 1*, and type in your class's serial number to see how students are doing in their digital application. Students can also e-mail their lesson summary to you directly or, if you prefer, they can print out a lesson summary and bring it in to class.

What's Next?

Ask: What are some other things for which we might thank God? (*Answers may include: health; good food; my family*) Tell students that in the next chapter they will learn בְּרָכוֹת, blessings, that are recited to thank God for various foods.

ABOUT THE PRAYER

A בְּרָכָה is a blessing that praises and thanks God for specific spiritual and material gifts.

Reciting a בְּרָכָה shows our appreciation for the world around us. The בְּרָכוֹת—"blessings"—express a direct relationship between the worshiper and God. Tradition teaches that God is both our partner and our ruler.

LEARNING OBJECTIVES

Students will be able to:

- Identify the six words that always appear at the beginning of a blessing.
- Fluently recite blessings said over various foods.
- Define key words found in and related to blessings said over foods.
- Match foods with their appropriate blessings.
- Explain why and when "Amen" is said.

NEW WORDS AND PHRASES

Prayer Words:

blessed, praised	בָּרוּךְ
you (for a boy or man)	אַתָּה
the world	הָעוֹלָם
bread	לֶחֶם
earth	אֲדָמָה
fruit(s)	פְּרִי, פֵּרוֹת
tree	עֵץ

Additional Prayer Words:

Adonai	יְיָ
our God	אֱלֹהֵינוּ
Amen	אָמֵן

Related Words:

blessing(s)	בְּרָכָה, בְּרָכוֹת

INSTRUCTIONAL MATERIALS

Text Pages 10–19
Word Cards #8–18

Digital application: Lesson 2—in the Kitchen (see page 7 for a list of games and activities)

WHERE WE ARE

Dad and Batya use a recipe to remind them of the ingredients and the steps as they bake brownies together. בְּרָכוֹת also serve as reminders. But בְּרָכוֹת are reminders that can help us turn everyday events into meaningful moments.

INTRODUCING THE LESSON

Ask: What are some things you do when you receive a gift? (*Answers may include: say thank you; write a thank you note; show the gift to others*) Why do you take these actions? (*Answers may include: to show appreciation; it's polite; so the person who gave the gift knows I like it*)

According to our tradition, we also receive gifts from God, such as the food we eat. There are special blessings, בְּרָכוֹת, that are recited when we are about to use one of these gifts. That is our way of saying thank you to God for this gift. Tell students that in this lesson they will learn to recite the blessings said over various foods.

INTO THE TEXT

As a class, read aloud the title of the chapter: בְּרָכוֹת. Explain that בְּרָכוֹת is the plural form of בְּרָכָה and that it means "blessings." Write the word בָּרוּךְ on the board. Challenge students to identify the letters that form part of both בְּרָכוֹת and בָּרוּךְ. Remind students that כ looks like this at the end of a word: ךְ. (*Both have the letters ברכ.*) Inform students that traditional blessings begin with the word בָּרוּךְ.

Ask: Why do you think we recite blessings? What are some things you would like to say a blessing for? List students' responses on the board or on a large sheet of paper. Save these lists for reference at the end of the lesson.

Focus students on the illustrations of Dad and Batya baking. Ask: Do you ever bake or cook with a parent, grandparent, brother, or sister? What do you like to bake or cook? What makes this a fun activity? How does this activity bring you closer to the person you are working with?

Direct students to read and discuss the opening paragraph on page 10 with a partner. Partners should share with one another their responses to the questions in the paragraph.

Reading Rounds

Have students read these words and word parts aloud. Vary the reading style. For example, divide the class into two groups: א and ב. Direct group א to read the first word part (בָּ), group ב to read the next word part (רוּךְ), and both groups together to read בָּרוּךְ. Continue reading the remaining word parts and words in this same fashion (group א, then group ב, then groups א and ב together).

Call on individuals or rows of students to read various lines. For example, ask student א or the front row of students to read line 5, and then ask student ב or the second row to read line 2.

Inform students that these words are all part of the traditional Hebrew blessing.

Blessing Formula

Ask students to silently read the opening paragraph. Choose volunteers to write math formulas on the board. (*Simple formulas include: A + 0 = A; B x 1 = B; C x 0 = 0*) Direct all students to write a math formula in their text.

Write the word "formula" on the board. Challenge students to define the word. (*a general fact, rule, or principle usually written with math symbols*) Write this definition of formula under a math formula.

Inform students that they are about to learn a new kind of formula, a blessing formula. Write the word בְּרָכוֹת on the board and two additional meanings for "formula." (*a set form of words for use in a ceremony or ritual; an exact statement of religious faith*)

Display Word Cards 4, 8, 9, 10, 17, and 29. Ask students to identify and define the word they learned in Chapter 1 (מֶלֶךְ = *king*). Present remaining words one at a time. Have students read each word and look up the meaning for Word Cards 8, 9, and 10 on page 14. Invite students to create hand signals or to draw pictures that will help them remember the meaning of each word.

Focus students on the terms יְיָ and אֱלֹהֵינוּ. Remind students that יְיָ is God's name, that it is not read the way it is written, and that it is pronounced "Adonai." Inform students that the word אֱלֹהֵינוּ is not God's name. Rather אֱלֹהֵינוּ means "our God."

Have students silently read the rest of the passage on the blessing formula. Then have the class chorally read the blessing formula with you. Call on students to respond to the closing questions. Ask students to write their own responses in their text. Encourage students to share their responses.

Digital Application

Tell students that at home, before the next class, they should click on בְּרָכוֹת in the digital application and enter the kitchen. There students should click on "Practice Reading בְּרָכוֹת" and review the blessing formula. Challenge students to read the prayer without mistakes. Remind students that how they pronounce the words is more important than how fast they recite them. In the next class, ask students to read the prayer out loud to a partner.

Doug the Fish

Hand the Doug puppet to a student and have him or her read Doug's question. Call on volunteers to respond. Ask: What do you like to bake or cook with your family? What is your favorite cooking job? How do you decide who does which part of the recipe? For fun, have groups of three to five students prepare and present a short skit depicting a family baking brownies. After the presentations, create a class list of ways to cooperate with family members.

Figure the Formula

Have the class chorally read the words from right to left. Direct students to complete the activity individually. Walk around the room to assess how well students are able to put the words in the proper order.

God's Menu

Plan what you will eat today by choosing one type of bread, one vegetable, one fruit, one dessert, and grape juice. Circle your choices. Then practice saying the blessing for each type of food.

1. בָּרוּךְ אַתָּה, יְיָ אֱלֹהֵינוּ, מֶלֶךְ הָעוֹלָם, הַמוֹצִיא לֶחֶם מִן הָאָרֶץ.

Praised are You, Adonai Our God, Ruler of the world, who brings forth bread from the earth.

2. בָּרוּךְ אַתָּה, יְיָ אֱלֹהֵינוּ, מֶלֶךְ הָעוֹלָם, בּוֹרֵא פְּרִי הָאֲדָמָה.

Praised are You, Adonai Our God, Ruler of the world, who creates the fruit of the earth (vegetables).

  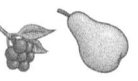

3. בָּרוּךְ אַתָּה, יְיָ אֱלֹהֵינוּ, מֶלֶךְ הָעוֹלָם, בּוֹרֵא פְּרִי הָעֵץ.

Praised are You, Adonai Our God, Ruler of the world, who creates the fruit of the tree.

God's Menu

Have students work in pairs and follow the directions described at the top of page 12.

Direct students to underline the blessing formula each time it appears on these pages. As a class, recite the blessing formula.

Divide the class into five groups. Assign each group the task of teaching one blessing to the rest of the class. Allow five minutes for groups to prepare their lesson. Encourage students to include drawing, acting, singing, and/or dancing. Have all groups present their lessons to the class.

Chanting the בְּרָכוֹת

Teach your students how to chant הַמוֹצִיא and בּוֹרֵא פְּרִי הַגֶּפֶן.

Name That בְּרָכָה

To prepare: Create 24 different game cards by affixing a picture of a food or drawing it on an index card. You may wish to display the Hebrew endings for the five blessings found on pages 12 and 13.

To play: Divide the class into two or three teams. Lay the index cards upside down on a table. Have a member of team א choose an index card. Team א must recite the correct blessing for the food illustrated or named on the card. If team א says the correct blessing, they receive a point. If team א does not say the correct blessing, then team ב must recite the blessing for the food shown or named on the card chosen by team א. Groups continue taking turns until the correct blessings have been recited for each of the cards. Teams win points for each correct blessing. The group with the most points is the winner.

Digital Application

Invite students to play "Unpack the Groceries" in the kitchen. Students put away "groceries" (such as fruit, vegetables, Shabbat wine, and ḥallah) by connecting that food object to the correct blessing, which is written in the correct storage place. For example, students click on a glass bowl that displays the blessing "בּוֹרֵא פְּרִי הָעֵץ." Students then place an apple in the glass bowl.

Invite students to play a similar game the next class. Fill a grocery bag with food. Let students remove one food item and announce which blessing they would say before eating it.

Did You Know?

Direct partners to discuss the question at the bottom of page 13 and to write their responses in their books. Invite students to share their responses with the class. (*Responses may include: because bread is a staple; because bread can be eaten at any meal*) Inform students that according to our tradition bread has a special status. The rabbis of the Talmud teach that we must treat bread with respect (*B'rachot* 50b). Bread also represents the partnership between God and people: God provides the rain and good soil needed for wheat to grow; people harvest and grind the wheat and combine it with other ingredients to make bread.

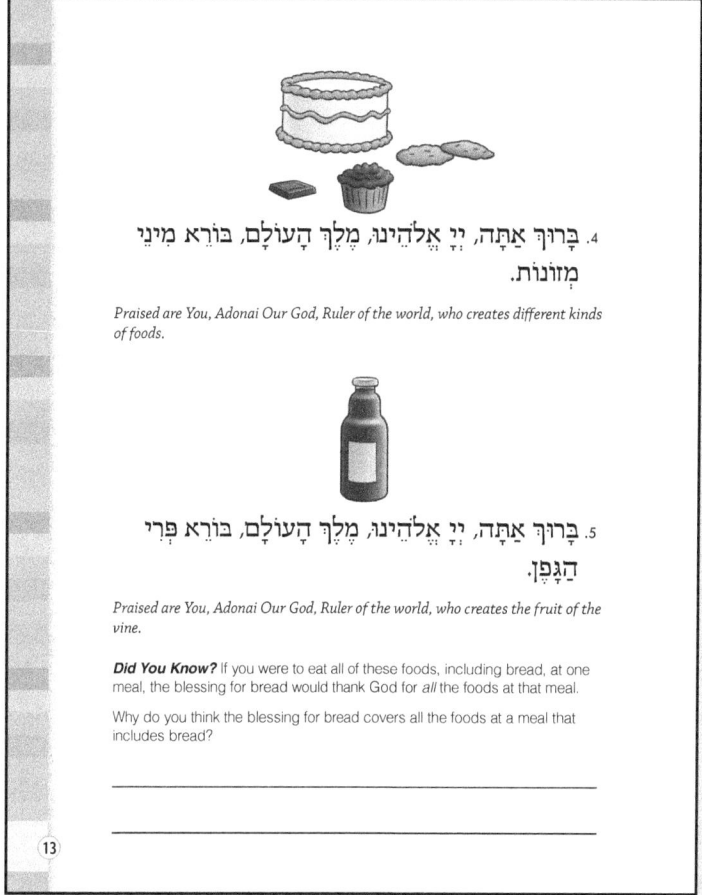

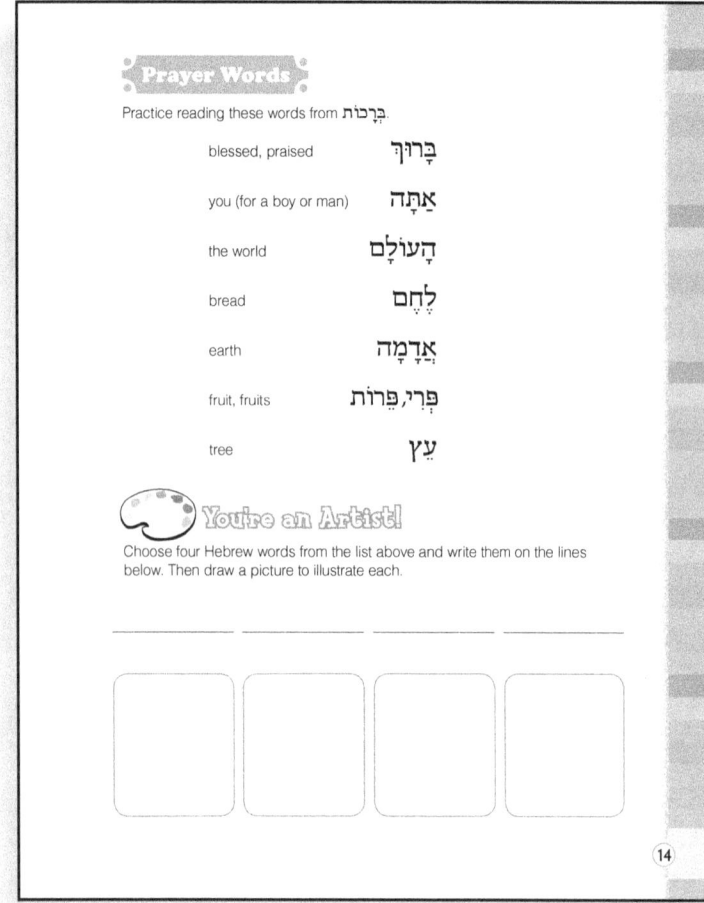

Prayer Words

Display Hebrew Word Cards #1 to 18. Provide a clue about one of the words. For example, say:

"I'm thinking of a word for something that grows on trees." (פְּרִי, פֵּרוֹת) Call on a volunteer to find the Word Card, read it correctly, and say its English meaning. Have that student then provide a clue about another Word Card. Continue until all Word Cards have been reviewed.

Digital Application

In the kitchen, students can play "Prayer Word Concentration" to review new vocabulary, which includes the Hebrew words: עֵץ (tree), הָעוֹלָם (the world), לֶחֶם (bread), מֶלֶךְ (ruler), פְּרִי (fruit), and אַתָּה (you, for a boy). For the next class, create your own Concentration word cards with the same words used in the digital game. Play Concentration in class.

One Hundred Blessings

Inform students that according to the ancient rabbis, each person should say at least one hundred blessings each day (*Menachot* 43b). Many of these blessings are recited in the daily prayers.

Distribute prayer books to your students. Challenge students to count the number of blessings, for example, in the first five pages of the morning service. Remind students that they can identify a blessing by the words בָּרוּךְ אַתָּה יְיָ.

Divide the class into groups of five to six students. Direct each group to create a list of 36 (double חַי) items or events over which a blessing might be recited. Have each group read its list aloud to the class.

You're an Artist!

Allow students to choose four Prayer Words and illustrate each word.

Tally how many students chose each word. Chances are very few students chose to illustrate בָּרוּךְ. If this is so, ask students why they did not choose this word. Use this as an opportunity to discuss the meaning of בָּרוּךְ.

What's Missing

Display Hebrew Word Cards #4, and 8 to 18. Have students close their eyes. Remove one word from the display. Invite students to open their eyes. Call on a student to announce the missing word and its meaning.

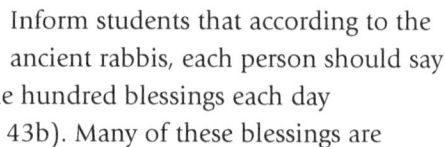

# At the Root

Write the letters כ, ב, and ך on the board. Tell students that these three letters are actually the same letter in different forms. Explain that just as English has different letter forms (upper case and lower case) for the same letter, Hebrew has different letter forms for five letters when they appear at the end of a word. Therefore ך is the form כ takes as a final letter. While ב may sound different from כ and ך—ב, כ, and ך are the same letter (just like the letter "c" in "cat" and "city").

Direct students to silently read "At the Root." Ask: How many letters does a root usually consist of? (3) What is the basic meaning of the root ברך? (bless, praise, knee) Write the words בָּרוּךְ, בֶּרֶךְ, and בְּרָכָה on the board. Circle the three root letters of these words and write ברך below the words. Ask students what they notice about the way the root letters are written. (*No final forms are used; there are no dots in the letters; there are no vowels.*)

To help your students understand Hebrew roots:

- Draw a tree with three roots and four branches.
- Write ברך on the roots—one letter on each root.
- Write בָּרוּךְ on one branch and בֶּרֶךְ on a second branch.

Allow students to complete the activity at the end of "At the Root."

Call on volunteers to write בְּרָכָה and בְּרָכוֹת on the remaining branches of your ברך tree.

A Secret Word

Have students silently read the directions to "A Secret Word." To ensure that students understand the directions, complete the first item as a class. Direct students to complete the remaining items with a partner. Call on volunteers to read the answers aloud as students check and correct their own work.

You may wish to challenge students to name the correct blessing for pizza and for an apple.

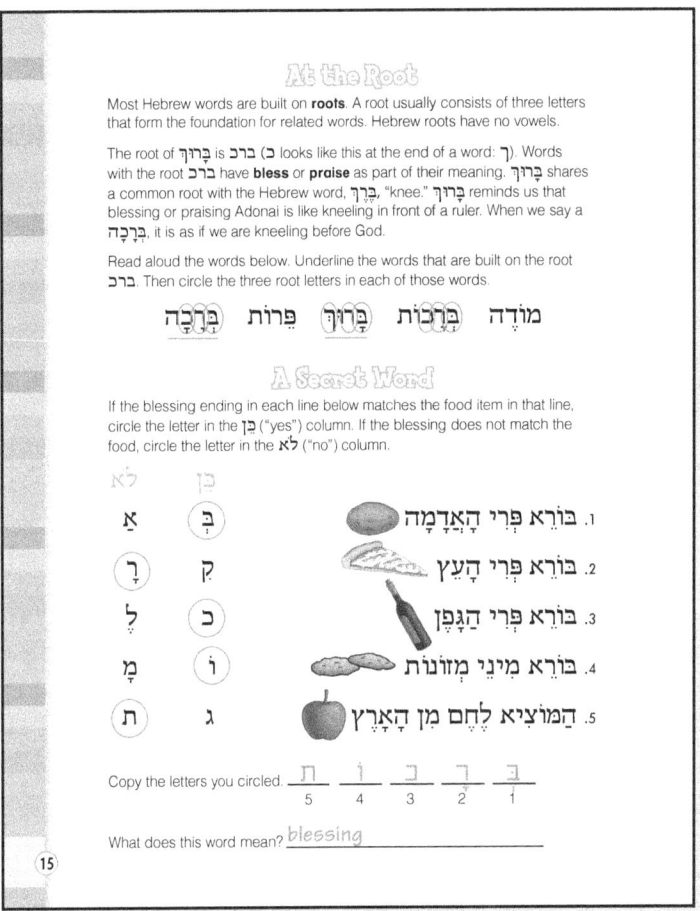

Explain that knowing which blessing to recite over pizza is a bit complicated. According to our tradition, if you eat only one slice of pizza and it is a snack, the blessing is בּוֹרֵא מִינֵי מְזוֹנוֹת, but if you eat more than one slice and it is your meal, the blessing is הַמּוֹצִיא. The blessing for the apple is much simpler: it is always בּוֹרֵא פְּרִי הָעֵץ.

 **Amen!**

Choose three volunteers to read, or dramatize, the parts of Ben, Batya, and Doug.

Direct students to circle the letters in אֵל מֶלֶךְ נֶאֱמָן that are related to the word אָמֵן. Check that students have circled the first letter of each word rather than the final three letters of נֶאֱמָן.

To have the class practice saying Amen:

- Name, or have a student name, a food or drink.
- Call on another student to recite the appropriate blessing.
- Direct (motion with your hands) the entire class to respond Amen.
- Repeat this, varying the foods and drinks. (*Suggested items include: apples, grape juice, ḥallah, potatoes, and cookies.*)

Have students individually complete the challenge at the bottom of page 16. Walk around the room, making sure that students have correctly identified the word נֶאֱמָן. Invite a student to the board to draw a tree representing words with the root אמנ. The tree should include the words נֶאֱמָן and אָמֵן.

Distribute *siddurim* to your students. Direct students to turn to a prayer, such as the Kaddish Shaleim, in which אָמֵן appears multiple times. Have students count the number of times אָמֵן appears. Ask: Why do you think אָמֵן appears more than one time? Why does it appear at the end of a sentence? (*Answers may include: we say אָמֵן at the end of each statement to show that we agree with that statement; there are lots of important statements in the Kaddish.*)

Review the idea that אָמֵן is a way of saying "I or we agree with your בְּרָכָה." Ask: How does saying Amen—we agree with you—help people get along with one another? How can people disagree with one another without risking hurting each other's feelings? (*Suggestions may include: speak to one another respectfully; listen thoughtfully to each other's words.*)

THE PRAYERS OF OUR PEOPLE I • כָּל יִשְׂרָאֵל

Picture Perfect

Have students complete this activity individually. Walk around the room to assess students' recognition of the various blessings. Review the answers as a class.

Divide the class into five groups. Assign each group one of the five food blessings presented in this chapter. Have each group create a collage of the foods over which its blessing is recited. Supply each group with poster board, glue, scissors, magazines, and markers. Direct each group to include the blessing or the ending words of the blessing on the collage.

Photo Op

Challenge students to locate and circle the Hebrew words for All-Bran Flakes. (*Top left box, Hebrew is directly below the English*) Invite students to read some of the words on these cereal boxes. Point out that the Hebrew words on these boxes do not have vowels. Inform students that in Israel most words are written without vowels. To demonstrate how people are able to read Hebrew words without vowels write ברוך אתה (without vowels) on the board and challenge students to read the words aloud. Repeat this with other familiar words until students understand how a person who knows Hebrew can read it without vowels.

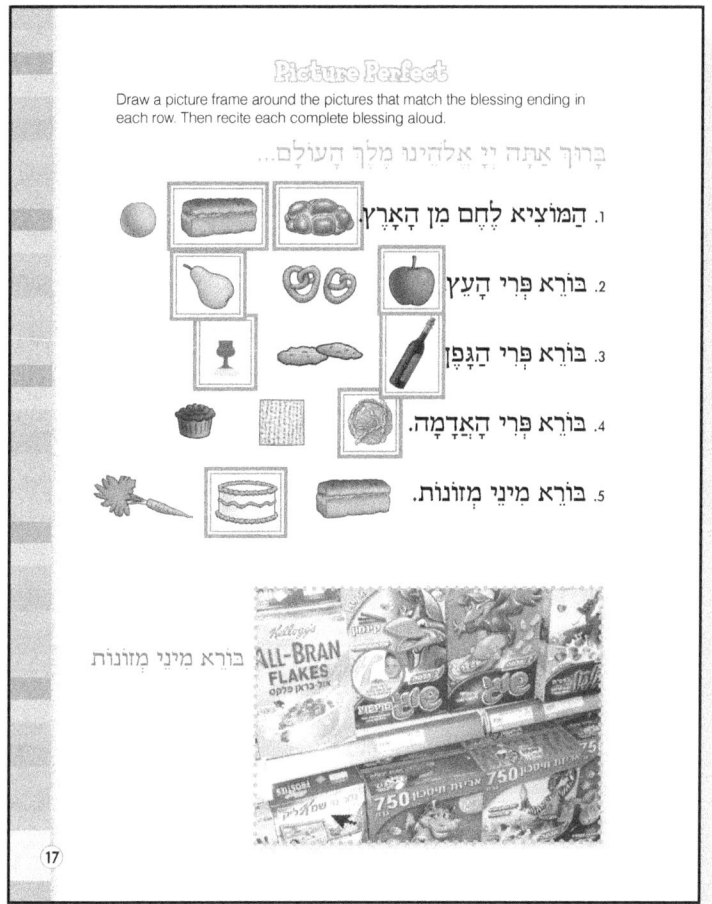

33 CHAPTER 2

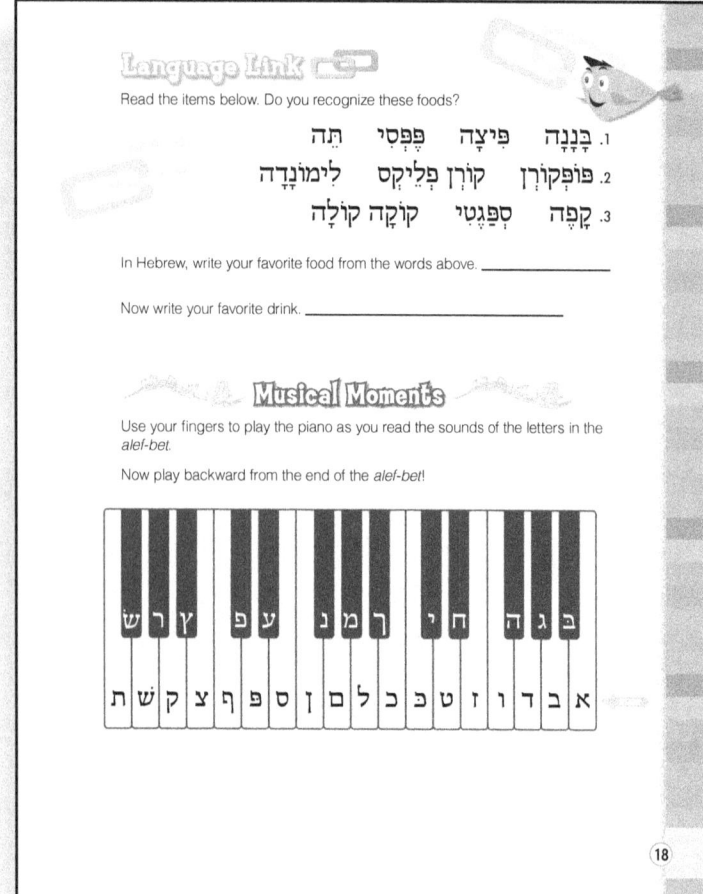

Language Link

Direct students to read "Language Link" with a partner. Have students underline all the foods they recognize. Ask students to record their personal favorite food and drink.

Inform students that there is a blessing over food that they have not yet learned. This blessing is recited over drinks, fish, meat, and cheese.

בָּרוּךְ אַתָּה, יְיָ אֱלֹהֵינוּ, מֶלֶךְ הָעוֹלָם,
שֶׁהַכֹּל נִהְיֶה בִּדְבָרוֹ.

Praised are You, Adonai Our God, Ruler of the world, by whose word all things come into being.

Write the Hebrew ending words of this blessing on the board and invite students to practice saying the blessing.

Blessing Endings

Challenge students to work with a partner and, on a separate sheet of paper, write the blessing ending for each of the foods found in "Language Link." As a class, review each of the foods and its proper blessing. Students receive a point for each correct blessing. The pair with the highest number of points is the winning pair.

בָּנָנָה; פּוֹפְּקוֹרְן: בּוֹרֵא פְּרִי הָאֲדָמָה

פִּיצָה: בּוֹרֵא מִינֵי מְזוֹנוֹת or הַמּוֹצִיא
לֶחֶם מִן הָאָרֶץ

קוֹרְן פְלֵיקְס; סְפָּגֶטִי: בּוֹרֵא מִינֵי מְזוֹנוֹת

פֶּפְּסִי; תֵּה; לִימוֹנָדָה; קָפֶה;
קוֹקָה קוֹלָה: שֶׁהַכֹּל נִהְיֶה בִּדְבָרוֹ

Musical Moments

Invite your class to share "Musical Moments" together. Have all students move their fingers as you say the sounds of the *alef bet* together. For fun, speed up the pace of the "piano playing" as well as the reading of the sounds. Repeat this playing and read the *alef bet* backward.

Invite students to pick a tune, such as "Twinkle, Twinkle," and sing the sounds of the *alef bet*, forward and then backward to that tune.

Fluent Reading

Have students take turns reading all the blessings to a partner. Consider having students time their reading. Challenge students, for example, to read all the blessings on page 19 in less than one minute. Shorten the amount of time to encourage students to read at a quicker pace. Have students compete against their own best time.

Use the reading of these blessings as an informal assessment of your students' reading. Go around the room and listen to individual students read various blessings.

You may choose to inform students that these blessings are said on the following occasions: (1) At the beginning of the evening service (after Bar'chu); (2) After the Torah reading; (3) Near the beginning of the morning service (after Bar'chu); (4) Before reciting the Haftarah; (5) In the middle of both the morning and evening services (after Mi Chamochah, before the Amidah).

Clue to Cyberspace

Have students work with a partner to discover the clue for "Ben's Skateboarding Street Course." (3,100) Remind students to use this clue to score bonus points in the online game. Motivate students about the digital application by asking them if they skateboard. If so, have they ever "ollied" (jumped) while on the skateboard? In the next class, ask students their scores in the skateboarding game. Who scored the highest? Ask that student to offer tips for succeeding at the game.

Review Game

Play one of the Word Card games described on page 11 to review the words and concepts of this chapter. Questions might include: What is the fifth word of the blessing formula? What is the blessing said when eating an orange?

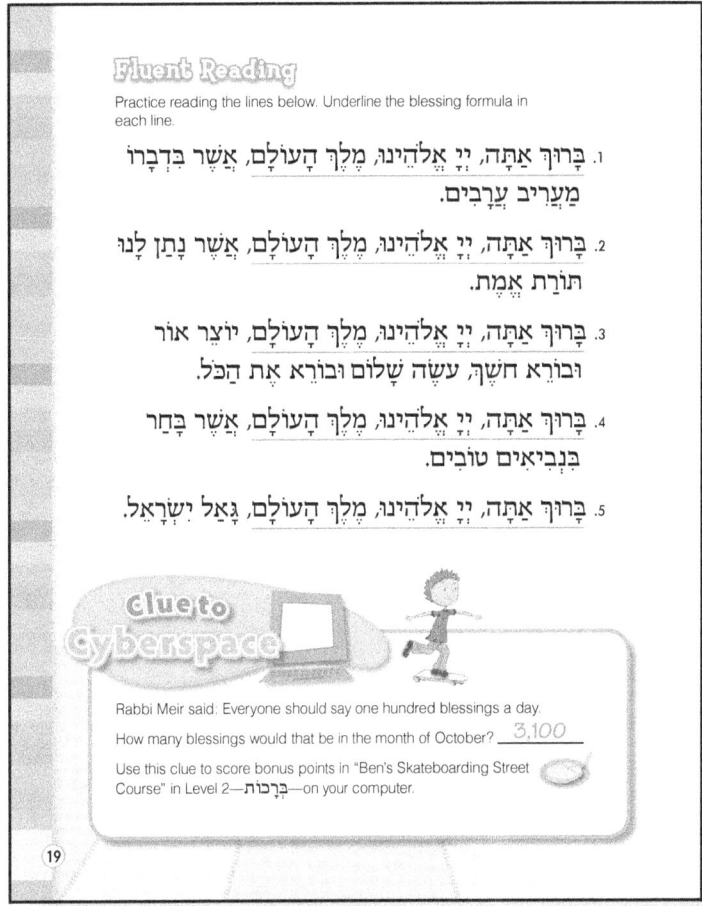

My Own Siddur

If students are creating their own siddur, prepare a page by copying the five food blessings, leaving space for illustrations, onto a white sheet of paper. Give each student a copy of this page, and instruct students to draw an illustration that represents each blessing or to write a few sentences that give the blessings personal meaning. Store this page with the מוֹדָה/מוֹדֶה אֲנִי personal siddur page.

Assessment

Assess students' reading fluency and knowledge of prayer content as you did in Chapter 1, using the chart on page 15 of the Teacher's Edition to track progress. You can also assess students' progress online at www.behrmanhouse.com. Click on the blue Assessment button at the bottom of the screen, select *Kol Yisrael 1*, and type in your class's serial number to see how all students are doing in their digital application.

What's Next?

Ask: After studying this chapter, why do you think we say blessings? Aside from foods and drinks, what else might we say blessings over? List students' responses on the board. Take out the list that you compiled at the beginning of this chapter (see page 26) and compare it to the new list. (Save the lists for use in Chapter 3.) Inform students that in the next chapter they will learn about another kind of blessing: they will learn בְּרָכוֹת that are recited before performing various מִצְוֹת.

בִּרְכוֹת שֶׁל מִצְוָה 3

ABOUT THE PRAYER

Blessings of mitzvah—בִּרְכוֹת שֶׁל מִצְוָה—remind us that we are fulfilling מִצְוֹת, commandments in the Torah. These commandments lead us to actions that help us fulfill the greater commandment to be a holy people.

LEARNING OBJECTIVES

Students will be able to:

- Define the word מִצְוָה.
- Identify the ten words that comprise the blessing formula for בִּרְכוֹת שֶׁל מִצְוָה.
- Fluently recite the blessings said when affixing a mezuzah and when studying Torah.
- Define key words found in and related to blessings when affixing a mezuzah and when studying Torah.
- Determine when וֹ is pronounced as "oh" and when it is pronounced as "voh."
- Identify the root letters קדש and recognize that words with this root have "holy" or "set apart" as part of their meaning.

NEW WORDS AND PHRASES

Prayer Words:

makes us holy	קִדְּשָׁנוּ
with God's commandments	בְּמִצְוֹתָיו
and commands us	וְצִוָּנוּ
to engage	לַעֲסוֹק
in the words of	בְּדִבְרֵי
Torah	תּוֹרָה
to affix	לִקְבֹּעַ
mezuzah	מְזוּזָה

Related Words:

commandment(s)	מִצְוָה, מִצְוֹת
blessing(s) over the commandments	בְּרָכָה, בִּרְכוֹת שֶׁל מִצְוָה
who, that	אֲשֶׁר

INSTRUCTIONAL MATERIALS

Text Pages 20–27
Word Cards #19–29

Digital application: Lesson 3—in the Study (see page 7 for a list of games and activities)

WHERE WE ARE

Batya and Ben are doing homework in the study. Batya helps Ben with his homework, and he thanks her for doing what he refers to as "a mitzvah."

INTRODUCING THE LESSON

Display the lists students created in Lesson 2 with occasions when blessings might be recited.

Challenge students to identify which of these actions are part of a Jewish ritual or have to do with studying Jewish texts. Put a check next to all the actions that have a בְּרָכָה שֶׁל מִצְוָה associated with them. (*Suggestions may include: lighting Ḥanukkah candles or lighting Shabbat candles*) If you are not certain, check with your rabbi, cantor, or education director.

Explain that there are blessings recited over specific מִצְוֹת, actions that, according to our tradition, God has commanded us to perform. Inform students that in the upcoming chapters they will learn blessings that are recited before performing specific מִצְוֹת, such as blowing the shofar and putting up a mezuzah.

INTO THE TEXT

Focus students' attention on the illustration of Batya and Ben. Call on students to describe the illustration. Ask: Why do you think Batya and Ben are studying in the same room? Where do you like to do your reading and studying? When do you read or study with your family?

Direct students to read and discuss page 20 with a partner. Ask: When have you done a good deed for someone or when has another person done a good deed for you? How did you feel?

Explain to students the difference between ritual מִצְוֹת and those between people. Make sure students understand that these are all commandments written in the Torah.

Direct students to complete the questions at the bottom of page 20, then have students share their responses with the class. Ask: What מִצְוָה have you recently performed for someone in your family? How does performing מִצְוֹת for family members help your family to get along and appreciate one another?

On the board, draw a vertical line to create two columns. Ask students to name or describe various מִצְוֹת. List ritual מִצְוֹת, such as lighting Ḥanukkah candles, saying prayers, or reciting Kiddush, in one column. List non-ritual מִצְוֹת—those that could be described as good deeds, such as visiting the sick or helping a friend with his or her homework—in the second column.

After listing at least three מִצְוֹת in each column, ask students to describe the difference between the two types of מִצְוֹת.

Point out that, in general, there is no blessing recited for a mitzvah that is done for the sake of another person.

Inform students that in this chapter they will learn several blessings that are recited before performing specific מִצְוֹת, such as lighting Shabbat candles.

THE PRAYERS OF OUR PEOPLE I • כָּל יִשְׂרָאֵל

Reading Rounds

Write וֹ on the board. Call on a volunteer to read its sound (oh). Explain that at times וֹ has the sound "vo." Direct students to read the introduction to "Reading Rounds" with a partner.

Using two different colored pieces of chalk or dry-erase markers, write the word בְּמִצְוֹתָיו on the board. Write all consonants (במצותיו) in one color and all vowels (ְ ִ ְ ָ) in a second color.

Explain that consonants and vowels generally alternate in Hebrew words. This means that we rarely see or pronounce two vowels in a row. Since the צ has a vowel under it, the ו must be a consonant, and וֹ has to be the consonant-vowel combination "vo."

Write the word מַצוֹת (plural of מַצָּה), again using one color for consonants (מצת) and a second color for vowels (וֹ ַ). Students will see that since there is no vowel under the צ, the וֹ must be the vowel "oh."

Have students practice reading the words and word parts with a partner. Next, ask the class to read all five lines chorally. For variety, divide the class into two groups, א and ב. Direct group א to read the word and word parts in line 1. Have group ב echo each word or word part after it is read by group א. For line 2, switch roles. Have group ב read the word or word parts and group א echo it.

Word Find

Allow students to find and circle the words מִצְוֹת and תּוֹדָה. Challenge students to find and translate other words in these strings of letters. Words found in the first string: פְּרִי (fruit), בְּרָכָה (blessing), אֲדָמָה (earth), לוֹמֵד (learns), מוֹדֶה (thank), מֶלֶךְ (king). Words found in the second string: הַמּוֹצִיא (who brings forth), בְּבַקָּשָׁה (please), אֲנִי (I), חַי (living), שַׁבָּת (Shabbat), בָּרוּךְ (praised, blessed).

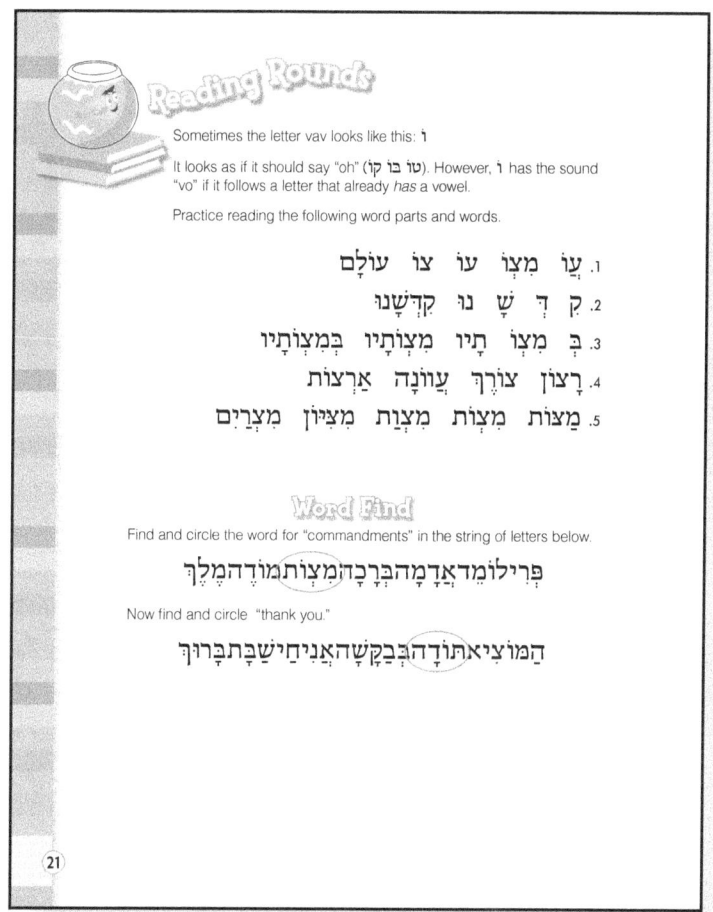

Direct students to draw lines separating each of the words in the strings of letters. As a class, chorally read the words contained in each of the strings.

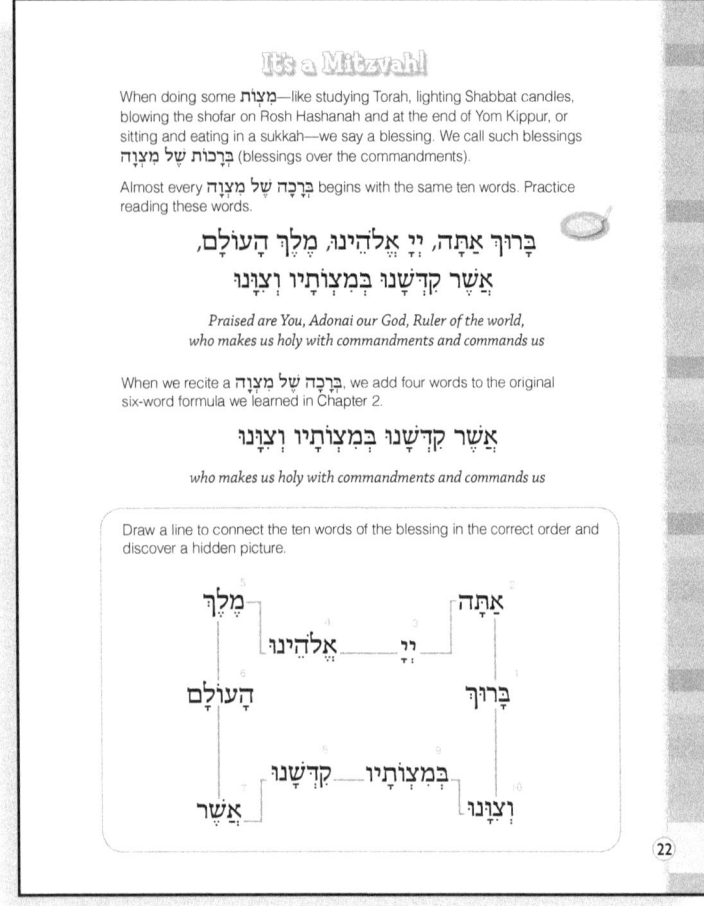

when moving into a new house) If there is a מְזוּזָה in your classroom, ask students to locate it.

Hidden Picture

Have students connect the words at the bottom of the page to discover the hidden Torah. Invite the class to chorally read the words in their proper order while tracing the lines with their fingers.

It's a Mitzvah!

Have partners read the first paragraph describing בְּרָכוֹת שֶׁל מִצְוָה. Ask: When are some occasions that we say a בְּרָכָה שֶׁל מִצְוָה? (*studying Torah; lighting Shabbat candles; blowing the shofar; sitting in a sukkah*) How many words are in the opening formula of a בְּרָכָה שֶׁל מִצְוָה? (*10*)

Direct students to chorally read the ten words, in Hebrew and then in English, that begin a בְּרָכָה שֶׁל מִצְוָה. Ask students questions to help them understand the meaning of these words. Sample questions include: According to the formula of a בְּרָכָה שֶׁל מִצְוָה, whom does God command? (*us*); What does God make us? (*holy*); How does God make us holy? (*with commandments*). Tell students that the class will soon take a closer look at the meaning of "holy" and the root letters קדש.

Introduce students to the new words from the בְּרָכָה שֶׁל מִצְוָה formula. Present Word Cards #19, 20, 21, and 29 one at a time. Give students the meaning of אֲשֶׁר, and direct students to page 26 for the meanings of the other words. Place these four cards plus Word Cards #4, 8, 9, 10, 16, and 17 in mixed order on the board ledge. Invite a student to unscramble the word cards and to place the words in the order of a בְּרָכָה שֶׁל מִצְוָה.

Choose ten students to come to the front of the room. Give each of the students one card. Challenge students to arrange themselves in the בְּרָכָה שֶׁל מִצְוָה word order. From the class's perspective, the student holding בָּרוּךְ should be standing on the far right, and the student holding וְצִוָּנוּ should be on the far left.

Digital Application

Tell students that at home, before the next class, they should click on בְּרָכוֹת שֶׁל מִצְוָה at the bottom of the screen to enter the study. Once in the study, students should click on "Practice Reading Mitzvot" and locate the blessing recited when hanging a מְזוּזָה. In the next class, ask students when they might recite this blessing. (*Answers may include:*

THE PRAYERS OF OUR PEOPLE I • כָּל יִשְׂרָאֵל   40

 **Blessing Circle**

Read the first sentence of "Blessing Circle" aloud to the class. Pause as students form a circle. Continue reading one sentence at a time, pausing as students follow the directions. As an alternative, pick a student to act as "teacher" and to get the activity underway. After students have completed reciting the ten-word formula once, encourage them to repeat it, gaining speed and fluency with each repetition.

Vary the activity by having each person recite two words. The first person says בָּרוּךְ אַתָּה and so on.

 **At the Root**

Call on a volunteer to explain how most Hebrew words are built on root letters. If you have a word tree with the root letters ברכ, focus students on this display. Inform students that in בְּרָכוֹת שֶׁל מִצְוָה they encounter another root: קדשׁ. Direct students to silently read the first two sentences of "At the Root." Ask: What word in the בְּרָכוֹת שֶׁל מִצְוָה formula has the root letters קדשׁ? (קִדְּשָׁנוּ) What is the meaning of words with the root letters קדשׁ? (*holy; set apart*)

Direct students to circle the root letters in each of the Hebrew words. Ask: Which of these words or phrases is what we call: the ancient Temple in Jerusalem? (בֵּית הַמִּקְדָּשׁ); the prayer recited over wine? (קִדּוּשׁ); where the Torah is kept? (אֲרוֹן קֹדֶשׁ).

Have students individually write why they think the Jewish marriage ceremony has "holy" as its root. Invite students to share their responses with the class. (*Responses may include: a married couple has entered a relationship that sets them apart from other people; a married couple's relationship with one another is holy.*)

Direct students to complete the exercise at the bottom of the page and to read each prayer sentence aloud with a partner.

Word Tree

Create a tree based on the root קדשׁ, as you did for ברכ. Include the five words and phrases found in "At the Root."

41 CHAPTER 3

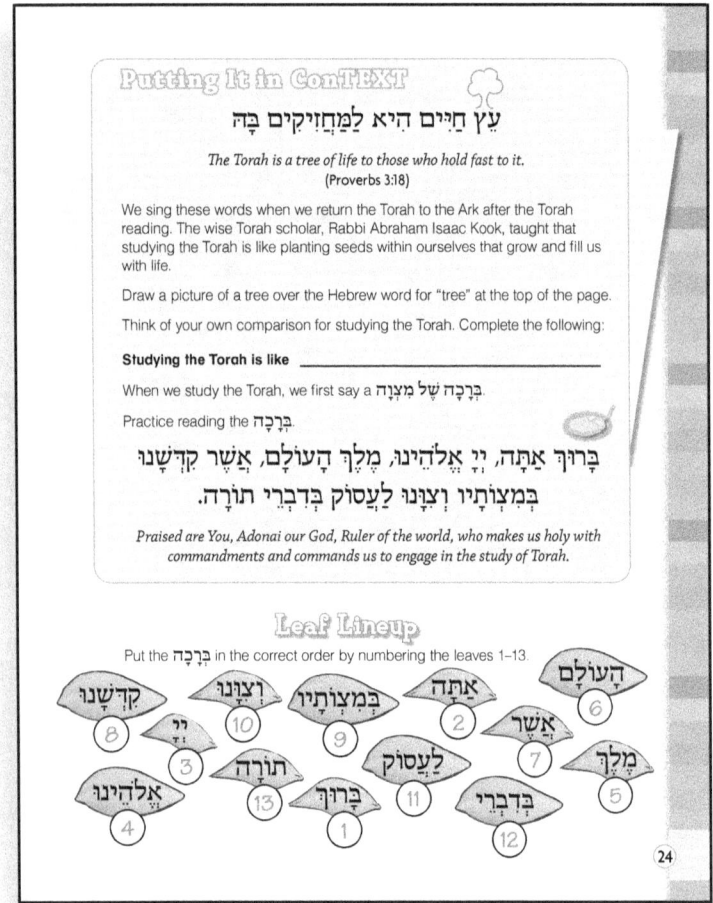

Leaf Lineup

Have students complete the exercise individually. Invite volunteers to the front of the room to say numbers from one to thirteen. Direct the class to respond by chorally reading the word with that number. For example, if the student says "six," all students read aloud הָעוֹלָם. Tell students to correct their own work and to put a check next to each number that has been called.

Putting It in ConTEXT

As a class, chorally read the Hebrew words of עֵץ חַיִּים. Focus students on the phrase "The Torah is a tree of life," and ask students to explain what the phrase means to them. (*Responses may include: the Torah is strong like a tree; the laws of the Torah tell us how to live our lives; the Torah gives us wonderful things all our life.*) Call on a volunteer to explain the meaning of "to those who hold fast to it." Pantomime holding tightly onto a tree, and invite students to do the same. Ask: What happens if we let go? (*Responses may include: We wouldn't have the Torah; we could lose our knowledge of our history and our laws.*)

Direct students to read the first two paragraphs with a partner. (You may wish to tell students that Rabbi Kook was born in Europe in 1865. He later moved to Israel, where he became the first chief rabbi of Israel.) Allow students to write and then share their own comparisons for studying Torah. Give each student a sheet of construction paper. Direct students to write their comparison at the bottom of the page and to illustrate what they have written. Display these illustrations on a bulletin board.

Invite the music teacher or cantor to teach your students to sing עֵץ חַיִּים to one or more tunes.

Present Word Cards #22, 23, and 24, and direct students to refer to page 26 to learn their meanings.

Explain that since it is a מִצְוָה to study Torah, we say a בְּרָכָה שֶׁל מִצְוָה before studying Torah.

As a class, chorally read the blessing, first in English and then in Hebrew, recited before studying Torah. Ask: Why do you think it is a מִצְוָה to study Torah? (*Answers may include: we are reminded that it is important to learn about our history, about being Jewish, and about Jewish laws.*)

Digital Application

In the study, students should click on "Practice Reading Mitzvot" to review the blessing recited before studying Torah.

Tic-Tac-Toe

Invite students to play Tic-Tac-Toe with a partner.

Challenge students to identify different words on the Tic-Tac-Toe board. Questions may include: What is the third word in the blessing formula? (יְיָ) Which word means "tree"? (עֵץ)

Digital Application

In the study, students should click on "Tic-Tac-Toe" to review the new vocabulary, such as מִצְוָה (commandment) and אֲשֶׁר (who). Some of the vocabulary is reviewed from previous chapters, such as עֵץ (tree) and מֶלֶךְ (ruler). In the next class, divide students into two teams and play Tic-Tac-Toe using words from Chapters 1–3. Ask students if it is easier to play against the computer or fellow students. Why or why not? Which is more fun?

Putting It in ConTEXT

Bring the parchment from a mezuzah to show your class. (Your education director or rabbi may have a parchment available.) Explain that the parchment is prepared from the skin of a kosher animal. A scribe, known as a *sofer*, copies words taken from two sections of the Torah onto the parchment. The Sh'ma and V'ahavta (Deuteronomy 6:4-9) make up the first section. The second passage is comprised of Deuteronomy 11:13-21. Have your students locate the words of the Sh'ma on the parchment.

As a class, read the Hebrew and then the English for Deuteronomy 6:9. Challenge students to find these words on the mezuzah parchment.

If there is a mezuzah on your classroom door, ask students to describe how the mezuzah is positioned. If there is no mezuzah, demonstrate where one would be placed (*on the right side as you enter the room, about shoulder height for an adult, in a "5 minutes-to-5 o'clock" angle*)

Present Word Cards #25 and 26. Direct students to page 26 to learn their meanings.

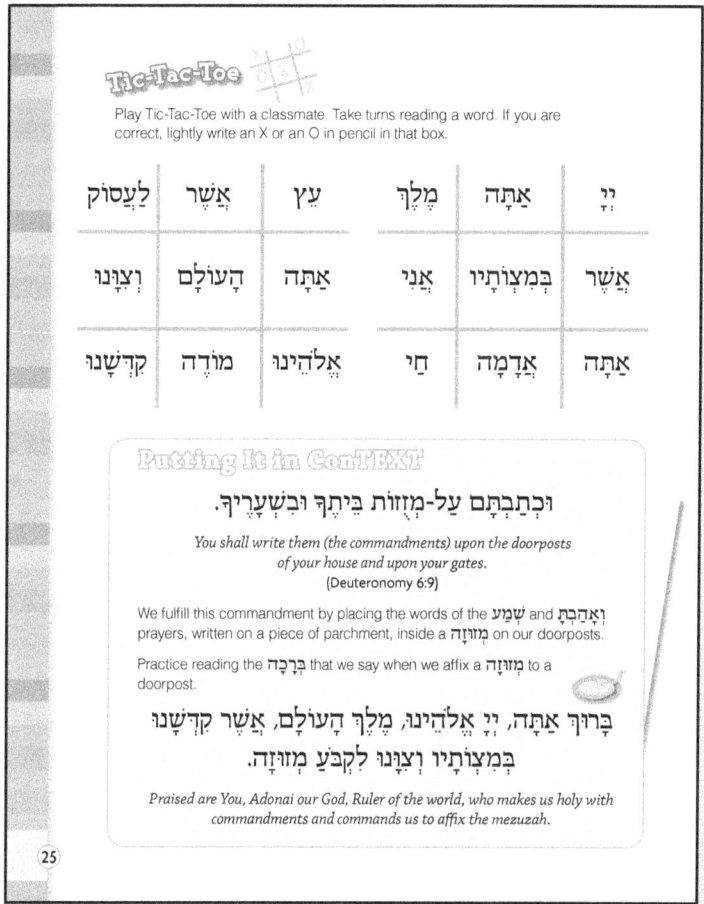

As a class, read aloud—in Hebrew and in English—the blessing recited when affixing a mezuzah.

Explain that when a person moves into a new home it is a mitzvah to hang a mezuzah. There is a special ceremony for hanging the mezuzah for a new home called a חֲנֻכַּת הַבַּיִת, which means dedication of the house. Challenge students to identify the word that is very similar to the name of one of our holidays. (חֲנֻכָּה) Tell students that people often invite friends and family to celebrate with them at the חֲנֻכַּת הַבַּיִת.

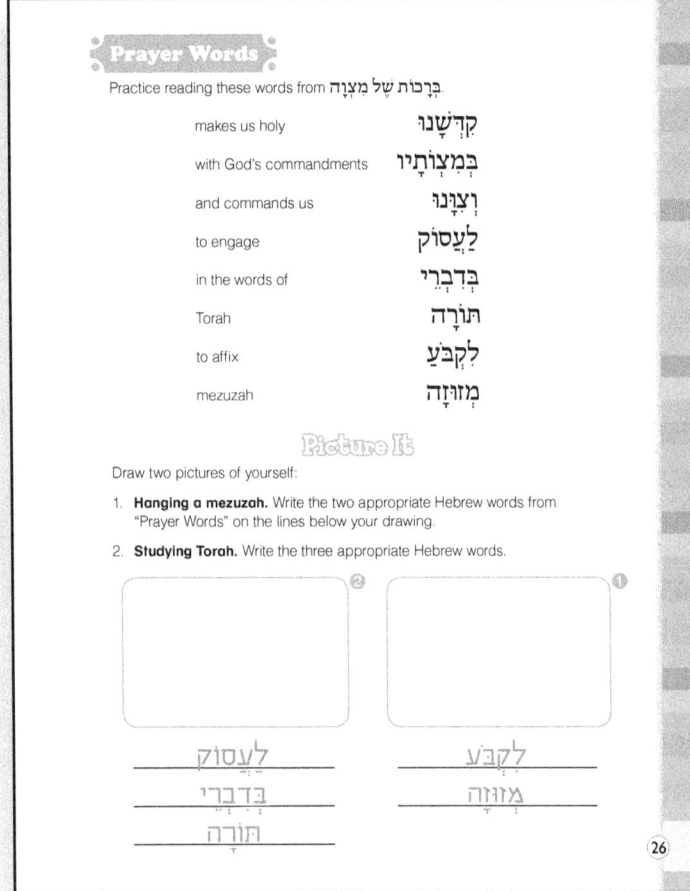

Prayer Words

Play מַה הַמִּלָּה?—What's the Word? using Word Cards #19 through 26. Have a student choose a Word Card. The other students must guess what the word is, based on questions they ask. They can ask any question that will help them guess the word.

Sample questions:

- Is the word part of the blessing formula?
- Is the word recited when we hang a mezuzah?
- Does the word have five letters?

The class may ask as many questions as they like, but each student may guess only once. The student who guesses correctly receives a point and chooses the next word. The student with the most points at the end of eight rounds is the winner.

For an even greater challenge, play this game using Word Cards #1 through 29.

Digital Application

In the study, students can play the "Arrange Your Books" matching activity to review vocabulary, which includes the Hebrew words בְּמִצְוֺתָיו (with God's commandments), קִדְּשָׁנוּ (makes us holy), וְצִוָּנוּ (and commands us), and אֲשֶׁר (who). Before students complete the activity at home, ask them if their families have any Jewish books on their shelves. What kind? What type of book might have the blessings in it? (*siddur*)

Picture It

Allow students to complete the activity. Use this as an opportunity to informally assess students' knowledge of these two blessings and their ability to write Hebrew letters.

THE PRAYERS OF OUR PEOPLE I • כָּל יִשְׂרָאֵל

Book Search

As a class, read aloud from right to left the Hebrew words on each book. Challenge students to complete this activity individually. Walk around the room to check students' recognition and understanding of these words.

Clue to Cyberspace

Direct students to work with a partner to determine which statements are true and which are false. Add up the numbers for a clue. (4) Call on a volunteer to change the false statement into a true statement. (הַמּוֹצִיא *thanks God for bread.*)

Digital Application

Ask students if they have ever played ping pong before. If so, when? Ask students to click on the image of the ping pong ball on Batya's desk in the study to play the "Ping Pong" game, which reviews the vocabulary of בְּרָכוֹת שֶׁל מִצְוָה. Remind students to use the clue (4) to gain bonus points. Challenge students to see who can score the highest. Ask the high scorer if he or she has ever played ping pong in real life.

Ask students to complete Review 1 on their computer to assess what they have learned in Lessons 1 through 3. In the next class, divide students into two teams and challenge teams to write and ask their own review questions. (*Some questions might include: What blessing do you say over chocolate cake?* בּוֹרֵא מִינֵי מְזוֹנוֹת; *Who says* מוֹדֶה אֲנִי *and who says* מוֹדָה אֲנִי*? boy says* מוֹדֶה אֲנִי *and a girl says* מוֹדָה אֲנִי; *What blessing do you say when hanging a* מְזוּזָה*?* לִקְבֹּעַ מְזוּזָה...)

Concentration

Review students' knowledge of prayers and blessings from chapters 1 through 3. Create ten pairs of matching cards, twenty cards in total. Suggestions for pairs:

- The ending of the blessing said when affixing a mezuzah: לִקְבֹּעַ מְזוּזָה

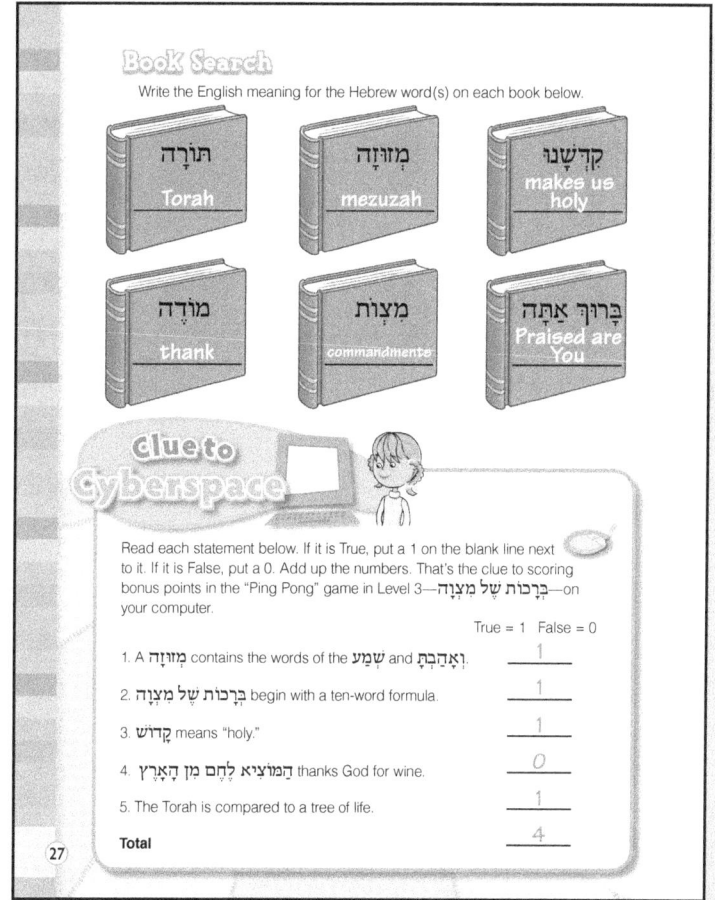

- The first three words of the blessing formula: בָּרוּךְ אַתָּה יְיָ
- The way a boy says "I give thanks…": מוֹדֶה אֲנִי

Play a game of Concentration following the directions on page 12.

My Own Siddur

If students are creating their own siddur, prepare a page by copying the two new blessings, leaving space for illustrations, onto a white sheet of paper. Give each student a copy of this page, and instruct the students to draw an illustration that represents each blessing or to write a few sentences that give the blessings personal meaning. Store this page with their other personal siddur pages.

Assessment

As students are working on any of the above activities, meet individually with students to assess reading fluency and knowledge of prayer content. Use the chart on page 15 of the Teacher's Edition to keep track of students' progress. You can also assess students' progress online at www.behrmanhouse.com. Click on the blue Assessment button at the bottom of the screen, select *Kol Yisrael 1*, and type in your class's serial number to see how all students are doing in their digital application.

What's Next?

Challenge students to list with a partner seven things they know about Shabbat. Call on pairs to read their lists. Record on the board any rituals mentioned, such as lighting Shabbat candles or eating ḥallah. Congratulate your students on knowing so much about Shabbat, and tell them that in the next chapter they will study בְּרָכוֹת that are recited on Shabbat when performing rituals such as those listed on the board.

בִּרְכוֹת שֶׁל שַׁבָּת 4

ABOUT THE PRAYER

At the conclusion of the six days of creation, God "blessed the seventh day and called it holy" (Genesis 2:3). Every Friday night we sanctify Shabbat with a special ceremony: we recite blessings over candles, over wine, and over bread. Shabbat is a day set aside for rest from our weekday activities—it is the sanctification of time.

LEARNING OBJECTIVES

Students will be able to:

- Recite fluently three blessings said at the Friday night table.
- Explain why we cover our eyes when lighting Shabbat candles.
- Define key words found in and related to Friday night blessings.
- Give examples of ways to create *sh'lom bayit*.
- Name different occasions when ritual candles are lit.

NEW WORDS AND PHRASES

Prayer Words:

candle	נֵר
who creates	בּוֹרֵא
the vine	הַגֶּפֶן
who brings forth	הַמּוֹצִיא

Related Words:

bridegroom	חָתָן
bride	כַּלָּה
tzedakah	צְדָקָה
remember	זָכוֹר
observe	שָׁמוֹר
peace, hello, good-bye	שָׁלוֹם
a peaceful Shabbat	שַׁבָּת שָׁלוֹם
peace at home	שְׁלוֹם בַּיִת

INSTRUCTIONAL MATERIALS

Text Pages 28–39
Word Cards #30–42

Digital application: Lesson 4—Dining room (see page 7 for a list of games and activities)

WHERE WE ARE

It is Friday evening and we join Ben, Batya, and their parents in the dining room as they are about to welcome Shabbat.

INTRODUCING THE LESSON

The Story of Creation

Read the story of creation with the class (Genesis 1–2:4; or *The Explorer's Bible, Volume I*, pages 9–13). Invite a volunteer to list on the board what God does each of the days. (*On days 1 through 6 God creates the following: 1: light; 2: heavens; 3: earth and vegetation; 4: sun, moon, stars; 5: fish and birds; 6: land animals and people; on day 7 God rested.*) Ask: How was the seventh day different from the first six days of creation? (*God did not work on the seventh day; God put aside the seventh day to rest; God declared the seventh day to be holy.*) What does it mean to be holy? (*set apart; having to do with God*) What does it mean that the seventh day is holy? (*Responses may include: it is unlike any other day of the week; it is a day that is special and has special rituals.*)

Explain that in this lesson students will learn בְּרָכוֹת for this holy day, Shabbat.

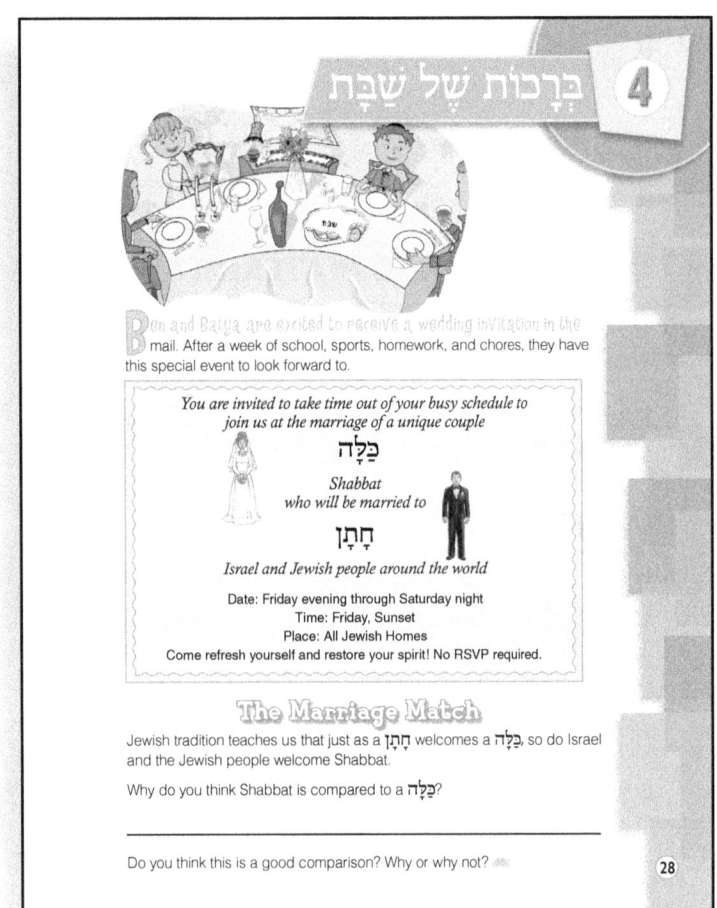

INTO THE TEXT

Call on students to describe the illustration of Batya and Ben's family celebrating Shabbat. Ask questions such as: What is Batya doing? (*lighting Shabbat candles*) What is the father doing? (*reciting Kiddush*) What special items are on the table? (*flowers, wine, ḥallah*) Why do you think Batya and Ben are smiling?

Explain that in Judaism Shabbat is compared to a bride, and the Jewish people to a bridegroom. Ask: In what ways is the joining together of Shabbat and the Jewish people like a marriage? (*Answers may include: like a husband and wife, Shabbat and the Jewish people need each other; like a husband and wife, Shabbat and the Jewish people are joined together; just as we celebrate a marriage, we celebrate Shabbat.*)

Call on a volunteer to do a dramatic reading of the "marriage invitation."

The Marriage Match

Have students read the sentence and write responses to the questions independently. (*Responses may include: because they are both beautiful; because they are both loved*) Invite students to share their thoughts with the class.

THE PRAYERS OF OUR PEOPLE I • כָּל יִשְׂרָאֵל

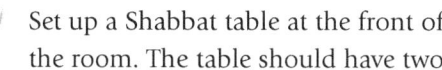

Welcoming Shabbat

Set up a Shabbat table at the front of the room. The table should have two candlesticks with candles, a glass of grape juice, and two ḥallahs or ḥallah rolls. Ask: What is special about the table setting? (*Responses may include: candlesticks with Shabbat candles; two ḥallot*)

Read the opening lines on page 29. Invite students to read the first blessing aloud with you, in Hebrew and in English. Ask: Which commandment do we fulfill after we recite this blessing? (*lighting Shabbat candles*) Direct students to read the blessing twice to a partner. After students have practiced reading, demonstrate how candles are lit. Have all students stand and copy you as you pretend to light the candles, wave your hands three times back and forth from the candles to you, and then cover your eyes. As a class recite the blessing over the candles.

Invite students to be seated. Call on a volunteer to read the description for the blessing over the wine or grape juice. As a class, read the blessing aloud in Hebrew and then in English. Direct each student to read the blessing once to a partner. Students learned this blessing in Chapter 2 and should be able to read it fluently. If possible, give each student a small glass of grape juice. Ask students to recite the blessing with you, and then drink the juice.

Call on a volunteer to read aloud the description of the blessing recited over the ḥallah. Chorally read the blessing in Hebrew and in English. Remind students that they have already learned this blessing in Chapter 2. Direct students to read the blessing once to a partner. As a class recite the blessing then give each student a piece of ḥallah.

Allow students to complete the question at the bottom of the page and to check their answer with a partner.

Teach, or invite the cantor or music specialist to teach, the tune for each of these Shabbat blessings.

Digital application

Tell students that at home, before the next class, they should click on בְּרָכוֹת שֶׁל שַׁבָּת at the bottom of the screen to enter the dining room. Once in the dining room, students can click on the wine cup to practice reading the three בְּרָכוֹת שֶׁל שַׁבָּת. You might also invite students to practice these blessings with their parents.

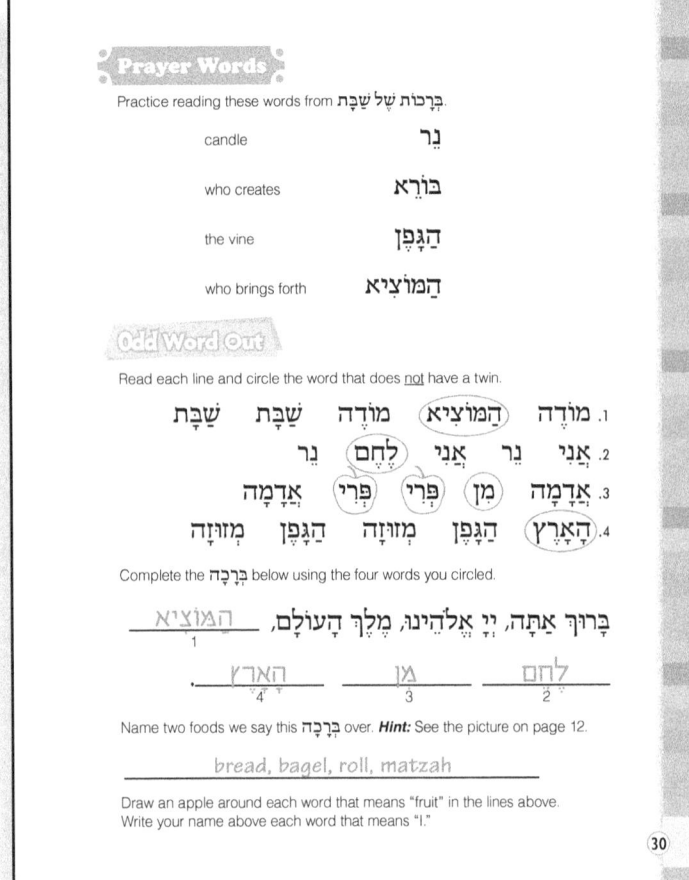

English meaning of the word הַגֶּפֶן. (Note: Do not ask for the meaning of מִן or הָאָרֶץ as students have not yet learned their meanings.)

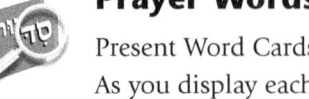

Prayer Words

Present Word Cards #30 through 33. As you display each card, call on students to read the word in Hebrew and to say its English meaning.

Invite a student to the front of the room. Direct the student to stand in front of you, facing the class. Standing behind the student, show the rest of the class one of the words. Challenge the student standing in front of you to guess which word is being displayed by asking the class "yes" and "no" (or כֵּן and לֹא) questions about the word. Once the student has guessed the word and said its meaning, invite another student to guess a second word.

As an alternative, display the four words and have students play charades while the rest of the class guesses the word. For example, for הַגֶּפֶן, a student may twist and curl his or her body.

Digital Application

In the dining room, students can click on the hutch to review Shabbat and general vocabulary, which includes מֶלֶךְ (ruler), לֶחֶם (bread), מְזוּזָה (mezuzah), פְּרִי (fruit), נֵר (candle), and הַגֶּפֶן (the vine). In the next class, list these six words on the board. Ask students which of these words are recited in the Shabbat blessings? (מֶלֶךְ, לֶחֶם, פְּרִי, נֵר, הַגֶּפֶן)

Odd Word Out

As a class, chorally read line 1. Direct students to individually identify and circle the word that does not have a twin. Repeat this with the remaining three lines. Have students work with partners to complete the blessing and the activities at the bottom of the page. Some foods that students may list are rolls, ḥallah, or matzah.

As a class, sing the מוֹצִיא blessing.

Word Review

Choose one of the games on pages 11 through 13 and play a quick game reviewing these words. Challenges may include: Recite a blessing that includes a word from line 3; read all of line 2 fluently (no errors); say the

THE PRAYERS OF OUR PEOPLE I • כָּל יִשְׂרָאֵל 50

What's Missing?

Display Word Cards #11, 30, 31, 32, and 33 on the ledge of the board. Direct students to put their heads down and close their eyes. Remove one of the cards. Challenge students to say the Hebrew and the English for the missing card. Have the first student who pronounces the correct word place the missing card back on the ledge and then remove another card while the other students have their eyes closed. Continue until all cards have been played.

Encourage students to complete this page individually. Walk around the room to assess how well students fill in the missing Hebrew words and correctly illustrate the item associated with each blessing.

A Tale about Shabbat

Share the following story from Midrash:

When Rabbi Yehudah entertained Antoninus (who was probably the Roman emperor from 138–161 CE) on a Shabbat, Rabbi Yehudah served him cold dishes, which Antoninus ate and liked. On another occasion, Rabbi Yehudah entertained Antoninus on a weekday, when he served him hot dishes. Antoninus said, "I found the cold dishes tastier than the hot dishes." Rabbi Yehuda responded, "The hot dishes are missing one seasoning." Antoninus asked, "Can there be something that we do not have in the emperor's pantry?" Rabbi Yehuda answered, "The hot dishes lack Shabbat. Does your pantry have Shabbat?"

(adapted from *Genesis Rabbah* 11:4)

Ask: What are some of the "ingredients" of Shabbat that might have made cold dishes special and tasty? (*Suggestions might include: Shabbat is a day of rest—people can take time to enjoy their food; Shabbat is a day of celebration—people may enjoy their food more when they are happy; Shabbat is a day spent with family and friends—people may enjoy food more when they know the person who prepared it for them.*) Do you have any special foods you like to eat on Shabbat or other holidays?

Picture Match

Ask students to read the directions and complete the activity with a partner. Have partners take turns reading each line aloud as they look for the matching words. To review, call on pairs of students to read aloud a line and to then repeat the matching word. For example, students called upon to read line 1 would read all of line 1 and then repeat the word פְּרִי. Direct students to check and correct their work.

Giving Tzedakah

Inform students that according to Jewish tradition there are eight levels of giving tzedakah. These were written down by the great Jewish philosopher, Moses Maimonides, who was born in Spain around 1135.

Divide the class into groups of four to five students. Copy only the right two columns of the list below and distribute it to all students. (Note: Maimonides' order is presented in the far left column.) Direct groups to number the levels from the best (1), in their opinion, to the least (8) recommended way to give tzedakah. Groups should be able to explain why they chose the order they are suggesting.

Invite a representative from each group to come forward, read their listing of least to most recommended ways to give tzedakah, and explain their reasons for this order.

Compare Maimonides' order with the orders suggested by the class groups.

	Number the levels of giving tzedakah from the best, in your opinion, to the least recommended way
5	When someone gives directly to the poor without being asked to do so.
3	When the person who gives knows who is receiving the tzedakah, but the receiver does not know who gave the tzedakah.
1	When someone helps a person before they become poor by offering a gift or a loan, or by helping them find employment so that the person does not become dependent on others.
7	When someone gives less than he should, but is happy to give.
4	When the receiver of the tzedakah knows who gave the tzedakah, but the person who gave does not know the receiver.
6	When someone gives directly to the poor after being asked for the donation.
8	When someone gives, but does not really want to.
2	When the person who gives does not know who receives the tzedakah, and the person who receives it does not know who gave it.

THE PRAYERS OF OUR PEOPLE I • כָּל יִשְׂרָאֵל

Let There Be Light

Direct students to silently read the first paragraph. Ask: Do we generally say a בְּרָכָה before or after we do the action? (*before*) As a class, chorally read the blessing recited before affixing a mezuzah. Direct students to complete the sentence in the text that follows the blessing. Chorally read the blessing recited before studying Torah and direct students to complete the next sentence in their text.

Name other actions we do, and challenge students to recite the blessing said before each of the actions. For example, ask, "What do we say before eating a carrot?" Students respond, בָּרוּךְ אַתָּה...בּוֹרֵא פְּרִי הָאֲדָמָה.

Present the following problem to your students: Since we generally say a blessing before we do the act, would you expect to say the blessing over the Shabbat candles before or after lighting the Shabbat candles? (*Students will most likely say "before."*) But if Shabbat begins the moment we say the בְּרָכָה over the candles, and traditional Jewish law prohibits lighting a fire on Shabbat, how are we able to light Shabbat candles? Allow students to give suggestions. Some students may already know that we light the candles before we say the blessing and cover our eyes as we say the blessing.

Direct students to read the description of how Shabbat candles are lit and recite the blessing with a partner. Ask: Why do we cover our eyes while reciting the blessing over the Shabbat candles? (*So that we won't begin to enjoy the candlelight until after we have said the blessing.*) Invite students to read the blessing with you chorally. Challenge students to stand, cover their eyes, and recite the blessing with you by heart.

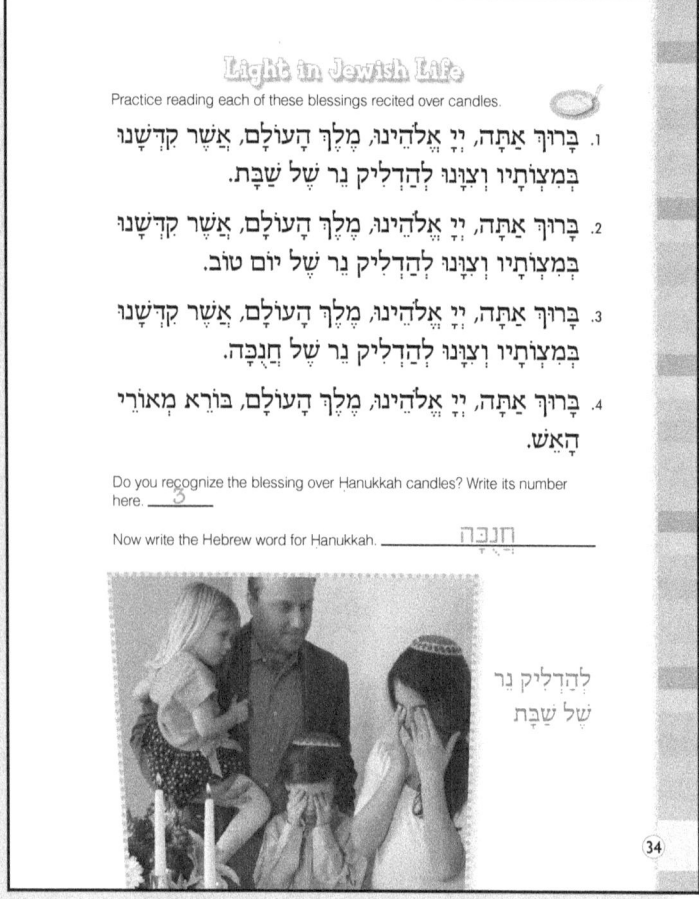

asking: How do you feel when you see the Shabbat candles? What do you think about when you see lit Shabbat candles?

Light in Jewish Life

As a class chorally read each blessing. Divide the class into three groups. Have each group read one blessing. Group 1 reads blessing 1, group 2 reads blessing 2, group 3 reads blessing 3, group 1 reads blessing 4, and so on. Continue until all groups have read each of the four blessings.

Direct students to individually complete the exercises below the blessings.

Challenge students to identify when each of these blessings is recited. (*1: Friday evening; 2: the evening of a holiday, such as Passover; 3: Ḥanukkah; 4: Saturday night at Havdalah, at the close of Shabbat and the beginning of a new week*)

Digital Application

In the dining room, students can click on the matches to light the candles and then practice reading the blessings said over various ritual candles. In the next class, ask students to name other times in the Jewish year when we light candles. (*Answers may include: on Ḥanukkah, at the Passover seder, on a yahrtzeit*)

Reading Fluency

Challenge students to read words and phrases from these blessings by asking questions such as:

1. In which word is ו pronounced "vo"? (בְּמִצְוֹתָיו)

2. Which of the blessings on page 34 is not a בְּרָכָה שֶׁל מִצְוָה? (בּוֹרֵא מְאוֹרֵי הָאֵשׁ, #4)

3. Which four words help us to identify a בְּרָכָה שֶׁל מִצְוָה? (אֲשֶׁר קִדְּשָׁנוּ בְּמִצְוֹתָיו וְצִוָּנוּ)

Photo Op

Ask: If this photo had sound, what do you think you would hear? (*the blessing over Shabbat candles*) What do you think the people will say after the blessing? (*Suggestions may include: Shabbat Shalom; Amen; let's eat!*) Invite students to chorally recite the blessing together. Call on a volunteer to explain why the two people are covering their eyes. Consider

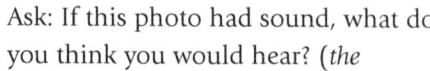

Picture Match

As a class, create a list of ways that candles are used in Jewish rituals. (*Answers may include: Shabbat candles, holiday candles, havdalah candles*) On the board write: נֵר תָּמִיד. Ask students to define נֵר. (*candle*) Explain that נֵר also means lamp or light. Take students to the sanctuary and have them locate the נֵר תָּמִיד. Tell students that נֵר תָּמִיד means "eternal light" and that it is always lit. In most synagogues the light is electric; in some places it is lit with burning oil. The נֵר תָּמִיד reminds us of the menorah that stood in the Holy Temple and had a continuously burning light. It also symbolizes God's presence. Another interpretation is that the נֵר תָּמִיד symbolizes the light of Torah.

Return to the classroom and focus students on page 35. Have students identify the נֵר תָּמִיד and the *ḥanukkiyah*. Write the word *yahrtzeit* on the board. Explain to students that the *yahrtzeit* candle, lit in memory of a loved one who has died, burns for at least twenty-four hours. We light the *yahrtzeit* candle on the anniversary of that person's death and at sundown before certain holidays (Pesaḥ, Shavuot, Sukkot, and Yom Kippur) during which we say Yizkor, the memorial prayer service.

Write on the board: A commandment is a lamp, and Torah is light. (כִּי נֵר מִצְוָה וְתוֹרָה אוֹר)

Inform students that this is written in the Bible in the Book of Proverbs (6:23). As a class, discuss ways that commandments and Torah are lights. (*Suggestions may include: they help us to see things better; they help us to find the right path.*)

A Story

Direct students to silently read the first paragraph. Ask: According to the story, why do we cover the ḥallah? (*So the ḥallah won't feel hurt that the candles and wine were blessed before the ḥallah.*) Do you think this is a true story? (*No!*) What can we learn from the story? (*Suggestions may include: Don't put someone in an embarrassing situation; we should be sensitive to others' feelings.*)

Ask students, individually or with a partner, to write their own explanation about why we light

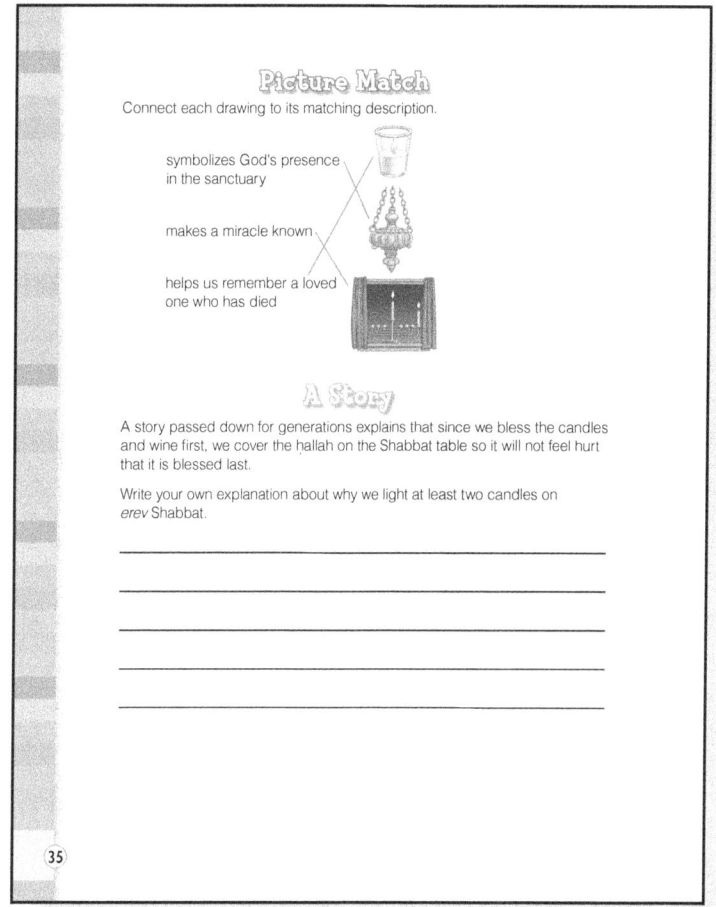

at least two Shabbat candles. Encourage them to write a story that has a moral. Invite students to share their stories with the class. Consider compiling these stories and sending them home to share with families. Or post the stories on a bulletin board in the hall with the heading "Why Two Candles?—Our Students' Interpretations."

An Opening Toast

Read the opening question and invite students to respond. Encourage students to describe or give examples of what people say in toasts and in speeches honoring someone.

Have students read the next paragraph with a partner. Ask: How many בְּרָכוֹת do we say over wine on Shabbat evening? (*2*); Which בְּרָכָה sets Shabbat apart and helps make it holy? (*the second בְּרָכָה*); Which בְּרָכָה is the blessing over the wine or grape juice? (*the first בְּרָכָה*)

As a class, practice reading the בְּרָכָה over wine. Challenge students to identify various Hebrew words in the בְּרָכָה. For example, ask: Which Hebrew word means "fruit of"? (פְּרִי)

Allow students to fill in the answer at the bottom of the page. Have students share their answers. (*Possible answers are: Rosh Hashanah; Sukkot; Sh'mini Atzeret; Simḥat Torah; Pesaḥ; Shavuot*)

Photo Op

Call on volunteers to describe the photo. Focus students on the cup the boy is holding. Write *hiddur mitzvah* (הִדּוּר מִצְוָה) on the board. Explain that *hiddur mitzvah* means that we make the act of performing a mitzvah pleasing and beautiful. Ask: How is this Kiddush cup an example of *hiddur mitzvah*? (*It is a beautiful silver cup, not just an ordinary drinking cup.*) As a class, brainstorm other examples of *hiddur mitzvah*. (*Suggestions may include: decorating a sukkah, a silver menorah, a painted mezuzah, a pretty tablecloth for the Shabbat table*)

Ask students to imagine themselves practicing *hiddur mitzvah*. Give students markers and construction paper. Invite students to illustrate and write a short sentence describing how they could practice *hiddur mitzvah*. A student might, for example, draw herself blowing a long, curvy shofar and write, "Miriam is blowing a very large and beautiful shofar." Hang students' illustrations on the bulletin board. Display the term הִדּוּר מִצְוָה on the board.

THE PRAYERS OF OUR PEOPLE I • כָּל יִשְׂרָאֵל   56

The Matter of Manna

Ask students to read "The Matter of Manna" with a partner.

Read Exodus 16:11–16, 21–26, and 27–36 out loud to the class. Alternatively, read the summary of Exodus 15:23–16:35 found on page 11 of *The Explorer's Bible, Volume 2* (Behrman House).

Ask: Why is it important for us "to remember the Exodus from Egypt and the double portion of manna"? (*Suggestions may include: to remind us of God's miracles described in the Torah; to remind us what God did for the Jewish people*)

Digital Application

In the dining room, students can click on the hallah to review the מוֹצִיא blessing. The exercise challenges students to recognize and organize the words of the מוֹצִיא.

Spot the Difference

Direct students to read the Hebrew words aloud to a partner and to complete the activity. As a class, chorally read the lists of words.

Challenge students to identify other prayer words that begin with הַ or הָ. (*Answers may include:* הַגֶּפֶן, הָאֲדָמָה, הָאָרֶץ)

Hebrew Baseball

Play Hebrew Baseball on page 12 to review the meaning of הַ. Challenge students by asking the meaning of words such as הַמֶּלֶךְ, הָאֲדָמָה, and הַמְזוּזָה.

57   CHAPTER 4

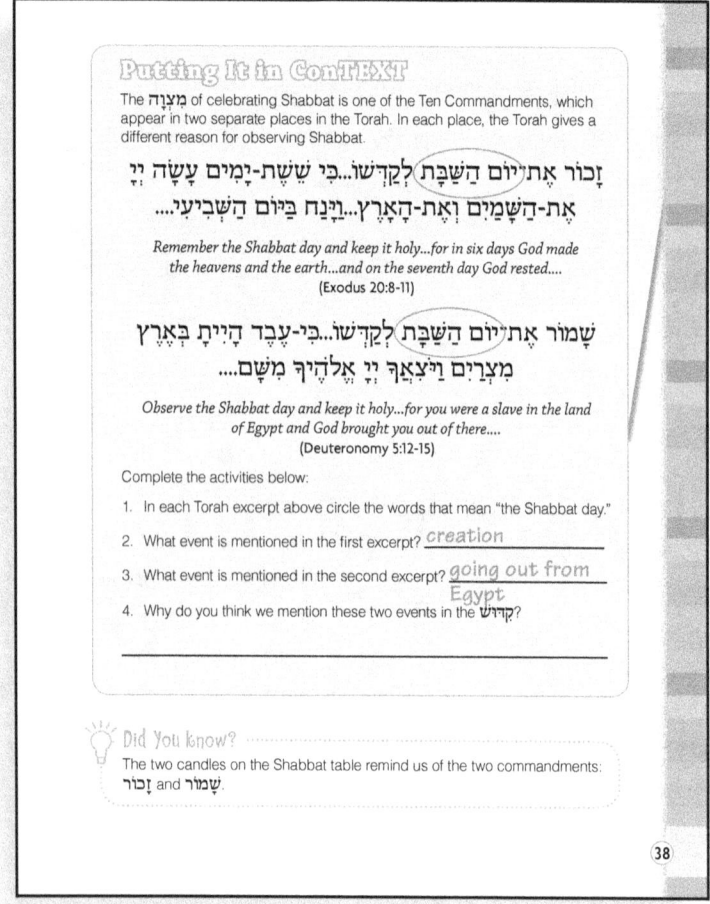

Putting It in ConTEXT

Direct students to silently read the first paragraph. Ask: How many times does the Ten Commandments appear in the Torah? (*twice*) What is one difference between the two sets of commandments? (*They give different reasons for observing Shabbat.*)

As a class, chorally read the Hebrew and English for Exodus 20:8–11. Ask: According to this verse, what two things do we need to do in regard to Shabbat? (*Remember it and keep it holy.*) Why must we remember Shabbat and keep it holy? (*Because, according to the Torah, God rested on Shabbat, the seventh day.*)

Invite students to join you in reading Deuteronomy 5:12–15 in Hebrew and English. Ask: According to this verse, what two things do we need to do in regard to Shabbat? (*Observe Shabbat and keep it holy.*) How is the verse from Deuteronomy the same as Exodus? (*Both say to keep Shabbat holy.*) How are they different? (*Deuteronomy says to "observe" Shabbat; Exodus says to "remember" Shabbat.*) According to Deuteronomy, why must we observe Shabbat and keep it holy? (*Because we were slaves in Egypt and God freed us from Egypt.*) Why wouldn't we be able to observe Shabbat if we were still slaves? (*Slaves must work all the time; they are not free to worship when and where they please.*) What does God freeing us from slavery have to do with observing Shabbat? (*We were able to observe Shabbat because God freed us from slavery.*)

Direct students to individually complete the activities and to compare their answers with a classmate. As a class, have students share their responses to the last question. (*Responses may include: they are two of the greatest events in Jewish history; each set of the Ten Commandments has a specific commandment about Shabbat, so we include both.*)

Did You Know?

Write the words שָׁמוֹר and זָכוֹר on the board. Challenge students to give their English meanings. (*Observe and remember*) Ask: What is the difference between observing and remembering something? (*Suggestions may include: Observing requires action; remembering only requires thinking. Observing may require following rules; remembering is up to the individual.*)

Distribute *siddurim* and have students turn to the first verse of לְכָה דוֹדִי. Challenge students to find the words that mean "Observe and remember." (שָׁמוֹר וְזָכוֹר) Teach, or invite the cantor or music specialist to teach, the first verse of לְכָה דוֹדִי. You may wish to tell your students that this verse is based on the traditional view that when God gave the Ten Commandments, God caused the Children of Israel to hear the words שָׁמוֹר and זָכוֹר at the exact same time. (Shevuot 20b) Challenge students to find the word for bride (כַּלָּה) in לְכָה דוֹדִי. (*refrain and last verse*)

THE PRAYERS OF OUR PEOPLE I • כָּל יִשְׂרָאֵל

At the Root
Write the word שָׁלוֹם on the board. Encourage students to guess its three root letters. Circle the letters שלם.

Direct students to silently read the paragraphs about the root letters שלמ. Allow students to individually write how "wholeness," "completeness," and "peace" are connected. Invite students to share their explanations with the class. (*Suggestions may include: When something is complete or whole it can be perfect—peace is a perfect time or a perfect state. When something is complete or whole, we don't have to do anything to fix it—we can feel peaceful.*)

Language Link
Have students read "Language Link" with a partner. Ask: How do we wish each other a peaceful Shabbat? (שַׁבָּת שָׁלוֹם) What is the Hebrew for "peace in the home"? (שָׁלוֹם בַּיִת) Allow students to write how they can help create שָׁלוֹם בַּיִת in their own homes. Invite students to share their responses.

Divide the class into groups of three. Direct each group to create a short skit that demonstrates a way to help achieve שָׁלוֹם בַּיִת. Have groups present their skits to the class.

Doug the Fish
Invite a student to use the Doug puppet and ask Doug's question. Have that student call on volunteers to respond. (*Suggestions may include: Good morning; nice to see you; can I help you?*)

Clue to Cyberspace
Have students work with a partner to discover the clue. (2)

Digital Application
In the dining room, students can click on the image of the skateboard to play "Batya's Vert Skate" game and review vocabulary, which includes the Hebrew words אַבָּא (father), אִמָּא (mother), סַבָּא (grandfather), סַבְתָּא (grandmother), יֶלֶד (boy), יַלְדָּה (girl), חָתָן (groom), and כַּלָּה

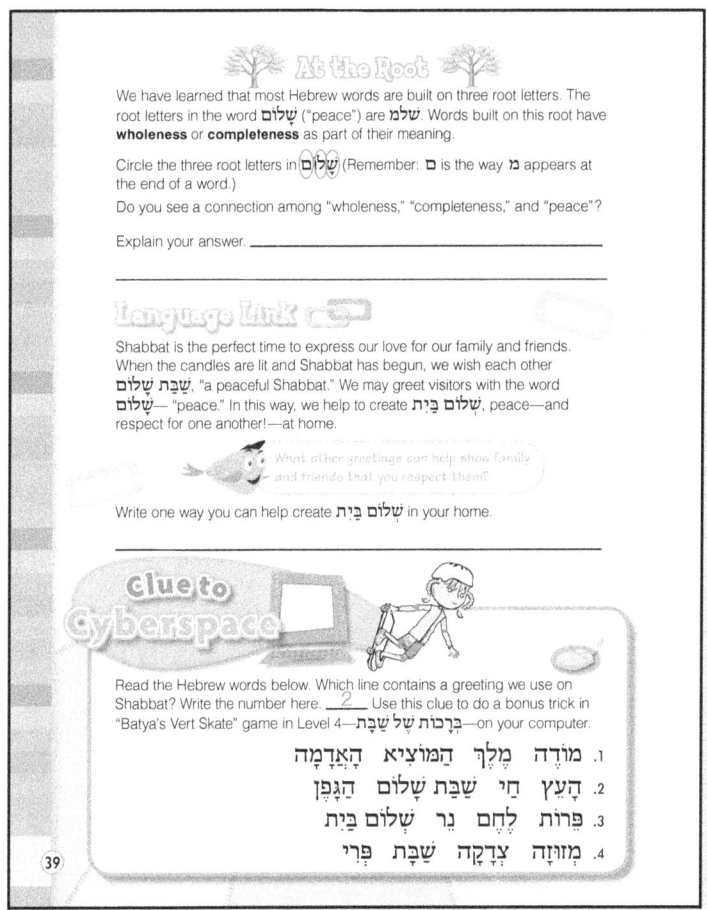

(bride). Remind students to use their clue (2) to do a bonus trick in the game. In the next class, ask students who received the highest score. Which Hebrew word was the hardest to recognize? Which was the easiest?

My Own Siddur
If students are creating their own siddur, prepare a page by copying the blessing for lighting Shabbat candles. Students can illustrate or write sentences as they have done for previous blessings.

Assessment

As students are working on any of the above activities, meet individually with them to assess reading fluency and knowledge of prayer content. You can mark students' progress using the assessment chart and check their progress online at www.behrmanhouse.com.

What's Next?

Refer students to page 36, and ask: How many בְּרָכוֹת are recited on Shabbat and holidays before drinking wine or grape juice?(*two*) What is the difference between the two blessings? (*The first is the blessing over wine or grape juice; the second sets the day apart and helps to make it holy.*)

Inform students that in the next chapter they will learn the second blessing and will soon know the entire קִדּוּשׁ.

ABOUT THE PRAYER

The Hebrew word קִדוּשׁ means "sanctification," "making holy," or "setting apart." A commandment in the Torah tells us to "remember the Sabbath day and keep it holy" (Exodus 20:8). One of the ways we perform this commandment is by reciting the קִדוּשׁ. Shabbat is considered a time of joy ("If you call the Sabbath a joy, God's holy day is honored" [Isaiah 58:13]), and wine is a symbol of joy ("Wine makes glad the human heart" [Psalms 104:15]), and so we recite the קִדוּשׁ with wine on Shabbat.

LEARNING OBJECTIVES

Students will be able to:

- Describe the two moments to remember mentioned in the קִדוּשׁ for Shabbat.
- Recite the קִדוּשׁ fluently.
- Define key words found in and related to the קִדוּשׁ.
- Describe the commemoration of יוֹם הַזִכָּרוֹן in Israel.

NEW WORDS AND PHRASES

Prayer Words:

holiness	קִדוּשׁ
memory	זִכָּרוֹן
memory	זֵכֶר
(of the) work of creation	(לְ)מַעֲשֵׂה בְרֵאשִׁית
(of the) going out from Egypt	(לְ)יְצִיאַת מִצְרַיִם
(in/with) love	(בְּ)אַהֲבָה
(and in/with) favor	(וּבְ)רָצוֹן

Related Words:

the Day of Remembrance	יוֹם הַזִכָּרוֹן
Israel's Independence Day	יוֹם הָעַצְמָאוּת
secretary (man/woman)	מַזְכִּיר, מַזְכִּירָה

INSTRUCTIONAL MATERIALS

Text Pages 40–45
Word Cards #43–52

Digital Application: Lesson 5—Dining room (see page 7 for a list of games and activities)

WHERE WE ARE

The Kiddush cup, filled with wine, is sitting on the dining room table. Doug the fish is ready to celebrate Shabbat…in a Kiddush cup!

INTRODUCING THE LESSON

As a class, brainstorm and create a list of everything students know about the creation story as told in Genesis. Next, as a class create a list describing what students know about the Israelites' exodus from Egypt. Encourage students to tell their favorite parts of these accounts or act them out.

Remind students that they have learned the first blessing in the Shabbat Kiddush. Inform students that in this chapter they will learn the second blessing, which mentions both the creation of the world and the Israelites' exodus from Egypt.

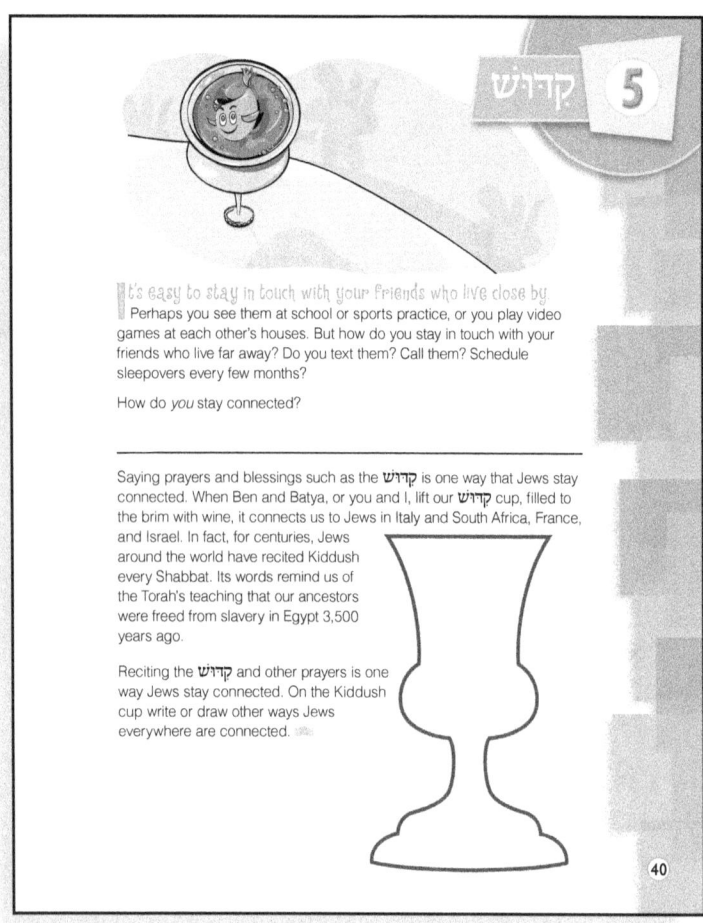

INTO THE TEXT

Write the word קִדּוּשׁ on the board. As a class, have students brainstorm a list of things they know about קִדּוּשׁ and the meaning of the word. (*Answers may include: it has the root letters קדשׁ; it has to do with being holy; it is said on Shabbat; it is said over wine.*) Inform students that in this chapter they will learn the meaning of the words in the קִדּוּשׁ.

Direct students to read and discuss the first paragraph with a partner. Have students write down how they stay connected. Ask students to raise their hands if they: IM friends; send e-mails; send texts; call on their cell phones. Ask students for other ways to stay connected.

Have students read and discuss the remaining paragraphs with their partner. Ask: How does saying the Kiddush connect us with Jews who lived a thousand years ago? (*They recited Kiddush, just as we recite it today; Kiddush reminds us of our ancestors who left Egypt.*) How does saying the Kiddush connect us with Jews throughout the world? (*Jews all over the world recite Kiddush, just as we do.*)

Allow students time to write or illustrate on the Kiddush cup other ways that Jews are connected.

Give each student two rectangular (1½″ × 8″) strips of construction paper. Direct students to illustrate ways that we are connected to Jews all over the world on one strip and to Jews throughout history on the second strip. Help them distinguish how these ways are different. For example, we might stay connected to Jews all over the world via the Internet by going to the same Jewish Web sites or by attending international Israel Day parades. We might stay connected to Jews throughout history by lighting Shabbat candles and reading the same prayers.

Create a paper chain: Loop one strip, overlapping one end over another, to form a circle. Glue or staple to hold. Insert another rectangle through the loop. Form that rectangle into a loop, then glue or staple it into place. Continue until you have a chain representing our connection to Jews all over the world as well as Jews from the past.

Reciting the Kiddush

Direct students to read "Reciting the Kiddush" with a partner. Challenge students to independently identify the two events included in the Kiddush. (*the work of creation and the going out from Egypt*) Call on a volunteer to name the two events.

Read for Speed

Focus students on line 7. Explain that the vowel has two different sounds. Usually its sound is "ah," but occasionally its sound is "oh." Inform students that the vowel in קָדְשׁוֹ is pronounced "oh." As a class, chorally read line 7. Challenge students to find this word in another line on page 41. (*line 11*)

Direct students to read all the lines out loud with a partner.

Divide the class into two teams. Have teams take turns reading the lines in "Read for Speed." Call out a number from one to eleven. For example, say "two," and challenge the first team to fluently read line 2. A team receives one point for reading a line fluently. Continue having teams take turns until all lines have been correctly read. The team with the most points is the winning team.

The Kiddush

Read aloud line 1 from the Kiddush. Have the class chorally read the line after you. Call on pairs of students to read the line. Have the class chorally read the English meaning for this line.

Repeat this for each line on page 42.

Before reading lines 4 and 9, challenge students to identify the words that have the vowel that is sounded as "oh." (קָדְשׁוֹ, קָדְשָׁךְ)

Have students practice reading the entire Kiddush with a partner.

Assign each student one line from the prayer. (If there are more than ten students have some students work in pairs. If there are fewer than ten students, assign a student two consecutive lines.) For each prayer line give students one sheet of light colored construction paper, a 3" x 8½" piece of lined paper, pencil or pen, glue stick, and markers. Direct students to (1) learn to recite the assigned line fluently, (2) copy the Hebrew and English of their assigned line onto the lined paper, (3) glue the phrase to the bottom of the construction paper, and (4) illustrate the meaning of the phrase on the construction paper.

Invite students, beginning with the student who illustrated line 1, to come to the front of the room, read the line in both Hebrew and English, and present and explain the illustration. Display these illustrations on a bulletin board labeled קִדּוּשׁ—Our Class Interpretation.

Digital Application

Tell students that at home, before the next class, they should click on the קִדּוּשׁ at the bottom of the screen to enter the dining room. Once in the dining room, students can click on the large wine glass and then on "Practice Reading" to practice reading the קִדּוּשׁ. Ask students to compare this קִדּוּשׁ with the blessing said over wine in the Shabbat blessings. How are they different? (*Answers may include: the full קִדּוּשׁ is longer; the Shabbat blessing is the last line of the קִדּוּשׁ; the full קִדּוּשׁ asks us to remember our history.*)

The Kiddush

Practice reading the קִדּוּשׁ.

1. בָּרוּךְ אַתָּה, יְיָ אֱלֹהֵינוּ, מֶלֶךְ הָעוֹלָם, בּוֹרֵא פְּרִי הַגָּפֶן.
2. בָּרוּךְ אַתָּה, יְיָ אֱלֹהֵינוּ, מֶלֶךְ הָעוֹלָם,
3. אֲשֶׁר קִדְּשָׁנוּ בְּמִצְוֹתָיו וְרָצָה בָנוּ.
4. וְשַׁבַּת קָדְשׁוֹ בְּאַהֲבָה וּבְרָצוֹן הִנְחִילָנוּ,
5. זִכָּרוֹן לְמַעֲשֵׂה בְרֵאשִׁית.
6. כִּי הוּא יוֹם תְּחִלָּה לְמִקְרָאֵי קֹדֶשׁ,
7. זֵכֶר לִיצִיאַת מִצְרָיִם.
8. כִּי בָנוּ בָחַרְתָּ וְאוֹתָנוּ קִדַּשְׁתָּ מִכָּל הָעַמִּים,
9. וְשַׁבַּת קָדְשְׁךָ בְּאַהֲבָה וּבְרָצוֹן הִנְחַלְתָּנוּ.
10. בָּרוּךְ אַתָּה, יְיָ, מְקַדֵּשׁ הַשַּׁבָּת.

1. Praised are You, Adonai our God, Ruler of the world, who creates the fruit of the vine.
2. Praised are You, Adonai our God, Ruler of the world,
3. who makes us holy with commandments and takes delight in us.
4. In love and favor, God has made the holy Shabbat, our heritage,
5. as a memory of the work of creation.
6. It is first among our holy days,
7. a memory of the going out from Egypt.
8. You chose us from all the nations and You made us holy,
9. and in (with) love and favor You have given us the Shabbat as a holy inheritance.
10. Praised are You, Adonai, who makes the Shabbat holy.

(42)

Chanting the Kiddush

Teach, or invite the cantor or music specialist to teach, students to sing the traditional melody for Kiddush.

Sh'lom Bayit

Ask: Do you ever sing with your family? If so, when? What kind of songs do you sing? How does it feel to sing together? How might singing the Kiddush with your family help create *sh'lom bayit*? (*Responses may include: creates a fun experience because it can be fun to sing together; everyone is doing the same thing.*)

Prayer Words

Present Word Cards #43 through 49 to the class. Ask questions about the new vocabulary, such as: Which two words share the root letters זכר? (זֵכֶר and זִכָּרוֹן) Which phrase is about the Israelites leaving Egypt? (לִיצִיאַת מִצְרָיִם) Challenge students to find and underline each of these words or phrases on page 42. Hold up a Word Card (except for Card #43) and challenge students to read the line on page 42 that contains that word or phrase.

Digital application

In the dining room, after clicking on the large wine glass, students should click on "קִדּוּשׁ Match" to review the new vocabulary, which includes the Hebrew words זִכָּרוֹן (memory), אַהֲבָה (love), קָדוֹשׁ (holiness), and רָצוֹן (with favor). In the next class, write each of the four Hebrew words and their English translation on a piece of construction paper. Divide students into four groups. Ask each group to write words or draw pictures that symbolize the word. You may wish to explain רָצוֹן (with favor) as "with pleasure" or "happily." Encourage students to be creative.

The זִכָּרוֹן group might draw Jewish memories (*the Israelites leaving Egypt*) and the קָדוֹשׁ group might draw a family celebrating Shabbat.

Missing Link

Have students work with a partner to complete the activity. Call on volunteers to read their answers. Invite students to chorally read or sing each line. Direct students to check and correct their own answers.

Putting It in Order

Distribute Word Cards #4, 8, 9, 10, 13, 19, 20, 31, 32, and 44 through 49, giving one card to each student. If you have more than fourteen students, distribute additional Word Cards that students learned in previous lessons. Challenge students to stand in a line according to the word or phrase's order of appearance in the Kiddush. Allow students to refer to the prayer in their book. Those students

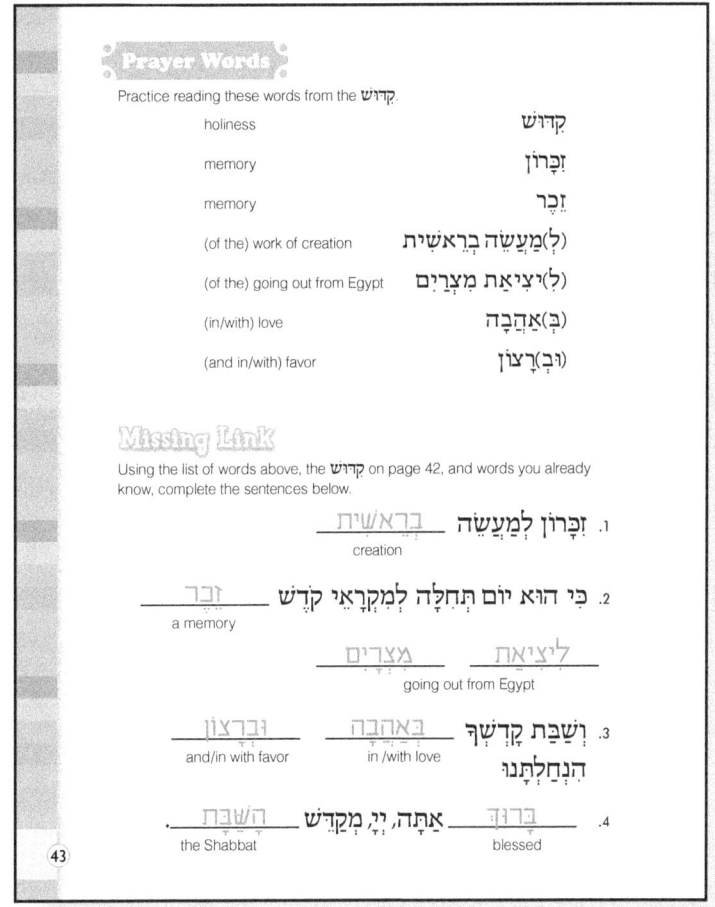

who have words that do not appear in the Kiddush should return to their seats. Have *all* students join in reciting or chanting the Kiddush. Direct Word Card holders to step forward and hold their card above their head as their word or phrase is said. Play the game again and ensure that students who did not get a word from the Kiddush do so this time.

At the Root

You have learned that the קִדּוּשׁ reminds us of two important events. Read them below in Hebrew then in English.

1. (זִכָּרוֹן) לְמַעֲשֵׂה בְרֵאשִׁית   2. (זֵכֶר) לִיצִיאַת מִצְרַיִם

a memory of the work of creation   *a memory of the going out from Egypt*

Underline the first Hebrew word of each phrase.

Circle the three letters that appear in both words. Write the letters. ז כ ר

These three letters form the root of the words זִכָּרוֹן and זֵכֶר and tell us that **remember** is part of a word's meaning.

Describe one place, person, or event you remember from when you were young. Why do you think it remains in your memory?

_____

_____

Holiday Link

In the Jewish calendar there is a day on which we remember soldiers who died defending Israel. We call this day יוֹם הַזִּכָּרוֹן, the Day of Remembrance. We observe יוֹם הַזִּכָּרוֹן on the day before יוֹם הָעַצְמָאוּת, Israel's Independence Day.

Name a Jewish holiday that is dedicated to remembering יְצִיאַת מִצְרַיִם.

Write its name in English here. _Passover_

Language Link

In Hebrew a secretary is a מַזְכִּיר (masculine) or a מַזְכִּירָה (feminine).

Circle the three root letters in מַזְכִּיר and מַזְכִּירָה. Write the root. ז כ ר

Why do you think מַזְכִּיר and מַזְכִּירָה are built on this root?

_____

44

---

festivities begin as everyone celebrates Israel's Independence Day.

Call on a student to name the holiday dedicated to remembering יְצִיאַת מִצְרַיִם. (פֶּסַח)

Language Link

Direct students to complete this activity with a partner. Call on a volunteer to explain why מַזְכִּירָה and מַזְכִּיר are built on the root letters זכר. (*Suggestions may include: a* מַזְכִּיר(ה) *records information that people need to remember; a* מַזְכִּיר(ה) *reminds the boss about meetings.*)

At the Root

Direct students to read and complete with a partner the activities in "At the Root." Invite students to join you and to chorally read the Hebrew phrases and their English meanings. Call on a volunteer to write the three root letters זכר on the board. Invite volunteers to share their early memories with the class. Ask: Why did you choose to write about this memory? What is special about this memory? Do you often think of this event? How does it make you feel when you think about it? What effect did this event have on you or your life? Why do you think the Jewish people need to remember "creation" and the "going out from Egypt"? (*Responses may include: so that we appreciate what we have; so that we remember what is written in the Torah.*)

Holiday Link

Direct students to follow along as you read "Holiday Link." Have all students join in and chorally read the Hebrew names of the holidays. Write יוֹם הַזִּכָּרוֹן on the board. Invite a student to the board to circle the three root letters that tell us "remember" is part of the word's meaning (זכר). Ask: Why do you think the Day of Remembrance is celebrated the day before Israel's Independence Day? (*Suggestions may include: we remember the soldiers who died in the War of Independence; we remember the soldiers who died so that Israel could be an independent country; we cannot be joyful for Israel's independence without remembering those who died for the country.*)

Inform students that the Day of Remembrance is a very solemn day in Israel. Places of public entertainment, such as theaters and nightclubs, are closed. Twice, once at 8:00 PM, on the eve of יוֹם הַזִּכָּרוֹן, and again at 11:00 AM during the day, a siren is sounded throughout the country.

The entire country comes to a standstill for one minute in the evening and two minutes in the morning. Pedestrians stop walking and all traffic stops. Throughout the day, television and radio programs are dedicated to soldiers who lost their lives fighting for Israel. At the close of the Day of Remembrance, the entire mood changes:

The Whole Holy Word

Have students work individually to complete this activity. Walk around the room to assess how well students (1) are able to identify words from a specific root, and (2) understand the significance of root letters repeating in a single prayer.

Call on volunteers to share their responses to the question. (*Suggestions may include: holiness is the most important idea in this blessing; there are different things that are holy.*)

Clue to Cyberspace

Ask students to read the blessing to a partner and to draw the ritual object (*Kiddush cup*). Ask students if they have Kiddush cups at home. What do they look like? How are they shaped?

Digital Application

In the dining room, after clicking on the large wine glass, students can click on "קִדּוּשׁ Slingshot" to review and practice spelling key vocabulary, which includes קָדוֹשׁ (holiness), הַשַּׁבָּת (the Sabbath), וּבְרָצוֹן (and in/with favor), and בְּרֵאשִׁית (Creation). Remind students to use the Kiddush cup clue to reset their timer in the "Kiddush Slingshot" game (by hitting the Kiddush cup, students' time clock will be reset). In the next class, ask students whether using the slingshot was easy or difficult. Ask students which Jewish hero was famous for his skill with a slingshot. (*King David*) What did he do? (*killed Goliath*)

Siddur Squares

Play "Siddur Squares" as described on page 13 to review Word Cards #1 through 52 and the content of blessings and prayers presented in chapters 1 through 5. Possible questions are:

What are the three root letters that tell us a word has to do with remembering? (זכר) How many blessings are in the Shabbat Kiddush? (*two*)

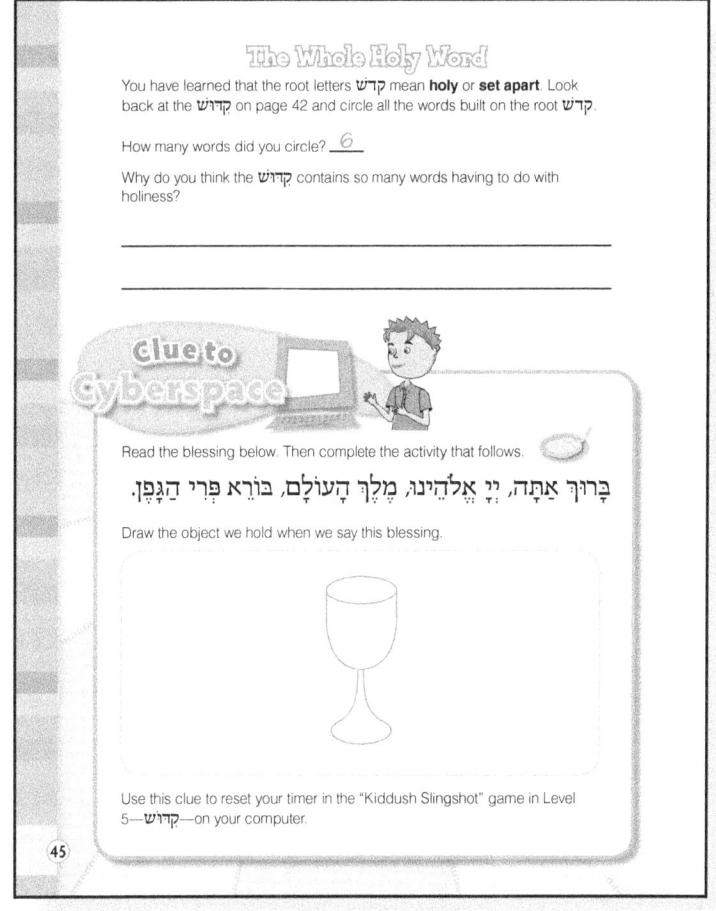

My Own Siddur

If students are creating their own siddur, prepare a page by copying the Kiddush. Students can illustrate or write sentences as they have done for previous blessings.

67 CHAPTER 5

Assessment

As students are working on any of the above activities, meet individually with them to assess reading fluency and knowledge of prayer content. You can mark students' progress using the assessment chart and check their progress online at www.behrmanhouse.com.

What's Next?

Direct students to turn back to page 34. Challenge them to identify the occasion on which each blessing is said. (*Shabbat; festivals—Rosh Hashanah, Sukkot, Pesaḥ, and Shavuot; Ḥanukkah; Havdalah*) Students will most likely be able to identify the occasions on which the first three blessings are recited. Explain that the fourth is recited over a braided candle that is lit during the Havdalah ceremony, when Shabbat has just ended and the new week begins. Inform students that in the next chapter they will learn this blessing and others that are recited during Havdalah.

ABOUT THE PRAYER

We welcome and say farewell to Shabbat with candles and wine. We conclude Shabbat with a special ceremony called Havdalah, which separates the holiness of Shabbat from the rest of the week. The Havdalah ceremony includes blessings over wine, fragrant spices, the flames of the Havdalah candle, and the separation of the holy from the everyday. Traditionally, Havdalah is recited after Shabbat, once three stars are visible in the night sky.

LEARNING OBJECTIVES

Students will be able to:

- Recite the four Havdalah blessings fluently.
- Explain when and how a Havdalah ceremony takes place.
- Define key words found in and related to the Havdalah blessings.
- Recite אֵלִיָּהוּ הַנָּבִיא and describe occasions when this is sung.
- Explain how we use all five senses during the Havdalah ceremony.

NEW WORDS AND PHRASES

Prayer Words:

spices	בְּשָׂמִים
fire	אֵשׁ
who separates	הַמַּבְדִּיל
holy	קֹדֶשׁ
everyday	חוֹל

Related Words:

separation	הַבְדָּלָה
a good week	שָׁבוּעַ טוֹב
week	שָׁבוּעַ
Elijah the Prophet	אֵלִיָּהוּ הַנָּבִיא

INSTRUCTIONAL MATERIALS

Text Pages 46–53
Word Cards #53–61

Digital Application: Lesson 6—Patio (see page 7 for a list of games and activities)

WHERE WE ARE

Shabbat has just ended. We join Batya and Ben on the patio as they recite Havdalah, saying good-bye to Shabbat and welcoming the new week.

INTRODUCING THE LESSON

Ask: Have you ever been to a closing ceremony? What was it like? (*Responses may include descriptions of closing ceremonies at the end of sports events, at the end of a school program, or at the end of camp.*) Why do you think we have closing ceremonies? (*Responses may include: to mark the end of an important event or occasion; to give us time to think about the experience; to help us transition to whatever we are doing next.*) Inform students that at the end of Shabbat there is a special closing ceremony, Havdalah. Havdalah helps us say goodbye to Shabbat and welcome the new week.

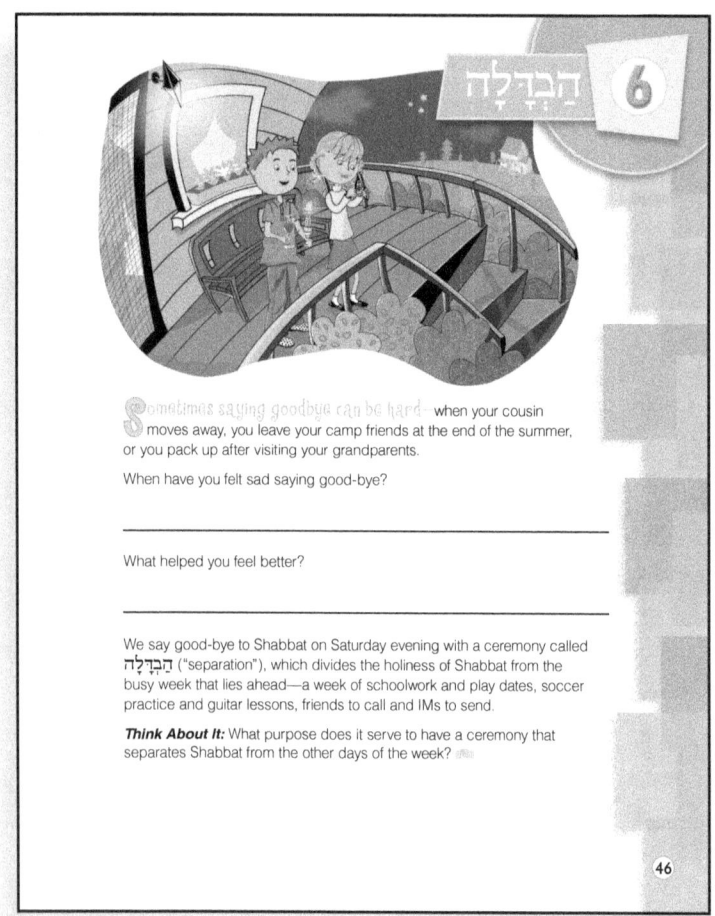

INTO THE TEXT

Focus students on the illustration at the top of page 46. Ask: What do you notice in this drawing? What are Batya and Ben doing? (*Standing outside; Ben is holding a glass with grape juice and a lit candle; Batya is holding a spice box. [You may need to tell students what Batya is holding.]*) What time of day is it? How do you know? (*early nighttime, only three stars are visible*)

Tell students that Batya and Ben are doing a special ceremony called הַבְדָּלָה. Write the word on the board. Explain that traditionally Havdalah is recited after Shabbat ends, once there are three stars visible in the sky. Inform students that they will be learning about Havdalah in this lesson.

Direct students to read and discuss page 46 with a partner. Allow students to write responses to the questions. Have students share times when they have felt sad saying good-bye (*Responses may include: at the end of camp; when a relative or friend moved; after visiting a friend who lives far away*) What helped them feel better? (*Responses may include: knowing they would soon talk or text; planning the next visit*)

As a class discuss the purpose of the Havdalah ceremony. (*Suggestions may include: reminds us that Shabbat is over and it is time to get back to the everyday schedule; extends the celebration of Shabbat; reminds us that Shabbat is different from all other days*)

The Four הַבְדָּלָה Blessings

Have students silently read the first paragraph. Ask: How many blessings are recited during הַבְדָּלָה? (*four*) What Hebrew greeting do we say at the end of הַבְדָּלָה? (שָׁבוּעַ טוֹב)

Havdalah—"How To"

Invite three volunteers to come to the front of the class. Give one student a cup of grape juice, one a spice box containing fragrant spices such as cloves and cinnamon, and one a Havdalah candle.

1. Wine

Ask the first student to hold up the cup of juice as the entire class recites the blessing over the juice. Dramatically tell the student not to drink the juice yet. Explain that during Havdalah we have more blessings to recite before we can enjoy the juice.

2. Spices

Ask the second student to hold up a spice box. Read the explanation of the spices and have all students join you in reciting the blessing over the spices. You may wish to recite the closing words of the blessing and have students repeat the words until they can say the words fluently.

Inform students that the word מִינֵי is plural and means "kinds of." Show students Word Card 53 and present the meaning of בְּשָׂמִים. Challenge students to explain why the Havdalah spice box needs to contain at least two different spices. (*Because* מִינֵי בְּשָׂמִים *means "kinds of spices," not just one spice.*)

3. Candle

Ask the third student to hold up the Havdalah candle as the class chorally recites the blessing over the candle. Have students repeat the closing words as they did for the blessing over spices.

Inform students that the word מְאוֹרֵי is plural and means "lights." Show students Word Card 54 and present the meaning of אֵשׁ. Challenge students to explain why the Havdalah candle needs to have at least two wicks. (*Because* מְאוֹרֵי הָאֵשׁ *means "fiery lights," not just one light.*)

71 CHAPTER 6

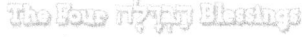

Digital application

Tell students that at home, before the next class, they should click on הַבְדָּלָה at the bottom of the screen to enter the patio. Once on the patio, students should click on the wine cup to practice reading the first three blessings of Havdalah. In the next class, ask students why they think הַבְדָּלָה was recited on the patio? (*Answers might include: to see three stars in the sky or to appreciate the darkness of the sky when Shabbat ends*) Remind students that הַבְדָּלָה need not be recited outdoors. It's just one way of making the end of Shabbat even more special. Ask students how else they might make the end of Shabbat feel special. (*Answers might include: saying* הַבְדָּלָה *with family; making your own* בְּשָׂמִים *box*)

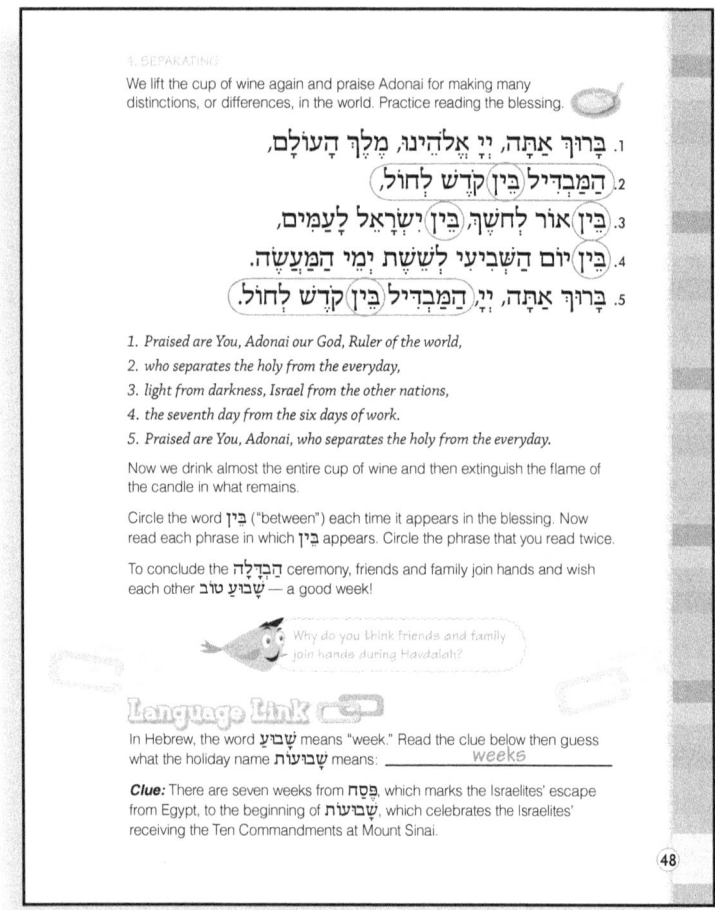

Tuesday (before dark), you may wish to incorporate Havdalah into your weekly schedule.

Language Link

Have students read and complete this activity with a partner. Call on a volunteer to explain the meaning of שָׁבוּעוֹת. Invite a student to look up the dates on which Passover and Shavuot will fall during the school year. As a class, use a calendar to count the (seven) weeks between the holidays.

4. Separating

Read the introduction to the fourth Havdalah blessing. Read each line of the blessing and ask students to recite it after you. Direct students to practice reading the blessing with a partner. Review the reading with the whole class, having students take turns. For example, divide the class into groups of three. Call on one group, and ask the students to read a specific line. Continue until each group has had several opportunities to read. Invite individual students to read a phrase or a line.

Direct students to identify the word בֵּין and to read the phrases that contain this word.

Write שָׁבוּעַ טוֹב on the board. Explain that it is traditional to wish friends and family a שָׁבוּעַ טוֹב as they start the new week. Encourage students to walk over to classmates and wish each other שָׁבוּעַ טוֹב.

Invite a volunteer to hold the Doug puppet and ask: Why do you think friends and family often join hands during Havdalah? (*Answers may include: to bring the warmth and friendship of Shabbat into the week; to show they feel close to one another.*)

The Four Blessings

To reinforce the concept that הַבְדָּלָה is comprised of four parts, give each student a blank sheet of paper and crayons or markers. Ask students to represent the four parts of Havdalah in any way they choose. For example, a student may choose to fold the paper into four (4¼" × 5½") rectangles and write a few words or draw simple illustrations to represent one of the blessings in each of the four rectangles. One quadrant would have the blessing over the juice or wine, another over the spices, another over the candle, and another for separating the holy from the everyday. Suggest students take home their works of art and explain the contents to their family.

Teach, or invite the cantor or music specialist to teach, the chanting of the Havdalah blessings, as well as the closing wish for a שָׁבוּעַ טוֹב. If you meet with your students on Sunday, Monday, or

THE PRAYERS OF OUR PEOPLE I • כָּל יִשְׂרָאֵל

Prayer Words

Present Word Cards #53 through 57. Direct students to find and circle each of the words in the blessings on pages 47 and 48.

Distribute Word Cards #4, 8, 9, 10, 13, 16, 17, 31, 32, and 53 through 57 to students. Name a blessing and invite the students who have Word Cards from that blessing to come to the front of the room and form a single line according to the order of the words in the blessing. The group should then recite the entire blessing. To increase the challenge, consider setting a time limit, such as 45 seconds, to form a line and correctly recite the blessing. Invite the entire class to recite the blessing after the group has said it correctly.

Digital Application

Ask students to play Tic-Tac-Toe to review the new vocabulary, which includes words from previous lessons, such as מֶלֶךְ (ruler), and new words, such as אֵשׁ (fire), שָׁבוּעַ (week), קֹדֶשׁ (holy), חוֹל (everyday), בְּשָׂמִים (spices), הַבְדָּלָה (separation), and יוֹם (day). In the next class, you may wish to play a class-wide Tic-Tac-Toe game using the same words.

Separation

Read the following phrase from Genesis 1:4, וַיַּבְדֵּל אֱלֹהִים בֵּין הָאוֹר וּבֵין הַחֹשֶׁךְ, then write the words on the board.

Explain that this phrase is taken from the account in the Torah of the first day of creation. Ask: Which word means "separated"? (וַיַּבְדֵּל) What other phrase in this verse is similar to a phrase in the fourth Havdalah blessing? (בֵּין הָאוֹר וּבֵין הַחֹשֶׁךְ) According to Genesis 1:4, what did God do? (*God separated the light from the darkness.*)

Direct students to look at the English meaning of the fourth Havdalah blessing. Ask: Which two phrases remind us of the Creation? (*light from darkness; the seventh day from the six days of work*) Which other prayer or blessing reminds us of creation? (*Kiddush*)

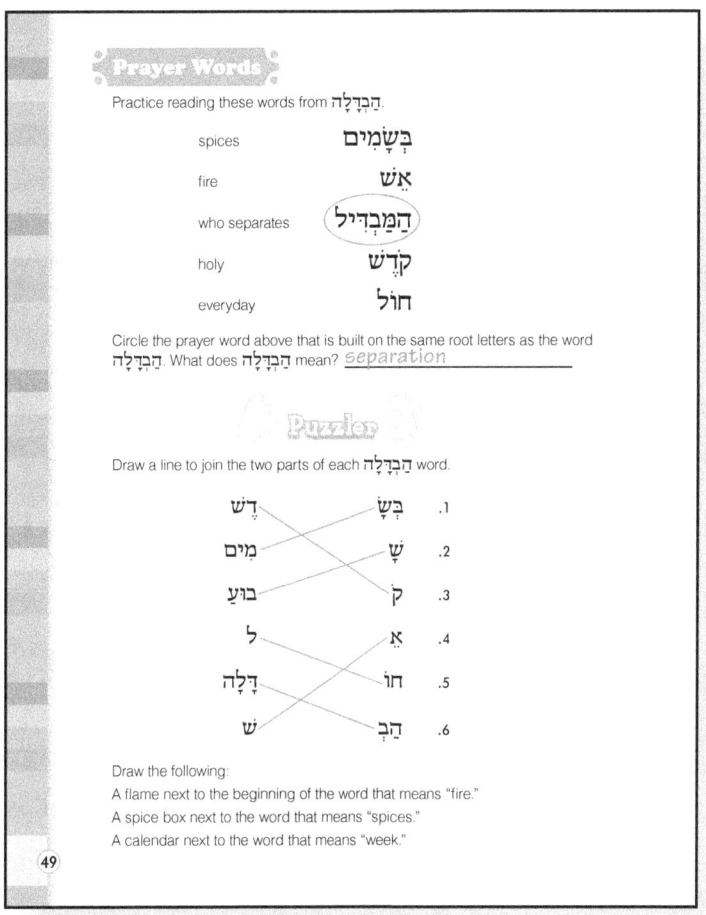

Puzzler

Have students complete the activity with a partner. Call on volunteers to read the first half of each word and others to read the second half. As students read their part of the word, they stand up. If you have more than twelve students in the class, repeat the activity with different students.

Digital Application

Once on the patio, students can click on the Havdalah candle to review the Puzzler, in which students will connect word fragments to form the words אֵשׁ (fire), שָׁבוּעַ (week), קֹדֶשׁ (holy), חוֹל (everyday), בְּשָׂמִים (spices), and הַבְדָּלָה (separation). Recreate the digital game as a classroom exercise. Before the next class, write each word on an index card. Then cut the card, and the word, into two puzzle pieces. Divide pieces among students and let them find their matching halves.

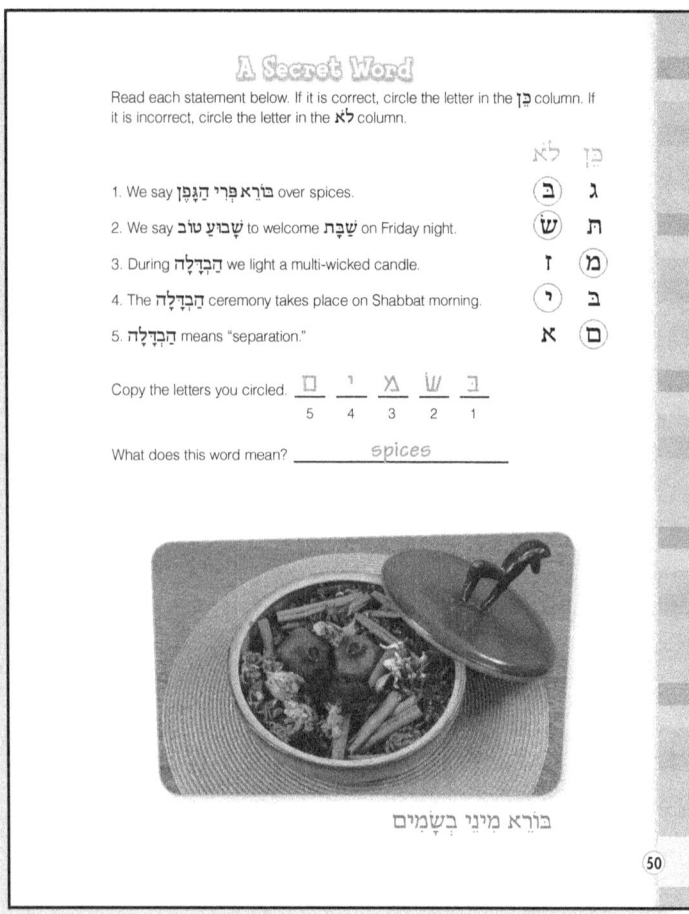

A Secret Word

Ask students to read and complete the "Secret Word" activity with a partner. Call on a volunteer to write the "secret word" and its meaning on the board.

 **Photo Op**

Invite the class to chorally read the words below the photograph. Challenge students to identify the words and say their meaning. (*The ending words of the second Havdalah blessing; "creator of various kinds of spices"*) Call on volunteers to describe the photo. Focus students on the decorative spice box. Write "*hiddur mitzvah*" (הִדּוּר מִצְוָה) on the board. Remind students that they learned about *hiddur mitzvah* in Chapter 4, page 36. Call on a volunteer to explain *hiddur mitzvah*. (*We make the act of performing a mitzvah pleasing and beautiful.*) Ask: How is this spice box an example of *hiddur mitzvah*? (*Responses may include: it is decorative; it is a piece of art.*)

Here is an easy way for each student to make his or her own "spice box." Each student needs:

- a circular piece of thin fabric (netting works very well), about 5" in diameter
- a 6" piece of narrow ribbon
- cloves (about 8) and 1 or 2 cinnamon sticks (broken in half)

To construct: Lay the circular piece of fabric on a table and place the cloves and cinnamon sticks in the center of the circle. Gather together the outside edges of the fabric so that the cloves and cinnamon sticks are enclosed, as if they are in a sack. Tie the fabric closed with the piece of ribbon.

For a more challenging craft project, students can also make their own Havdalah candles. Directions for making beeswax or paraffin Havdalah candles are available on the Internet. These are easy and fun to make. Students roll the beeswax or paraffin sheets around wicks to form their own Havdalah candles.

 **Havdalah with the Family**

As a class, plan a family Havdalah service. Encourage students to use their handcrafted spice boxes and candles with their families at the service.

Making "Sense" of הַבְדָּלָה

Have students work in pairs as they fill in the blanks to complete the sentence and match the blessing or phrase with each of the five senses.

Students can practice reading the blessings in a variety of ways. Have all students stand in a circle. Go around the circle having each student say one word of the blessing. Continue until all of the Havdalah blessings have been read. Read the blessings a second time. This time have each student read two words of the blessing.

Students can practice reading all four blessings with a partner. Walk around the room to check students' fluency. You may wish to ask students who have demonstrated fluency to listen to other students.

Have students share their ideas with the class about why we use all five senses during Havdalah. (*Suggestions may include: to be totally aware of the end of Shabbat and beginning of the new week; to make the experience of Havdalah more powerful*) Challenge students to name other occasions when they use all five senses. (*Responses may include: at a carnival where they see the roller coaster, hear the music and the noise, taste the cold ice cream, smell the roasting peanuts, and touch the animals*)

שָׁלוֹם בַּיִת

Ask: How can participating in a Havdalah service contribute to creating an atmosphere of *sh'lom bayit*? (*Answers may include: everyone wishes each other a good week; we join hands and feel close to one another; we share a pleasant experience as we look at the Havdalah candle and smell the spices.*) Alternatively, you may ask: How can sharing a fun, five-senses experience with your family help build שָׁלוֹם בַּיִת? (*Responses may include: It would be a rich experience with lots to talk about; because it involves all five senses, more people can appreciate it—some people like to sing, others like to tell stories, and others like to eat.*)

75 CHAPTER 6

Elijah the Prophet

Direct students to silently read the paragraphs about Elijah the Prophet. Ask: Who do we sing about at the end of the Havdalah ceremony? (*Elijah the Prophet*) What are four things our tradition teaches about Elijah? (*He fought for justice; he fought for the rights of the poor; he is a messenger of good news; he will bring peace to the world.*) Inform students that some people sing this song about Elijah at the beginning, rather than at the end, of Havdalah. Ask your rabbi or cantor when it is sung at your synagogue.

Ask students to describe the references to Elijah the Prophet on Passover. (*There is a special cup on the table called the Cup of Elijah; the door is opened for Elijah; some sing the song* אֵלִיָּהוּ הַנָּבִיא.) Invite students to share fun, family stories about opening the door for Elijah.

Read the words of אֵלִיָּהוּ הַנָּבִיא and have students repeat each line after you. Direct students to practice reading with a partner. Read the song chorally as a class. Teach, or invite the cantor or music specialist to teach, students the tune.

Explain to students that Tishbite means that Elijah was from Tishbi (or Tishbe) and that Tishbi was probably a town in Gilad (or Gilead), Israel, near the Sea of Galilee.

Tell students that according to the Bible, Elijah never died. Read your students the description in II Kings 2:11 of Elijah ascending to heaven. (An abridged version of these verses is found in *The Explorer's Bible, Volume 2*, page 102.) Today there are various traditions and customs that mention Elijah. According to our tradition, Elijah, who was brought up to heaven, will return and bring a time of peace for all.

Digital Application

On the patio, students can click on "More Practice Reading" to practice reading the words of אֵלִיָּהוּ הַנָּבִיא.

Did You Know?

Have students read these paragraphs with a partner. Allow students to individually write their own responses to the question. Encourage students to share their ideas with classmates.

Write on the board: בּוֹרֵא פְּרִי הָעֵץ. Ask: When would we say this? (*Before eating a fruit*) Write on the board: בּוֹרֵא פְּרִי הָאֲדָמָה. Again, ask when this blessing would be recited. (*Before eating a vegetable*) Inform students that just as we enjoy the fruit or vegetable after saying the blessing over it, after we say בּוֹרֵא מְאוֹרֵי הָאֵשׁ, we enjoy the light by making shadows. Traditional Jewish law teaches that once we have said a blessing, we need to complete the act for that blessing. If we were to simply say the blessing for light, but not make use of the light, then we would have said a blessing for no purpose. It would be like saying בּוֹרֵא פְּרִי הָעֵץ and not eating a piece of fruit. Ask students for other examples like this ("It would be like saying…and not….")

Clue to Cyberspace

Direct students to work with a partner to discover the clue for the "Ping Pong" game in Lesson 6 of the digital application (*3*).

Digital Application

Remind students that they have played digital Ping Pong before. Ask students who the previous Ping Pong champion was. In this chapter, they have the opportunity to be the next Ping Pong class winner. Challenge students to record their scores in Lesson 6 Ping Pong game. The game reviews the Hebrew words אֵשׁ (fire), קֹדֶשׁ (holy), חוֹל (everyday), and בְּשָׂמִים (spices). Remind students to use the clue (*3*) to gain extra points.

Ask students to complete Review 2 on their computer to assess what they have learned in Lessons 4 through 6. In the next class, divide students into two teams and challenge teams to write and ask their own review questions. (*Some questions and answers might include: What senses do we use in Havdalah? sight, smell, taste, hearing, and touch; What do the words זֵכֶר and זִכָּרוֹן mean?*

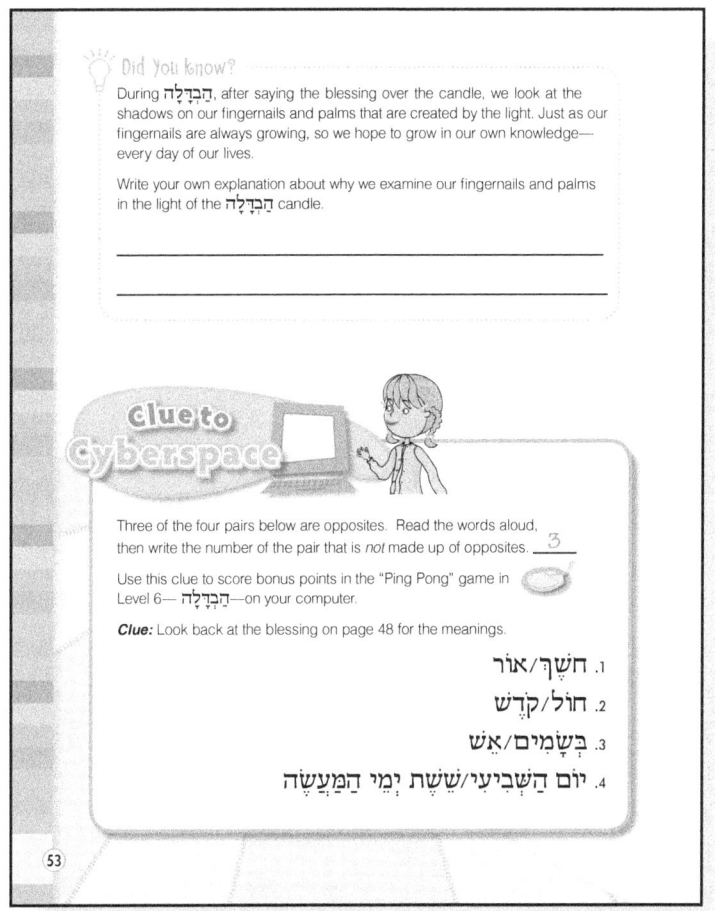

memory; how many words share the root קדשׁ in the Kiddush? 6—קִדְּשׁוֹ, קֹדֶשׁ, קִדַּשְׁתָּ, קָדְשְׁךָ, מְקַדֵּשׁ, קִדְּשָׁנוּ.*)

My Own Siddur

If students are creating their own siddur, prepare a page by copying the Havdalah blessings. Students can illustrate or write sentences as they have done for previous blessings.

77 CHAPTER 6

Assessment

As students are working on any of the above activities, meet individually with them to assess reading fluency and knowledge of prayer content. You can mark students' progress using the assessment chart and check their progress online at www.behrmanhouse.com.

What's Next?

Ask: Can you think of any blessings that we only recite a few times a year? (*Suggestions may include: the blessings over Ḥanukkah candles, before sitting in a sukkah, or hearing the shofar*) Inform students that in the next chapter they will learn special blessings recited on holidays, such as Rosh Hashanah, Sukkot, and Ḥanukkah.

בִּרְכוֹת שֶׁל יוֹם טוֹב

ABOUT THE PRAYER

Each יוֹם טוֹב—Jewish holiday—has its own traditions and its own blessings. These traditions connect us to our past. At the same time, we celebrate in the present and look ahead to the future.

The blessings we recite are an expression of our appreciation for the good in our lives. We recite blessings for specific holiday mitzvot, such as hearing the shofar, sitting in a sukkah, lighting a Ḥanukkah menorah, and eating matzah on Pesaḥ.

LEARNING OBJECTIVES

Students will be able to:

- Recite fluently the twelve holiday blessings presented in this chapter.
- Identify the twelve holiday blessings and describe when each is recited.
- Define key words found in and related to holiday blessings.
- Use and understand holiday and Rosh Hashanah greetings.
- Describe the order for lighting Ḥanukkah candles.
- Explain how helping to prepare for a seder can enhance שְׁלוֹם בַּיִת.

NEW WORDS AND PHRASES

Prayer Words:

to hear	לִשְׁמֹעַ
sound, voice	קוֹל
shofar	שׁוֹפָר
in the sukkah	בַּסֻּכָּה
lulav	לוּלָב
etrog	אֶתְרוֹג
Ḥanukkah	חֲנֻכָּה
miracles	נִסִּים
at this time	בַּזְּמַן הַזֶּה
the earth	הָאֲדָמָה
eating (of)	אֲכִילַת
matzah	מַצָּה
maror/bitter herbs	מָרוֹר

RELATED WORDS AND PHRASES:

a good and sweet New Year	שָׁנָה טוֹבָה וּמְתוּקָה
hear	שְׁמַע
booth(s), hut(s)	סֻכָּה, סֻכּוֹת
Welcome!	בְּרוּכִים הַבָּאִים
Ḥanukkah menorah	חֲנֻכִּיָּה
a great miracle happened there	נֵס גָּדוֹל הָיָה שָׁם
order, Passover seder	סֵדֶר
a good day, Jewish holiday	יוֹם טוֹב
holiday	חַג
happy holiday	חַג שָׂמֵחַ

INSTRUCTIONAL MATERIALS

Text Pages 54–65
Word Cards #62–84

Digital Application: Lesson 7—Family Room (see page 8 for a list of games and activities)

WHERE WE ARE

Rosh Hashanah is approaching. Batya and Ben are in their living room thinking about their favorite Jewish holidays. Ben listens as Batya blows the shofar.

INTRODUCING THE LESSON

Ask students to name all the Jewish holidays they can think of. Write students' responses on the board. Put a check next to Rosh Hashanah, Sukkot, Ḥanukkah, and Pesaḥ. Explain that in this chapter students will learn blessings that are recited on these holidays.

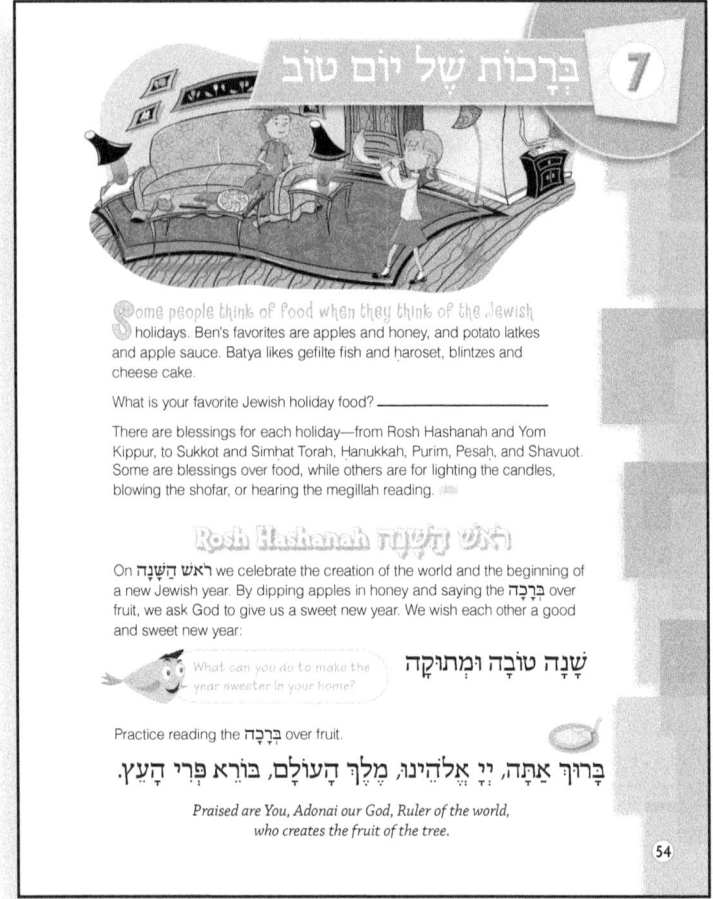

INTO THE TEXT

Focus students on the illustration at the top of page 54. Ask students to describe what they see. Ask: Do you or anyone in your family know how to blow a shofar? What do you think of or how do you feel when you hear the shofar? Encourage students to share personal stories about blowing a shofar or hearing its blast. Ask students what they see on the table in front of Ben. (*a dish with apples and honey*)

Invite a student to read the title of the chapter. Direct students to skim through the chapter and to guess the meaning of its title. Ask: Can you think of any special blessings for specific holidays? (*Answers may include: blessings for lighting the Ḥanukkah candles, for sitting in a sukkah, for eating matzah*) Remind students that in this chapter they will be learning special blessings for mitzvot associated with the holidays, including the blessing recited before hearing the shofar blast.

Have students silently read the introduction. Create a list on the board of students' favorite holiday foods. For fun, have students vote on the class's favorite food. Ask students for and list on the board words describing their associations with or feelings about these foods. (*Answers may include: Grandma, eating too much, yummy, sweet, ugh!*)

Rosh Hashanah רֹאשׁ הַשָּׁנָה

Direct students to silently read the paragraph about Rosh Hashanah. Ask: Why do we dip apples in honey? (*to ask God to give us a sweet new year.*) What is the greeting for a good and sweet year? (שָׁנָה טוֹבָה וּמְתוּקָה) Have the class practice saying שָׁנָה טוֹבָה וּמְתוּקָה. Invite half of the class to wish the other half a sweet and good year. Ask the others to respond in kind. Direct students to turn to students on each side of them and wish them a שָׁנָה טוֹבָה וּמְתוּקָה.

Before class, write Doug's question, "What can you do to make the year sweeter in your home?" on the top of a large sheet of poster paper. Have a volunteer hold the Doug puppet and ask Doug's question. Call on students to respond to Doug's question. List students' responses on the poster paper or have them write their responses on paper cut out in the shape of an apple. Display on the bulletin board.

Bring apples and honey to class. Invite students to dip apples in honey as they say the blessing, and then to enjoy the sweet treat.

Digital Application

Tell students that at home, before the next class, they should click on בִּרְכוֹת שֶׁל יוֹם טוֹב at the bottom of the screen to enter the family room. Once in the family room, students can click on "Practice Reading for רֹאשׁ הַשָּׁנָה" to practice reading the blessing said over apples and honey.

Shofar Blessing

Have students silently read about the blessing recited before blowing the shofar. Challenge students to underline the phrase that is unique to this blessing. (לִשְׁמֹעַ קוֹל שׁוֹפָר) Call on a volunteer to read the three underlined words and have the class chorally repeat this phrase. Ask students to practice reading the blessing and to circle the word for "shofar."

Prayer Words

Present Word Cards #62 through 64. Hold up cards one at a time, showing students the Hebrew word. Have the class chorally read the word and say its meaning. Mix the order of the cards and repeat several times.

Picture Match

Allow students to complete the "Picture Match" activity. Walk around the room to review their work.

Shofar Blasts

Write the following on the board:

תְּקִיעָה _____

שְׁבָרִים _____ _____ _____

תְּרוּעָה _ _ _ _ _ _ _ _ _

Ask students to make the sound of a shofar (be prepared for a cacophony!). Ask students if they noticed a varied number of sounds. Explain to students that there are three kinds of shofar blasts and that the lines on the board represent each of the shofar blasts: תְּקִיעָה is one long blast; שְׁבָרִים is three short blasts; and תְּרוּעָה is nine very short, quick blasts. Invite a volunteer to the front of the room to call out the names of the different shofar blasts. Have the class make the sounds of each blast after its name has been called out.

Ask: How does the shofar serve as a wake-up call? What does it remind us to do? (*Responses may include: it's like an alarm clock; it reminds us to think about and evaluate our actions; it reminds us to change our ways to be a better person; it reminds us to think about positive things we can do for others.*)

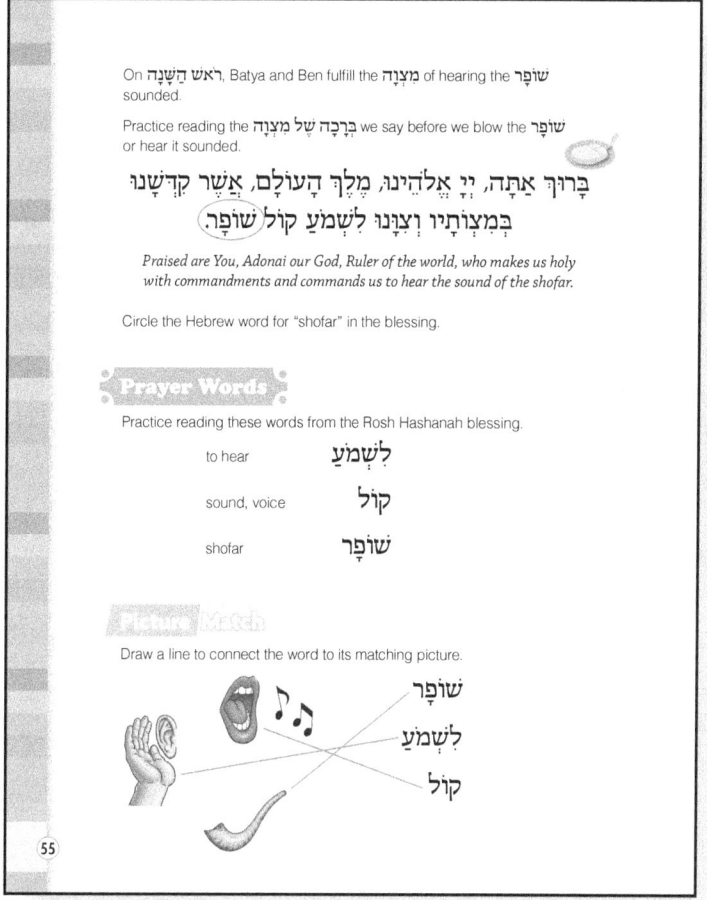

Digital Application

Once in the family room, students can click on "Practice Reading for רֹאשׁ הַשָּׁנָה" to practice reading the blessing recited before blowing the shofar. In the next class, ask students to recite this blessing. Challenge students by asking them on what other Jewish holiday we recite the shofar blessing. (*Yom Kippur*)

81 CHAPTER 7

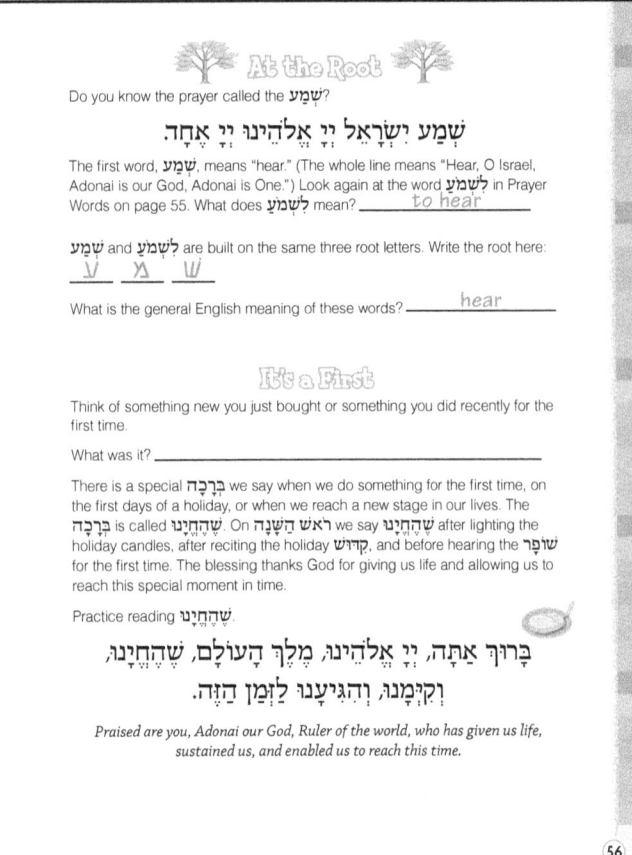

Direct students to circle the letters that tell us the word is about "living" or "life." (חַי)

Digital Application

Once in the family room, students should click on "Practice Reading for חֲנֻכָּה" to practice reading the שֶׁהֶחֱיָנוּ. In the next class, practice saying the blessing aloud together. Before doing so, ask students if anyone has experienced a "first" that week, such as "I scored a goal for the first time on my soccer team" or "I wore this t-shirt for the first time." Share in those students' "firsts" by reciting the שֶׁהֶחֱיָנוּ blessing as a class.

At the Root

Ask students to stand up if they've heard of—or heard—the שְׁמַע. Have students read the שְׁמַע aloud chorally. Direct students to work with a partner to read about the שְׁמַע and complete the activities.

Ask students to create hand motions for the phrase לִשְׁמֹעַ קוֹל שׁוֹפָר and for the שְׁמַע. Invite students to demonstrate the hand motions to the class as they recite the Hebrew words.

As a class, discuss the meaning of the שְׁמַע. Begin by asking, What is the difference between hearing someone and listening to someone? If a parent or a teacher asks you to listen to them, what might they want you to do? What do you think the people of Israel are being asked to do in the שְׁמַע? (*Answers may include: it does not simply mean the physical action of hearing something, but it implies listening, understanding, and obeying.*) Explain to students that "hear" is often used in English translations of this verse but that we understand it to mean "listen."

It's a First

Ask for volunteers to read their answers to the question about something new they bought or something they did for the first time.

Call on a volunteer to read aloud the paragraph about the שֶׁהֶחֱיָנוּ, encouraging the whole class to join in when a Hebrew word appears. Ask students if they can name any other times that the שֶׁהֶחֱיָנוּ is recited. (*Answers may include: wearing new clothes; sitting in a sukkah for the first time on Sukkot; using the lulav and etrog for the first time during Sukkot; at a bar and bat mitzvah ceremony*)

As a class, practice reading the שֶׁהֶחֱיָנוּ. Teach, or invite the cantor or music specialist to teach, students to chant this blessing.

Challenge students to identify the word meaning "who has given us life." (שֶׁהֶחֱיָנוּ) Remind students that they learned the word for "living" when they studied מוֹדָה/מוֹדֶה אֲנִי.

Sukkot סֻכּוֹת

Ask students to brainstorm words to do with Sukkot. What comes immediately to mind? List their suggestions on the board. (*Answers may include: sukkah, lulav, etrog, cold, decorations, carrying food in and out of the house*)

Have students read silently about Sukkot. Ask: How long ago is it thought that the Israelites left Egypt? (*around 3,500 years ago*) During what time of year does Sukkot fall? (*autumn*) What is a סֻכָּה? (*a booth*) When did the Israelites live in סֻכּוֹת? (*when they wandered in the desert for forty years*) When did Jewish farmers live in סֻכּוֹת? (*during the harvest season*)

Provide crayons or markers and ask students to decorate the word סֻכּוֹת on page 57, turning each letter into a fruit or vegetable. Allow students to be as creative as they like. Invite students to share their art work with the class.

Fluent Blessing Reading

As a class, read aloud, in Hebrew and in English, the blessing recited for sitting in a sukkah.

Direct students to underline the words that indicate that this is a בְּרָכָה שֶׁל מִצְוָה. Chorally read the underlined words. Ask students to circle the words related to sitting in a sukkah. Have a volunteer read the circled words.

Repeat these steps for the blessing recited over the lulav and etrog, having students circle and read the words related to waving the lulav and etrog.

Have students practice reading these blessings with a partner.

Digital Application

Once in the family room, students can click on "Practice Reading for סֻכּוֹת" to practice reading the Sukkot blessings. Challenge students to find the Sukkot-related words in these blessings. (סֻכָּה *and* לוּלָב)

Lulav and Etrog

It is difficult to obtain a lulav and etrog at any time other than just prior to Sukkot. Consequently, you will need to improvise in order to demonstrate how to wave the lulav and etrog. You might, for example, use a baton or short broom for the lulav and a handball for the etrog. Or, your synagogue may have a toy stuffed lulav and etrog. Or else try to bring in a photo or drawing of a lulav and an etrog and post them on the board.

Direct all students to stand, facing east, and to pretend that they are holding a lulav in the right hand and an etrog in the left. Hold your "lulav and etrog" to demonstrate for students, telling students that the tip, the pitam is facing down. As a class, recite the blessing for the lulav and etrog. With the class, pretend to turn the etrog so that the pitam is facing up. Wave the lulav three times in each of the following directions: east, south, west, north, upward, and downward.

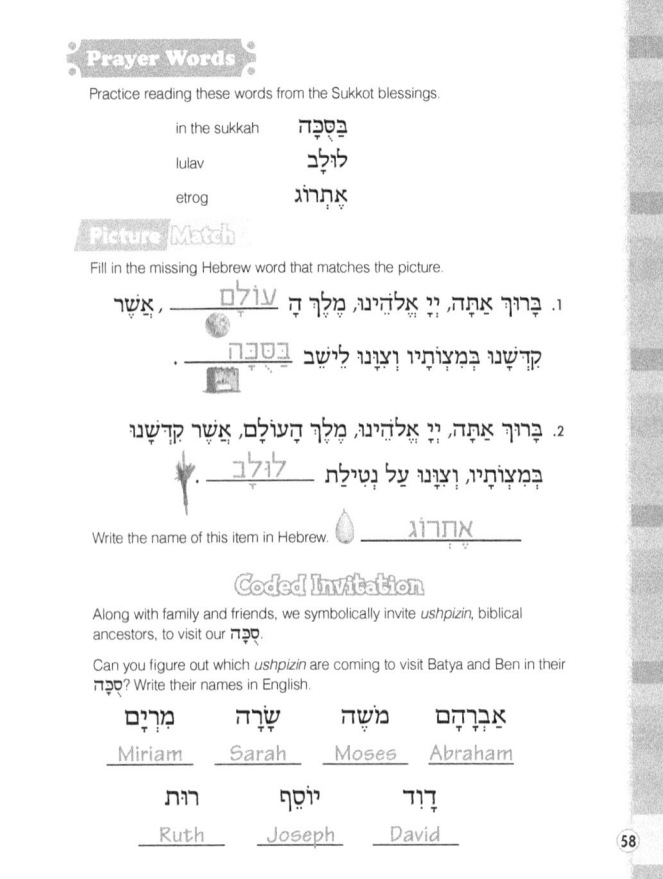

Prayer Words

Display Word Cards #65 through 67. Invite students to illustrate these words on the board. Point to the illustrations and have the class say their Hebrew names.

Picture Match

Direct students to read and complete this activity with a partner. Have pairs check their answers with other pairs.

Coded Invitation

As a class, discuss which biblical characters students would like to invite to their sukkah. Encourage students to explain their choices and to share what questions they would like to ask their guest.

You may wish to tell your class that in the past the traditional *ushpizin* (sukkah guests) were Abraham, Isaac, Jacob, Joseph, Moses, Aaron, and David. Today important women from the bible (Sarah, Rebecca, Rachel, Leah, Miriam, Abigail, Ruth, and Esther) are included as *ushpizin*.

Ask: How does the custom of *ushpizin* remind us of the mitzvah of "welcoming guests," *hachnasat orḥim*? (*Responses may include: we are reminded to invite guests to our home and to our sukkah; we invite different people from our community; it is a mitzvah to invite guests for meals.*)

Have students work in small groups to complete the activity.

Consider teaching your students the phrase used when welcoming guests: בְּרוּכִים הַבָּאִים (Word Card #78). Challenge students to identify the word meaning blessed or praised (בְּרוּכִים). Have students practice using this phrase as they act out greeting the *ushpizin*.

THE PRAYERS OF OUR PEOPLE I • כָּל יִשְׂרָאֵל 84

Ḥanukkah חֲנֻכָּה

Ask students to call out their favorite things about Ḥanukkah. (*Responses may include: candles, light, chocolate gelt, ḥanukkiyah, visiting family, gifts, blessings*) List their responses on the board.

Call on a volunteer to read the introduction aloud. As a class, chorally read the first and second blessings in Hebrew and in English. Ask: Which of these is a בְּרָכָה שֶׁל מִצְוָה? (*the first blessing*) Have students underline the words that indicate that this is a בְּרָכָה שֶׁל מִצְוָה.

Direct students to complete the activity with a partner. Call on a volunteer to describe the miracle God made for our ancestors. (*There were two different miracles: the miracle of oil lasting eight days and the miracle of a small army defeating a much more powerful one.*)

Encourage students to share their descriptions of a wonderful event they experienced. Ask: What made this event so wonderful? How did it make you feel? What did you want to do or say after this happened? As a class, chorally recite or chant the שֶׁהֶחֱיָנוּ. Remind students that they recently learned that the שֶׁהֶחֱיָנוּ is recited on Rosh Hashanah. Ask: On what other occasions is the שֶׁהֶחֱיָנוּ chanted? (*Answers may include: the first time sitting in the sukkah; wearing new clothing; at the first Passover seder*) Why don't we recite the שֶׁהֶחֱיָנוּ on all nights of Ḥanukkah? (שֶׁהֶחֱיָנוּ *is recited when we do something for the first time in a season.*)

Direct students to practice reading all three blessings with a partner.

Help students gain greater reading fluency by varying the reading task. You might ask students to alternate with a partner reading every other word of a blessing.

Digital Application

Once in the family room, students can click on "Practice Reading for חֲנֻכָּה" to practice reading the Ḥanukkah blessings.

חֲנֻכָּה Ḥanukkah

On the eight days of חֲנֻכָּה, Batya and Ben spin dreidels, eat crispy potato latkes, exchange gifts, and light candles in the חֲנֻכִּיָּה. They say the following בְּרָכוֹת on this Festival of Lights.

Practice reading the first blessing over the Hanukkah candles.

בָּרוּךְ אַתָּה, יְיָ אֱלֹהֵינוּ, מֶלֶךְ הָעוֹלָם, אֲשֶׁר קִדְּשָׁנוּ
בְּמִצְוֹתָיו וְצִוָּנוּ לְהַדְלִיק נֵר שֶׁל חֲנֻכָּה.

Praised are you, Adonai our God, Ruler of the world, who makes us holy with commandments and commands us to light the Hanukkah candles.

The second blessing praises God for making miracles.

בָּרוּךְ אַתָּה, יְיָ אֱלֹהֵינוּ, מֶלֶךְ הָעוֹלָם, שֶׁעָשָׂה נִסִּים
לַאֲבוֹתֵינוּ בַּיָּמִים הָהֵם בַּזְּמַן הַזֶּה.

Praised are you, Adonai our God, Ruler of the world, who made miracles for our ancestors in those days, at this time.

What miracle did God make for our ancestors?
<u>oil burned 8 days; few defeated many</u>

Describe a wonderful event (something like a miracle) that happened in your own life.

On the first night of Hanukkah, we recite a third blessing thanking God for allowing us to celebrate the holiday once again.

בָּרוּךְ אַתָּה, יְיָ אֱלֹהֵינוּ, מֶלֶךְ הָעוֹלָם, שֶׁהֶחֱיָנוּ,
וְקִיְּמָנוּ, וְהִגִּיעָנוּ לַזְּמַן הַזֶּה.

Praised are you, Adonai our God, Ruler of the world, who has given us life, sustained us, and enabled us to reach this time.

Circle the word in the blessing that is also its name.

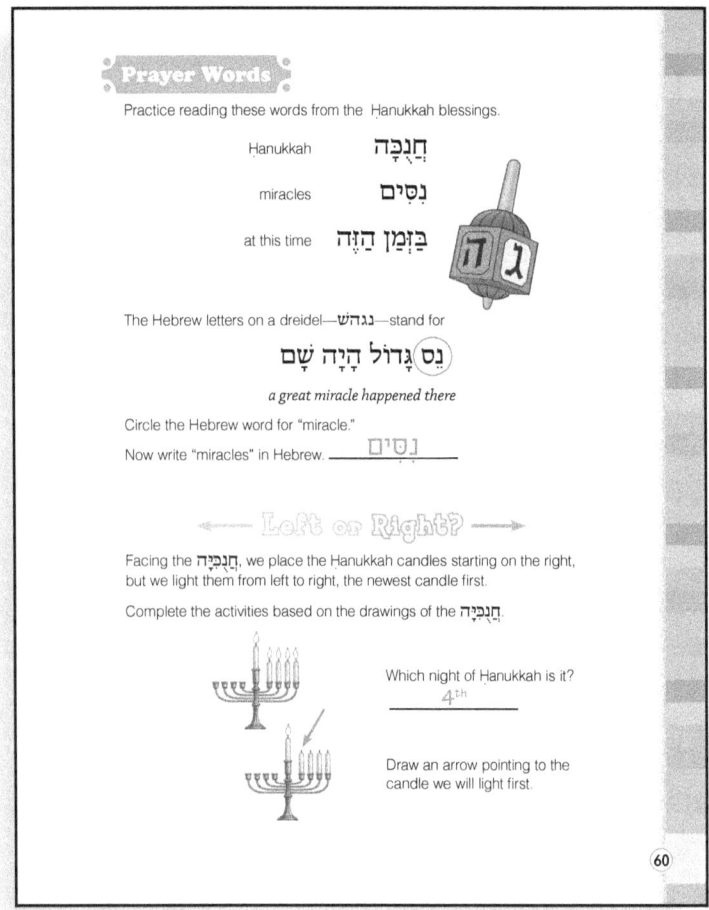

Prayer Words

Have students find and circle these words in the blessings on page 59. Display Word Card #70 and challenge students to identify the two-word phrase in שֶׁהֶחֱיָנוּ that is similar to בַּזְּמַן הַזֶּה. (לַזְּמַן הַזֶּה) Ask: What does לַזְּמַן הַזֶּה mean? (*to this time*)

Read aloud the Hebrew words that are represented by נ־ג־ה־שׁ. Call on a volunteer to read the Hebrew word for "miracle." Challenge students to explain the meaning of "ים" at the end of נִסִּים. (*makes it plural*)

Dreidel, Dreidel

If time allows, review the rules for playing dreidel, and allow students to play a game. You will need to bring several dreidels and pennies, buttons, or small, pre-cut squares of construction paper for the pot.

To play: Give each student ten game pieces (pennies or buttons). Have each player put one game piece into the "pot." Players take turns spinning the dreidel and do the following depending on which letter is facing up when the dreidel stops:

- *nun*, stands for *nisht* (in Yiddish) or "nothing": do nothing
- *gimmel*, stands for *gantz* or "everything": take the entire "pot"
- *heh*, stands for *halb* or "half": take half of the pot (or half plus one)
- *shin*, stands for *shtel* or "put in": put one piece in the pot

Note: If the pot ever has no pieces in it, everyone adds one piece.

A player is out when he or she has no pieces left. The winner is the person who gets all the game pieces or the person who has the most pieces after a designated time.

Left or Right

Direct students to complete the activity with a partner.

For fun, challenge students to calculate how many candles are needed to light a single ḥanukkiyah for all eight nights of Ḥanukkah. (*2 + 3 + 4 + 5 + 6 + 7 + 8 + 9 = 44 candles*)

Pesaḥ פֶּסַח

Ask students to call out words or phrases to do with Pesaḥ. (*Responses may include: matzah, no bread, cleaning the house, parsley, so many dishes!*) List their responses on the board.

Have students silently read the introduction to the Pesaḥ blessings. Ask: What are some of the ways the family members help to prepare for the seder? (*washing parsley; pouring wine; chopping ḥaroset, dishing out maror*) Invite a student to use the Doug puppet and to ask Doug's question. Encourage students to share stories about their favorite job in preparing for the seder.

Discuss how helping the family prepare for the seder is another way of enhancing שְׁלוֹם בַּיִת.

Focus students on the five Pesaḥ blessings. Ask: Which of these blessings have we already studied this year? (*drinking the wine, eating a green vegetable, Hamotzi*) Which of these blessings are בְּרָכוֹת שֶׁל מִצְוָה? (*the second blessing for eating matzah and the blessing for eating bitter herbs*) If students are surprised that we say Hamotzi on Pesaḥ when we do not eat regular bread, explain that matzah is a special kind of bread. It is unleavened bread. Hamotzi is followed by the blessing specifically said for eating matzah.

Direct students to underline the words that tell us a blessing is a בְּרָכָה שֶׁל מִצְוָה.

Fluent Blessing Reading

As a class, read aloud each of the blessings in Hebrew and then in English. Before you recite a blessing, encourage students to pretend they are about to eat or drink the item for which the blessing is recited.

Divide the class into groups of three. Review the blessings by pointing to a group and asking them to recite a particular blessing. For example, ask Group 2 to recite the blessing over the *maror*. After each group has read a few blessings, direct students to read the blessings with a partner.

Digital Application

Once in the family room, students can click on "Practice Reading for פֶּסַח" to practice reading the Pesaḥ blessings. In the next class, ask students which of the five Pesaḥ blessings are unique to Pesaḥ. (עַל אֲכִילַת מָרוֹר and עַל אֲכִילַת מַצָּה) Which are recited at Pesaḥ *and* at other times of the year? (בּוֹרֵא פְּרִי הַגֶּפֶן, בּוֹרֵא פְּרִי הָאֲדָמָה, and הַמּוֹצִיא לֶחֶם מִן הָאָרֶץ)

Blessing Review

To review the many blessings studied in this chapter, assign each student or pair of students a blessing. This chapter focused on the following blessings:

שֶׁהֶחֱיָנוּ, לִשְׁמֹעַ קוֹל שׁוֹפָר, בּוֹרֵא פְּרִי הָעֵץ, לְהַדְלִיק נֵר שֶׁל חֲנֻכָּה, נְטִילַת לוּלָב, לֵישֵׁב בַּסֻּכָּה, בּוֹרֵא פְּרִי הָאֲדָמָה, בּוֹרֵא פְּרִי הַגֶּפֶן, שֶׁעָשָׂה נִסִּים, עַל אֲכִילַת מָרוֹר, עַל אֲכִילַת מַצָּה, הַמּוֹצִיא

Give each student sheets of colored construction paper, markers, scissors, glue, and a copy of the blessing. Direct students to create a small poster about their blessing. The

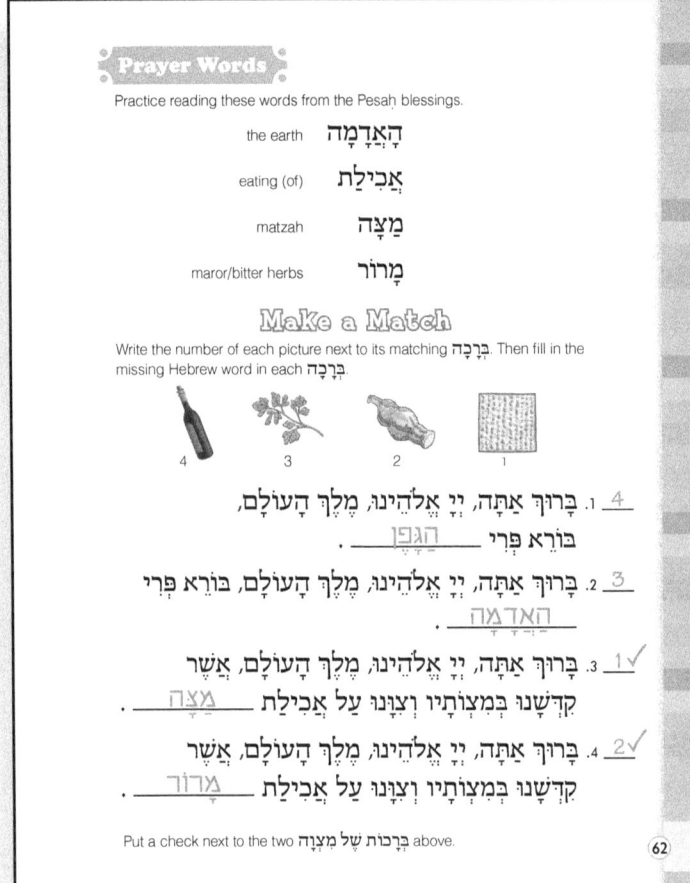

timing how quickly they can read the blessings without any errors. Have students compete against their own best time.

poster can include shapes, illustrations, and words that represent the meaning of the blessing and the occasion or occasions on which it is said. Invite each student to read his or her blessing, explain its meaning, tell about when it is said, and describe what they have created. Display these miniposters to create a blessings bulletin board.

Prayer Words

Display Word Cards #71 through 74. Focus students on the blessings on page 61. Challenge students to find and circle the words that are on display in the blessings. Pose questions to review these words and other vocabulary. Questions may include: Why does אֲכִילַת appear in two blessings? (*We are commanded to eat matzah and to eat maror.*) Which phrase describes a vegetable? (פְּרִי הָאֲדָמָה) What is the Hebrew for "bitter herbs"? (מָרוֹר)

Digital Application

Once in the family room, students can click on "Holiday Word Search" to review the holiday vocabulary words, which include חֲנֻכָּה (Hanukkah), בַּסֻּכָּה (in the sukkah), שׁוֹפָר (shofar), לוּלָב (lulav), שֶׁהֶחֱיָנוּ (who has given us life), נִסִּים (miracles), מַצָּה (matzah), הָאֲדָמָה (the earth), אֲכִילַת (eating of), מָרוֹר (bitter herbs).

Make a Match

Direct students to complete the exercise individually. Walk around the room to assess how well students recall these blessing words. Call on a volunteer to read the first blessing. Direct students to check their own work and then to chorally read the entire blessing. Repeat this for the next three blessings.

Ask students to underline the words that indicate that a blessing is a בְּרָכָה שֶׁל מִצְוָה.

Fluent Blessing Reading

Have students practice reading the blessings with a partner. Encourage students to read the blessings fluently. *Optional*: Challenge students to reach a "personal best" by

THE PRAYERS OF OUR PEOPLE I • כָּל יִשְׂרָאֵל

Order of the Seder

Ask students to share examples of ways they have "order" in their lives. (*Responses may include: I schedule my homework each night; school starts and ends at the same time every day; I play soccer three times every week; I keep all my white socks in one drawer and my colored socks in another.*)

Have students silently read the introduction. Ask: What is the meaning of the word סֵדֶר? (*order*)

As a class, read the order of the seder. To practice reading the names of each section, invite a student to the front of the room. Ask the student to say a number and have the class chorally read the name of that part of the seder. For example, if the students says, "five," the class responds, "מַגִּיד."

For additional practice, invite the class to stand in a circle. Call on a student to read the name of the first part of the סֵדֶר. Have the person next to that student read the name of the second part of the סֵדֶר. Continue around the circle, having students read the names of the seder parts in their correct order. Do the activity again, beginning with a different student.

Once students are familiar with the names of the parts of the סֵדֶר, have students work with a partner and complete the exercises below the list. Review the answers with the class, having students check their own work.

Singing the Seder

Challenge students to guess the Hebrew phrase for "order of the seder" (סֵדֶר הַסֵּדֶר).

Divide the class into groups of 3. Direct each group to think of at least two tunes to which they can sing סֵדֶר הַסֵּדֶר. Suggested tunes may include the beginning of: Adon Olam, Yankee Doodle, or Twinkle, Twinkle. Invite each group to sing סֵדֶר הַסֵּדֶר to the tune they have selected, and then have the class chorally join them as they repeat the tune.

Ask for a volunteer to drum along on the desk in time with the song. Perhaps a student would like to do a simple dance to accompany the music and chanting.

Fluent Blessing Reading

Read the holiday blessings below. Then, on the blank line at the end of each blessing, write the English name of the holiday on which we recite that blessing.

Put a big star ☆ next to your favorite holiday!

1. בָּרוּךְ אַתָּה, יְיָ אֱלֹהֵינוּ, מֶלֶךְ הָעוֹלָם, אֲשֶׁר קִדְּשָׁנוּ בְּמִצְוֹתָיו וְצִוָּנוּ עַל אֲכִילַת מָרוֹר. ___Passover___

2. בָּרוּךְ אַתָּה, יְיָ אֱלֹהֵינוּ, מֶלֶךְ הָעוֹלָם, אֲשֶׁר קִדְּשָׁנוּ בְּמִצְוֹתָיו וְצִוָּנוּ לֵישֵׁב בַּסֻּכָּה. ___Sukkot___

3. בָּרוּךְ אַתָּה, יְיָ אֱלֹהֵינוּ, מֶלֶךְ הָעוֹלָם, אֲשֶׁר קִדְּשָׁנוּ בְּמִצְוֹתָיו וְצִוָּנוּ לִשְׁמֹעַ קוֹל שׁוֹפָר. ___Rosh Hashanah___

4. בָּרוּךְ אַתָּה, יְיָ אֱלֹהֵינוּ, מֶלֶךְ הָעוֹלָם, אֲשֶׁר קִדְּשָׁנוּ בְּמִצְוֹתָיו וְצִוָּנוּ עַל אֲכִילַת מַצָּה. ___Passover___

5. בָּרוּךְ אַתָּה, יְיָ אֱלֹהֵינוּ, מֶלֶךְ הָעוֹלָם, אֲשֶׁר קִדְּשָׁנוּ בְּמִצְוֹתָיו וְצִוָּנוּ לְהַדְלִיק נֵר שֶׁל חֲנֻכָּה. ___Hanukkah___

6. בָּרוּךְ אַתָּה, יְיָ אֱלֹהֵינוּ, מֶלֶךְ הָעוֹלָם, אֲשֶׁר קִדְּשָׁנוּ בְּמִצְוֹתָיו וְצִוָּנוּ עַל מִקְרָא מְגִלָּה. ___Purim___

Fluent Blessing Reading

Focus students on blessing #6. Invite students to chorally read the blessing along with you.

Challenge students to guess the occasion on which this blessing is recited. If students have difficulty guessing the occasion, have the class read aloud the last word of the blessing. (מְגִלָּה)

Ask: On which holiday do we read a מְגִלָּה? (*Purim*) Explain that it is a mitzvah to hear מְגִילַת אֶסְתֵּר (Scroll of Esther) and that this is the blessing recited before performing that mitzvah.

Have students read all the blessings with a partner and then identify the holiday on which each blessing is recited. Remind students to indicate their favorite holiday with a star. They might even like to draw a simple picture in their book to illustrate their favorite holiday.

Challenge students to recite the appropriate blessing for various mitzvot. Ask, for example, what is the blessing recited over a food we eat instead of bread during Pesaḥ? (עַל אֲכִילַת מַצָּה)

Ask: Which is your favorite holiday? Why? What do you like best about the holiday?

Direct students to circle the blessing for the mitzvah they most like to perform. Ask students to form groups based on their favorite mitzvah from this list. Have each group prepare a short skit or advertisement that depicts why their mitzvah is their favorite. Invite each group to present their skit or advertisement to the class.

Duplicate enough copies of both the Bingo board and the Extra Word card for every student in your class. Have students cut up the six word boxes on the Extra Word card and place them at random in the empty boxes of the Bingo board. Give each student small objects, such as paper clips or pennies, to use as markers.

To play, call out one of the sixteen words or phrases for the students to find and cover. The first student to cover four squares in a row (horizontally, vertically, or diagonally), and read and translate the covered words correctly, wins.

Digital Application

Once in the family room, students should click on "Practice Reading for פּוּרִים" to practice reading the blessing recited before reading the Megillah.

Blessing Bingo

Select sixteen Hebrew words or phrases from any of the blessings studied this year. Prepare a Bingo board with sixteen squares. In ten of the squares, chosen at random, write Hebrew words or phrases from among the sixteen you selected, leaving the other six squares blank. On a separate piece of paper, draw six boxes (the same size as those on the Bingo board) and write in the remaining six Hebrew words or phrases. Call this card the Extra Word card.

Language Link

Ask students what makes a "good day" for them. (*Responses may include: I don't get homework; I get to sleep late; my favorite television show is on; it's the first day of camp.*) Read the introduction aloud to the class, having students chorally read the Hebrew phrases with you. Call on volunteers to share their response to the question.

Direct students back to page 54, and call on a volunteer to read and explain the meaning of the title of Chapter 7.

Challenge students to guess the meaning of the word יוֹם. Provide a clue by reminding them of the names יוֹם הָעַצְמָאוּת and יוֹם הַזִכָּרוֹן. Ask students to derive the meaning of the word טוֹב. Provide clues using the phrases שָׁנָה טוֹבָה וּמְתוּקָה and שָׁבוּעַ טוֹב.

Have your students practice wishing one another חַג שָׂמֵחַ.

Clue to Cyberspace

Have students work with a partner to complete the "Clue to Cyberspace" activity. (The phrase that appears twice is חַג שָׂמֵחַ.)

Digital Application

Once in the family room, students can click on "Holiday Slingshot" to review the objects used on the various holidays, such as an apple on Rosh Hashanah. The holiday objects relate to four holidays: Rosh Hashanah, Sukkot, Ḥanukkah, and Pesaḥ. Remind your students to use the clue (חַג שָׂמֵחַ) to reset their timer in the "Holiday Slingshot" game. You may wish to play a modified version of the game in the next class. Simply name a holiday and ask students to take turns describing objects used or foods eaten on that holiday. Give points for each object named.

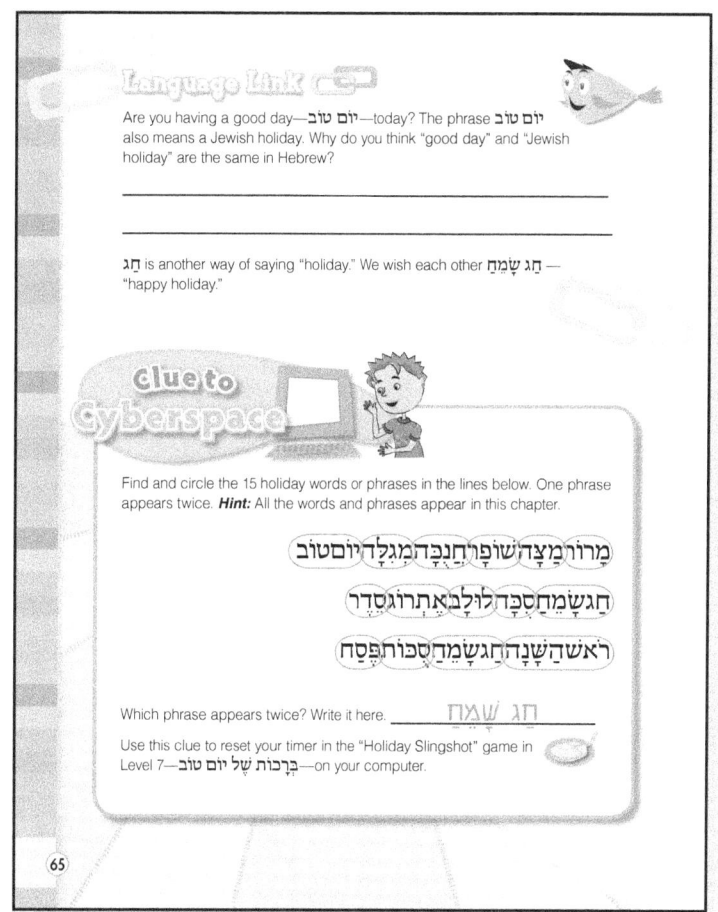

My Own Siddur

If students are creating their own siddur, prepare a page by copying the holiday blessings.

שֶׁהֶחֱיָנוּ, לִשְׁמֹעַ קוֹל שׁוֹפָר, בּוֹרֵא פְּרִי הָעֵץ,
לְהַדְלִיק נֵר שֶׁל חֲנֻכָּה, נְטִילַת לוּלָב, לֵישֵׁב בַּסֻּכָּה,
בּוֹרֵא פְּרִי הָאֲדָמָה, בּוֹרֵא פְּרִי הַגָּפֶן, שֶׁעָשָׂה נִסִּים,
עַל אֲכִילַת מָרוֹר, עַל אֲכִילַת מַצָּה, הַמּוֹצִיא

Students can illustrate or write sentences as they have done for previous blessings.

Assessment

As students are working on any of the above activities, meet individually with them to assess reading fluency and knowledge of prayer content. You can mark students' progress using the assessment chart and check their progress online at www.behrmanhouse.com.

Digital Application

Once in the family room, students can click on "Holiday Match" to review the blessing vocabulary of the various holidays, which includes לִשְׁמֹעַ (to hear), שׁוֹפָר (shofar), הָאֲדָמָה (the earth), לוּלָב (lulav), קוֹל (voice), and חֲנֻכִּיָּה (ḥanukkiyah). In the next class, you may wish to expand the activity. Divide students into pairs. Provide each pair with two pieces of paper and a word from a holiday blessing, such as מַצָּה (matzah) or נֵר (candle). Ask each pair to write the word on one piece and draw the word on the other. Collect the papers, redistribute them among students, and then challenge students to match their word with a drawing, or vice versa.

What's Next?

Ask the following open-ended questions: Why do people ask questions? When do you ask questions? Whom do you ask? Remind students that it is essential to ask questions in order to learn and that Judaism encourages us to ask questions. In fact, asking questions is a prominent part of the Pesaḥ seder. Inform students that in the next chapter they will study the Four Questions (מַה נִּשְׁתַּנָּה) that are recited at the Pesaḥ seder.

ABOUT THE PRAYER

It is customary for the youngest child to ask the Four Questions, מַה נִּשְׁתַּנָּה, at the beginning of the מַגִּיד section of the Pesaḥ seder. These questions focus on why this meal is different from ordinary meals. The four questions were originally presented as sample questions to be asked at a seder. Participants can ask any questions that are relevant to the seder.

LEARNING OBJECTIVES

Students will be able to:

- Fluently recite מַה נִּשְׁתַּנָּה.
- Define key words found in and related to מַה נִּשְׁתַּנָּה.
- Explain and answer each of the four questions from מַה נִּשְׁתַּנָּה.
- Explain the importance of imagining that each of us was freed from Egypt.

NEW WORDS AND PHRASES

Prayer Words:

| the night | הַלַּיְלָה |
| this | הַזֶּה |

Related Words:

the Four Questions	מַה נִּשְׁתַּנָּה
the	הַ־
night	לַיְלָה

INSTRUCTIONAL MATERIALS

Text Pages 66–71
Word Cards #85–89

Digital Application: Lesson 8—Dining Room (see page 8 for a list of games and activities)

WHERE WE ARE

Batya and Ben are seated at the Pesaḥ seder table in the dining room with their parents. Batya will chant the מַה נִּשְׁתַּנָּה as the rest of the family follows along in their *haggadot*.

INTRODUCING THE LESSON

Engage your students in a discussion about reciting the Four Questions by asking questions such as: Who in your family chants the Four Questions? Why does that person chant it? Do other participants join in? When and why?

Explain that in this chapter students will study the Four Questions and other parts of the haggadah.

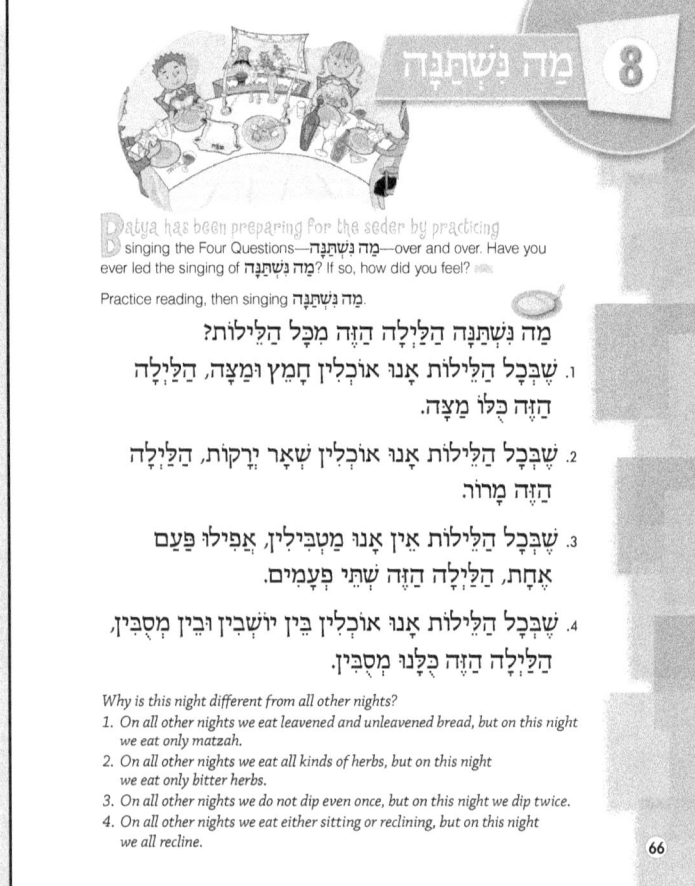

INTO THE TEXT

Call on a volunteer to read the introduction to the Four Questions as fellow students follow along. Invite students to tell about their own experiences reciting the Four Questions.

Reading Fluency

Direct students to follow along as you read aloud the first line of the מַה נִּשְׁתַּנָּה. Explain to students that the vowel ָ in מִכָּל is pronounced "oh." Direct students to page 42 and challenge them to identify the words in the Kiddush that, like מִכָּל, have a vowel ָ pronounced "oh." (קָדְשׁוֹ, קָדְשְׁךָ)

Reread the first line and ask students to chorally read the line after you. Have students read the Hebrew and its English meaning, found below the Hebrew, with a partner.

Repeat this for each of the four questions. Read a question aloud and have students chorally read it, then read the Hebrew and its English meaning with a partner.

Challenge students to answer the following questions without looking at the English translation: Which question asks about bitter herbs? (*second question*) Which question asks about matzah? (*first question*) Which question asks about how we sit as we eat? (*fourth question*) Which question mentions that on most nights we don't dip even once? (*third question*). In each case, ask students what their clue was.

Teach, or invite the cantor or music specialist to teach, students to chant the מַה נִּשְׁתַּנָּה.

Digital Application

Tell students that at home, before the next class, they should click on מַה נִּשְׁתַּנָּה at the bottom of the screen to enter the dining room. Once in the dining room, students can click on the wine cup to practice reading מַה נִּשְׁתַּנָּה. Ask students to count how many times the phrase מַה נִּשְׁתַּנָּה is written. (*only once*) Tell students to click on the musical note to practice chanting מַה נִּשְׁתַּנָּה. In the next class, you may wish to ask for a volunteer to sing מַה נִּשְׁתַּנָּה aloud.

THE PRAYERS OF OUR PEOPLE I • כָּל יִשְׂרָאֵל   **94**

The Answers

In preparation for this activity, bring to class *haggadot* and books about Passover that have information about the holiday. Divide the class into four groups. Direct each group to use their past knowledge, as well as the books and *haggadot*, to answer the questions on page 67.

As an added challenge, have students write the English meaning of each of the four Hebrew phrases.

Walk around the room to check students' work and help them locate the information needed.

Have each group present the information for one phrase. Invite other groups to share additional thoughts or information about the phrase.

Ask: Which two words appear in each of these phrases? (הַלַּיְלָה הַזֶּה) What do these words mean? (*this night*) You might suggest that students look back at the English on page 66 for their meaning.

Our Questions

Tell students that one of the original Four Questions asked why we eat only roasted meat at the seder. After the destruction of the Temple, when sacrifices were no longer performed, that question became irrelevant. Instead, we began to ask why we recline on this seder night.

Divide the class into groups of three. Ask each group to write up three original questions and answers about the Passover seder that might have replaced the original question. Have groups share their questions and answers with the class. Consider listing students' questions and answers on a chart or poster board and displaying the list of "Our Seder Questions" on the bulletin board.

Photo Op

Focus students on the photograph of the girls eating matzah. Direct students back to page 63 and review singing the order of the seder. Have students explain which part of the seder is being shown in this photograph. (מוֹצִיא מַצָּה—*because we eat the matzah*)

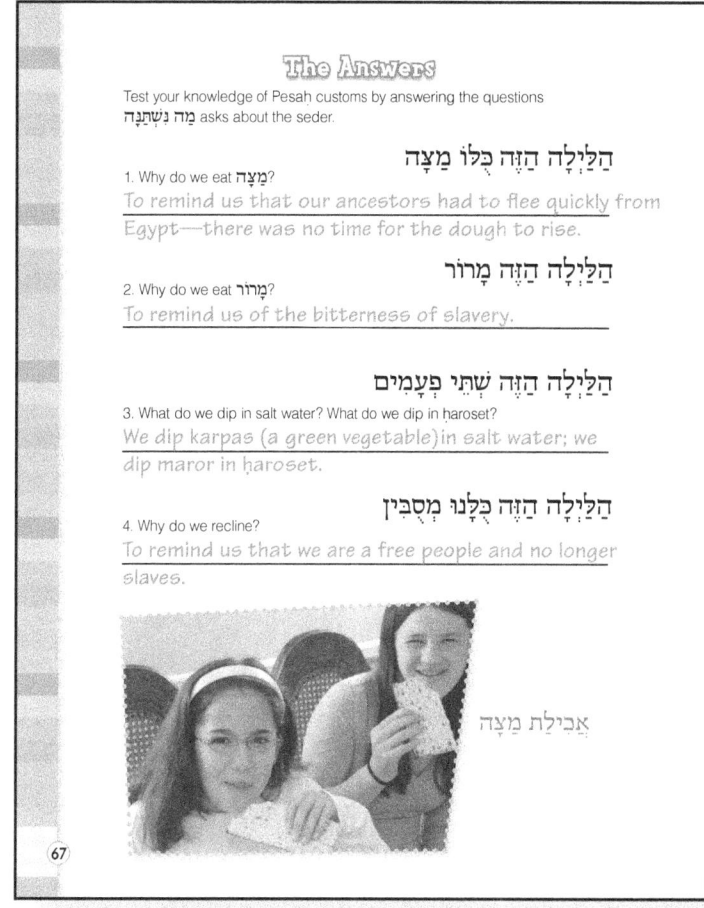

Ask: What blessing is recited before eating matzah? (עַל אֲכִילַת מַצָּה) What do the words אֲכִילַת מַצָּה mean? (*eating matzah*) What does matzah taste like to you? What does matzah sound like to you when it breaks? What do you like to put on your matzah?

Encourage students to bring in the recipe for a favorite meal that includes matzah. Recipes might include: matzah *brei*, matzah lasagna, matzah pizza. Have students include the name of the person who usually prepares this meal for them. Create a Matzah Passover cookbook for all students to bring home.

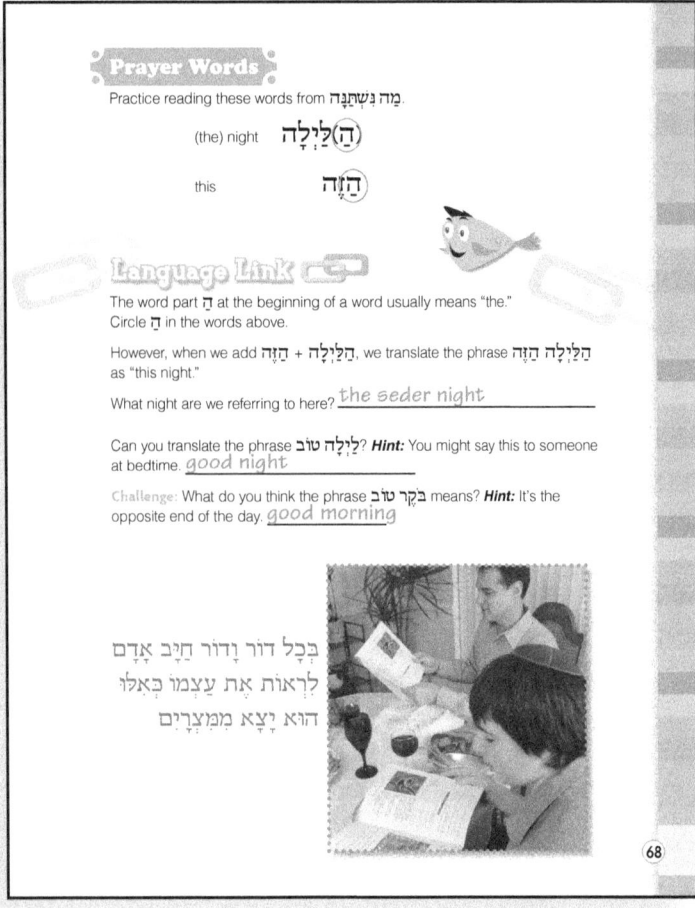

Thousands and thousands of tired people
Yelling and crying and laughing
Sweat and hot, dry air
Matzah, matzah, matzah and freedom
My family and the desert land.

 **Prayer Words**

Present Word Cards #85 and 86. Have students find and circle these words on page 66.

Language Link

Direct students to complete the activity with a partner. Review the answers as a class, having students check and correct their own work.

Have students practice using the phrases לַיְלָה טוֹב and בֹּקֶר טוֹב. Say, for example: If it is 8:00 in the morning, how should you greet your friends? (בֹּקֶר טוֹב) What should you say at 10:00 at night? (לַיְלָה טוֹב) Announce several different morning and night hours, encouraging students to chorally respond לַיְלָה טוֹב or בֹּקֶר טוֹב. You may choose to introduce the phrase עֶרֶב טוֹב for the early evening hours.

 **Photo Op**

Focus students on this photograph after they have studied page 69. Call on students to describe what they see in the photograph. Have the class chorally read the caption for the photograph.

Ask: What is the connection between this photograph and the caption? (*The photograph shows more than one generation celebrating the seder.*) Why do you think the photographer chose to show a young boy and a grown man? How can you tell they are celebrating Passover? How does reciting the same words as our parents and grandparents enhance שְׁלוֹם בַּיִת? Where do you usually have your Pesaḥ seder? Who is generally at your Pesaḥ seder?

As a class, discuss what it must have felt like to be among the Israelites who were freed from slavery in Egypt. Direct students to write a "Five Senses Poem" describing the experience of being freed. To write the poem, have students finish each of the following lines:

I see…; I hear…; I smell…; I taste…; I touch…

Students then copy only the endings of the sentences to create the poem. To the left is a sample poem:

Me Too!

Read the introduction and have students share stories about what their families do every year at the Pesaḥ seder. Ask if families add new customs from year to year.

Allow students to individually write down their family traditions and to write why Jews gather to retell and remember the exodus from Egypt. Invite students to share their responses.

Ask: How does celebrating the Pesaḥ seder help us to strengthen שָׁלוֹם בַּיִת in our home? (*Responses may include: we have a chance to spend time with friends and relatives; we all stop working to sit and eat a meal together; we sing fun songs together.*)

Invite students to join with you and to chorally read the Hebrew and English verse from the Haggadah. Ask: Who is this written for? (*all Jews, every generation*) What do we have to do? (*see ourselves as if we were freed from slavery in Egypt*) Do you think it is easy or hard to do this? Why?

Allow students to independently write why they think tradition tells us to imagine ourselves as being freed from slavery. Call on students to share their responses.

Challenge students to name the prayer that includes זֵכֶר לִיצִיאַת מִצְרָיִם. (קִדּוּשׁ)

Family Seder Lore

Encourage students to ask parents or grandparents to describe what their Pesaḥ seder was like when they were children. How is the family seder the same or different from the seders of their childhood? Have students share their family stories with the class. If possible, invite Ashkenazic and Sephardic guests to speak. It would be interesting to have someone who was not born in North America describe their family seder in the country of their birth.

Digital Application

Once in the dining room, students can click on the seder plate to review the Passover items, which include זְרוֹעַ (shankbone), חֲרוֹסֶת (lettuce), חֲזֶרֶת (haroset), כַּרְפַּס (parsley), מָרוֹר (bitter herbs), and בֵּיצָה (egg). Note that the words on the seder plate do not have vowels and may be difficult for students to read. Challenge students to read the word in the center of the plate: פֶּסַח (Pesaḥ). Bring in a seder plate to the next class. Let students point to the places where the various Passover foods are placed and explain the foods' symbolic value.

Me Too!

Describe two things your family does every year at the Pesaḥ seder.

1. _____
2. _____

If you ask a parent or grandparent, you're likely to find that they recited the same or similar words, performed the same rituals, and ate the same foods at their seders when they were young.

Why do you think Jews gather each year to retell the Pesaḥ story and remember our freedom from slavery in Egypt?

_____
_____

The Haggadah tells us:

בְּכָל־דּוֹר וָדוֹר חַיָּב אָדָם לִרְאוֹת אֶת־עַצְמוֹ כְּאִלּוּ הוּא יָצָא מִמִּצְרָיִם.

In every generation it is our duty to see ourselves as if we were freed from slavery in Egypt.

Why do you think it is important to "see ourselves as if we were freed from slavery in Egypt"?

_____
_____

The theme of our being freed from slavery in Egypt occurs in many prayers. Write in Hebrew the name of the prayer in which this phrase appears:

זֵכֶר לִיצִיאַת מִצְרָיִם

Hint: We say it over wine on Shabbat and holidays. Look back at Chapter 5.

קִדּוּשׁ

The Four Children

Inform students that each year in the haggadah we read about four different types of children. Ask: What else have we learned about that there are four of in the haggadah? (*the Four Questions*) Tell students that we also drink four cups of wine or grape juice at the Pesaḥ seder.

Have students silently read about the four children. Ask questions about the qualities of the four children. Ask, for example: Which child does not feel part of the Jewish people? (*rebellious*—רָשָׁע) Challenge students to identify the Hebrew word meaning "one." (אֶחָד)

Divide the class into four groups. Assign each group one of the four children. Have each group create a skit depicting their child at the seder table. As a reminder write on the board: How would your "child" relate to the Passover story? Have groups present their skits to the class.

Have students work with a partner to correctly label the pictures at the bottom of the page. Ask students to practice reading the Hebrew descriptions of each of the children with a partner.

Enrichment

Distribute a variety of *haggadot* and have students find different explanations about the symbolic meaning of the four children.

Digital Application

Once in the dining room, students can click on the hutch to review the four children, who include: אֶחָד חָכָם, אֶחָד רָשָׁע, אֶחָד תָּם, and אֶחָד שֶׁאֵינוֹ יוֹדֵעַ לִשְׁאוֹל. Students match each child with a representative picture: אֶחָד חָכָם to a drawing of a magnifying glass and eye; אֶחָד רָשָׁע to a drawing of a boy excluding other children; אֶחָד תָּם to a child who appears shy and has his head down; אֶחָד שֶׁאֵינוֹ יוֹדֵעַ לִשְׁאוֹל to a picture of a baby. In the next class, ask students how they matched each child with the picture, and why.

Clue to Cyberspace

Direct students to fill in the blanks in the מַה נִּשְׁתַּנָּה and then number the questions in their proper order. Walk around the room to assess students' knowledge and understanding of the Four Questions. The answer to the clue is 3.

As a class, practice chanting all of the מַה נִּשְׁתַּנָּה.

Digital Application

Once in the dining room, students can click on the image of the skateboard to play "Batya's Vert Skate" game and review vocabulary, which includes לַיְלָה (night), בֹּקֶר (morning), לֹא (no), כֵּן (yes), טוֹב (good), לֹא טוֹב (not good), לַיְלָה טוֹב (good night), and בֹּקֶר טוֹב (good morning).

Remind students to use the clue (3) to do a bonus trick in the game. In the next class, review the vocabulary. If your class ends in the evening, wave goodbye to students and say לַיְלָה טוֹב.

Make saying לַיְלָה טוֹב and בֹּקֶר טוֹב part of your classroom culture.

Concentration

Prepare a reading practice game for the מַה נִּשְׁתַּנָּה: Using 3" x 5" index cards, create twenty playing cards, comprised of two identical sets of ten different phrases. For example, write or copy and mount אָנוּ אוֹכְלִין חָמֵץ וּמַצָּה onto two index cards.

Place the cards face up. Allow students to see where each card is placed. Turn all the cards over and challenge students to make a match. Follow directions as described on page 12.

My Own Siddur

If students are creating their own siddur, prepare a page for the מַה נִּשְׁתַּנָּה. Students can illustrate or write sentences as they have done for previous blessings and prayers.

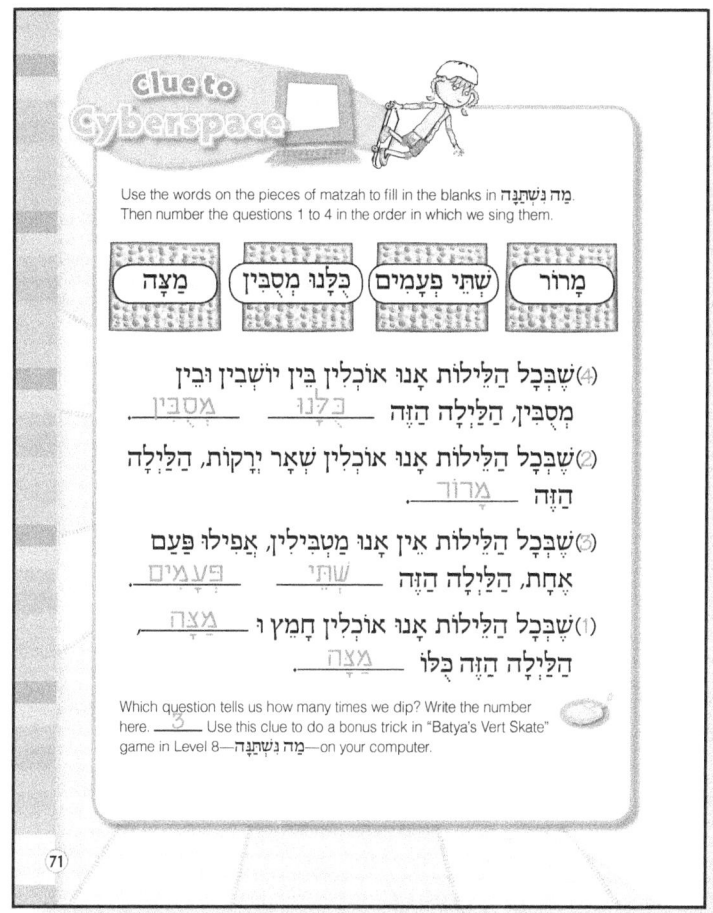

CHAPTER 8

Assessment

As students are working on any of the above activities, meet individually with them to assess reading fluency and knowledge of prayer content. Mark students' progress on the assessment chart and check their progress online at www.behrmanhouse.com.

What's Next?

Ask: Why are we taught to write thank you notes? (*Responses may include: it shows our appreciation; it's polite; we want the person to know we like the gift.*) Do you write thank you notes before or after receiving a gift? (*after*) Ask: When do we recite the blessings in which we praise and thank God for giving us food? (*before we eat fruit, vegetables, etc.*) Inform students that in the next chapter they will learn the blessing, בִּרְכַּת הַמָּזוֹן, that, unlike the other blessings, is recited after we eat. Just as we write a thank you note after receiving a gift, we recite בִּרְכַּת הַמָּזוֹן after eating a meal.

ABOUT THE PRAYER

בִּרְכַּת הַמָּזוֹן is the blessing recited after a meal at which bread has been consumed. בִּרְכַּת הַמָּזוֹן not only thanks God for providing us with the food we have just eaten, it also thanks God for the Land of Israel and the Torah, and it praises God's goodness and kindness.

LEARNING OBJECTIVES

Students will be able to:

- Identify Hebrew words related to "eating."
- Fluently recite the first blessing of בִּרְכַּת הַמָּזוֹן.
- Define key words found in and related to בִּרְכַּת הַמָּזוֹן.
- Describe when בִּרְכַּת הַמָּזוֹן is recited.
- Explain the role and importance of bread in Jewish tradition.

NEW WORDS AND PHRASES

Prayer Words:

who feeds	הַזָּן
(God's) goodness	טוּבוֹ
(with) kindness	(בְּ)חֶסֶד
food	מָזוֹן

Related Words:

בִּרְכַּת הַמָּזוֹן
the blessing after a meal, Grace after Meals

good	טוֹב
welcoming guests	הַכְנָסַת אוֹרְחִים
all	כָּל

INSTRUCTIONAL MATERIALS

Text Pages 72–79
Word Cards #90–97

Digital Application: Lesson 9—Kitchen (see page 8 for a list of games and activities)

WHERE WE ARE

Batya and Ben are in the kitchen with their mother preparing a meal for a food drive. They are acting as partners with God to help feed the hungry.

INTRODUCING THE LESSON

Ask students: If you were to write a prayer thanking God for a meal, what would you include?

List students' suggestions on the board for all to see and have a volunteer keep the same list on a large sheet of paper. Tell students that בִּרְכַּת הַמָּזוֹן is a prayer made up of four blessings recited after a meal. In this chapter, they will be studying the first blessing of בִּרְכַּת הַמָּזוֹן. Later, they will compare their own list to the contents of בִּרְכַּת הַמָּזוֹן.

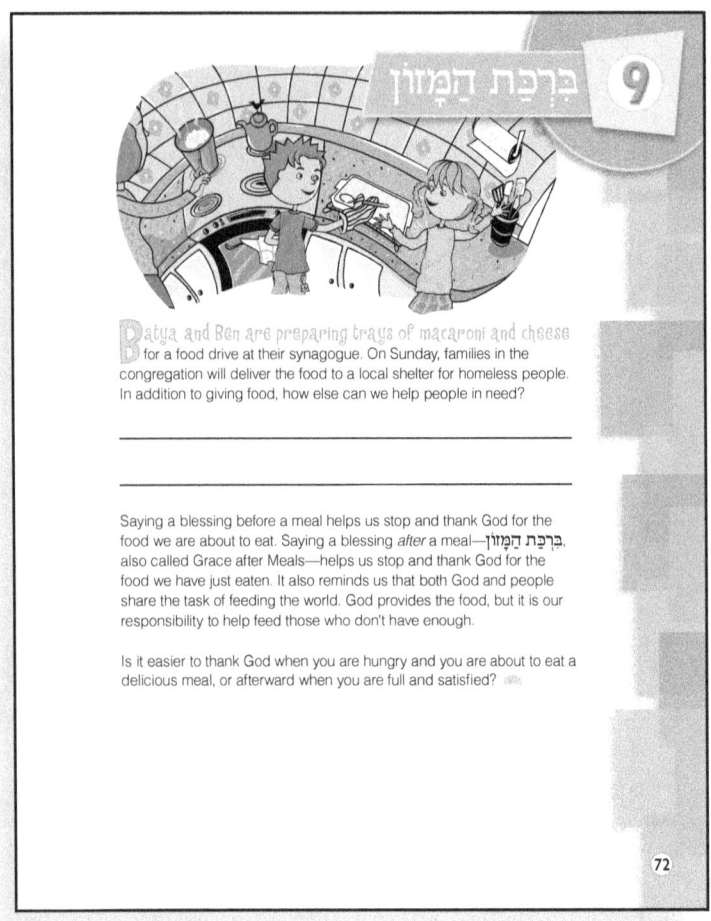

Goal: 100 food items

April 19: 25 items

April 12: 10 items

INTO THE TEXT

Call on a volunteer to read the introductory paragraph.

Allow students to individually write about other ways we can help people in need. (*Responses may include: raising money for a charity; donating used clothing; teaching people to read*) Invite students to share their responses with the class.

Have students silently read the rest of page 72. To check students' comprehension, ask:

- What do we thank God for when we say a blessing before we eat? (*We thank God for the food we are about to eat.*)
- When do we recite בִּרְכַּת הַמָזוֹן? (*after a meal*)
- According to our tradition, who shares the task of feeding the hungry? (*God and people*)
- What role does God play in feeding the hungry? (*God provides food.*)
- What role do people play in feeding the hungry? (*We help get food to people in need.*)

Ask students if they think it is more appropriate to thank God for food before or after they have eaten. Encourage students to explain their reasoning.

 **Feeding the Hungry**

Have your class organize a food drive at your school. Assign students different tasks such as creating posters, putting a notice in the school or synagogue bulletin, or setting up a drop-off box near an entrance in the synagogue. You may wish to have students create a poster, using a bar graph, that reflects a goal to be reached and the amount of food that has been collected. Assign students the task of counting the number of food items collected each week and indicating this number on the bar graph.

THE PRAYERS OF OUR PEOPLE I • כָּל יִשְׂרָאֵל   102

Fluent Blessing Reading

To practice reading בִּרְכַּת הַמָּזוֹן:
Read line 1 aloud as students follow along and then reread that line. Call on a volunteer to read the English translation. Continue reading each of the lines, one at a time, and have students follow along. Then chorally repeat each line and read its English translation.

Compare the contents of בִּרְכַּת הַמָּזוֹן with the list created by students when the chapter was first introduced.

Have students practice reading the prayer in a variety of ways. Divide the class into four groups. Assign each group three consecutive lines (1–3; 4–6; 7–10; 11–12) to read fluently. Allow the groups time to practice reading their three lines. After a few minutes, call on the groups to chorally read their three lines according to their order in the prayer. Reassign each group a different set of lines. Again, allow groups time to practice their lines before all groups chorally read their part of the prayer. Repeat this two more times until students have practiced reading all the lines from בִּרְכַּת הַמָּזוֹן.

Teach, or invite the cantor or music specialist to teach, students to chant בִּרְכַּת הַמָּזוֹן.

Digital Application

Tell students that at home, before the next class, they should click on בִּרְכַּת הַמָּזוֹן at the bottom of the screen to enter the kitchen. Once in the kitchen, students can click on the back cupboard to practice reading the first blessing of בִּרְכַּת הַמָּזוֹן. Challenge students to find two words they already know. Some answers might include: הָעוֹלָם (the world), אַתָּה (you, for a male), and אֲשֶׁר (who).

In Your Own Words

Allow students to individually choose and write a Hebrew line from בִּרְכַּת הַמָּזוֹן that they consider to be most important. Invite students to share the line they have chosen and to explain the meaning of their line and the reason they chose it.

Practice reading בִּרְכַּת הַמָּזוֹן

1. בָּרוּךְ אַתָּה, יְיָ אֱלֹהֵינוּ, מֶלֶךְ הָעוֹלָם,
2. הַזָּן אֶת הָעוֹלָם כֻּלּוֹ
3. בְּטוּבוֹ בְּחֵן בְּחֶסֶד וּבְרַחֲמִים.
4. הוּא נוֹתֵן לֶחֶם לְכָל בָּשָׂר
5. כִּי לְעוֹלָם חַסְדּוֹ.
6. וּבְטוּבוֹ הַגָּדוֹל תָּמִיד לֹא חָסַר לָנוּ,
7. וְאַל יֶחְסַר לָנוּ מָזוֹן לְעוֹלָם וָעֶד
8. בַּעֲבוּר שְׁמוֹ הַגָּדוֹל,
9. כִּי הוּא אֵל זָן וּמְפַרְנֵס לַכֹּל
10. וּמֵטִיב לַכֹּל, וּמֵכִין מָזוֹן
11. לְכָל בְּרִיּוֹתָיו אֲשֶׁר בָּרָא.
12. בָּרוּךְ אַתָּה, יְיָ, הַזָּן אֶת הַכֹּל.

1. Praised are You, Adonai, our God, Ruler of the world,
2. Who feeds the entire world
3. with goodness, with grace, with kindness and with mercy.
4. You give bread to all people,
5. for Your kindness lasts forever.
6. Because of Your great goodness we have never lacked food,
7. Nor shall we ever lack food in the future
8. because of Your great name,
9. for You support and assist all creatures
10. and bring goodness to all, and provide food
11. for all You have created.
12. Praised are You, Adonai, who gives food to everyone.

In Your Own Words

Choose one line from בִּרְכַּת הַמָּזוֹן that praises God, and write it in Hebrew.

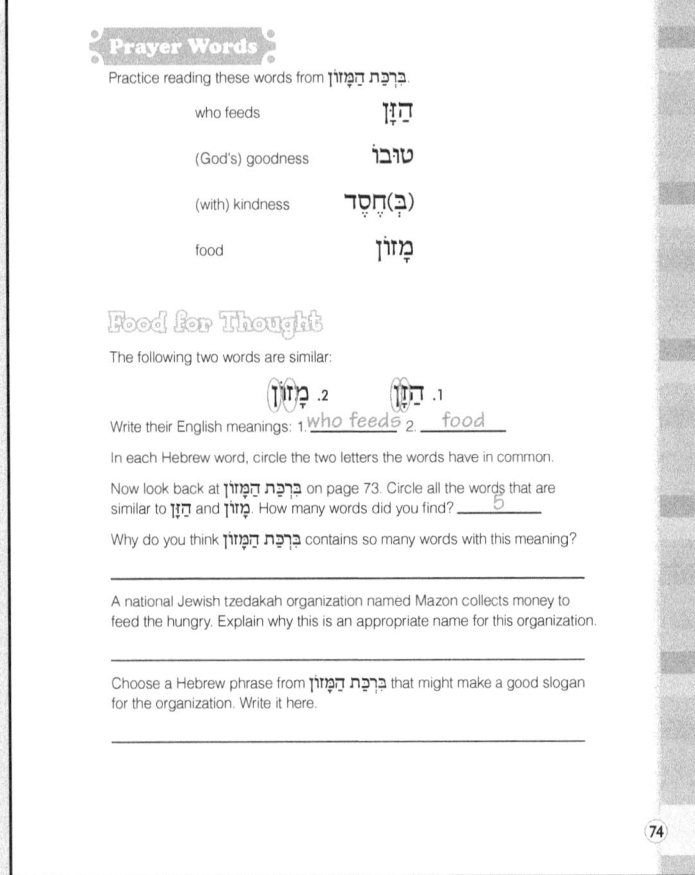

Prayer Words

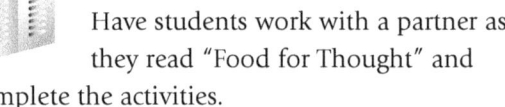

Present Word Cards #90 through 93. When presenting Word Card #90, challenge students to explain the meaning of הַ־ (*the*). Ask: What is the meaning of שָׁבוּעַ טוֹב? (*a good week*) Which new word is similar to one of the words in this phrase? (טוּבוֹ) What is the shared meaning of טוֹב and טוּבוֹ? (*good*)

Display Word Cards #4, 8, 9, 10, 11, 16, 17, and 90 through 93. Challenge students to put the words in order on the board ledge according to their appearance in בִּרְכַּת הַמָּזוֹן.

Food for Thought

Have students work with a partner as they read "Food for Thought" and complete the activities.

Invite students to share their responses with the class. Call students up to the board to write a phrase from בִּרְכַּת הַמָּזוֹן that would make a good slogan for the organization Mazon, which provides food for communities in need.

Encourage students to learn about Mazon on the internet (www.mazon.org). Have students, for example, find out: Who does Mazon help? What percentage of monetary gifts does Mazon encourage people to donate from life-cycle events like the bar and bat mitzvah?

As a class, study the following text from Leviticus 19:9-10: "When you reap [cut and gather] the harvest of your land, you shall not reap your field to its very border, neither shall you gather the gleanings [pieces that are left over and are collected bit by bit] after your harvest. You shall not strip your vineyard bare, neither shall you gather the fallen grapes of your vineyard. You shall leave them for the poor and for the stranger: I am Adonai your God."

Ask: Why do you think the Torah says that we should give food to the hungry? (*Responses may include: People may not do this unless they are told; we must remember to help people–even those we don't know.*) How can we observe this mitzvah today? (*Responses may include: Donate money to organizations like Mazon; take leftover food to soup kitchens; help serve food at a soup kitchen.*) Why do you think this section ends with "I am Adonai your God"? (*Responses may include that this phrase reminds us that according to our tradition this is a law given by God; what we do matters to God; God wants us to share the work of feeding the needy.*)

Digital Application

Once in the kitchen, students can click on "Food List" to learn and review the Hebrew names of various foods, including חָלָב (milk), לֶחֶם (bread), גְּלִידָה (ice cream), עוּגָה (cake), פָּלָפֶל (falafel), סוֹדָה (soda), פִּיצָה (pizza), and גְּבִינָה (cheese). In the next class, help students review this new vocabulary by asking "food ingredient" questions such as: What do we put on pizza? (גְּבִינָה) What is ice cream made of? (חָלָב) What do we put in pita? (פָּלָפֶל).

It's a Good Thing

Direct students to work with a partner to complete "It's a Good Thing." Have students practice saying the phrases with their partners. As a class, review the answers as students check and correct their work. Next, say the English meaning of a phrase and have students chorally respond by saying the phrase in Hebrew. Invite students to make up English sentences and include the Hebrew phrase. For example, a student might say, "Before I go to sleep, my mother always says לַיְלָה טוֹב to me."

Putting It in ConTEXT

Read the introduction aloud. Have students join with you and chorally read the biblical quote, Deuteronomy 8:10, in both Hebrew and English. Invite volunteers to act out the first three actions in this verse. (*eating, feeling full, reciting a blessing*) Ask: According to this verse, when do we have to bless God? (*when we eat and are satisfied*) What are we blessing God for? (*the good land*) What does "good land" have to do with eating? (*We need good land in order to grow fruits and vegetables and raise farm animals.*) According to our tradition, how can we partner with God to get food to the table from the good land? (*God provides good land, rain, and seeds; people tend the land and take in the harvest.*)

Direct students to complete the activity with a partner. Check the answers as a class. Challenge students to identify the word that is built on the root אכל (וְאָכַלְתָּ) and the word meaning "your God" (אֱלֹהֶיךָ).

Teach, or invite the cantor or music specialist to teach, students to chant this verse from בִּרְכַּת הַמָּזוֹן.

Challenge students to circle all the ךָ and תָּ endings. Inform students that these suffixes mean "your" or "you." Ask: Why do these endings appear so many times in this verse? (*Responses may include: according to our tradition, this law is for us; so we know that this law applies to everyone*)

Share the following story with your students: When Rabbi Eliezer was a young man he was determined to go and learn Torah from Rabban Yohanan ben Zakkai in Jerusalem. Despite his father's protests, Rabbi Eliezer went to Jerusalem. Rabbi Eliezer told Rabban Yohanan that he had never studied Torah before. So Rabban Yohanan began by teaching him the Sh'ma, the Amidah, Birkat Hamazon, and two rules of law every day. (*The Book of Legends—Sefer HaAggadah*)

Ask: Why do you think Birkat Hamazon was one of the first prayers that Rabban Yohanan taught Rabbi Eliezer? (*Suggestions may include: He thought it was one of the most important prayers; he felt that an educated Jew should know this prayer; it is a prayer that is said every day; it reminds us to give food to the hungry.*)

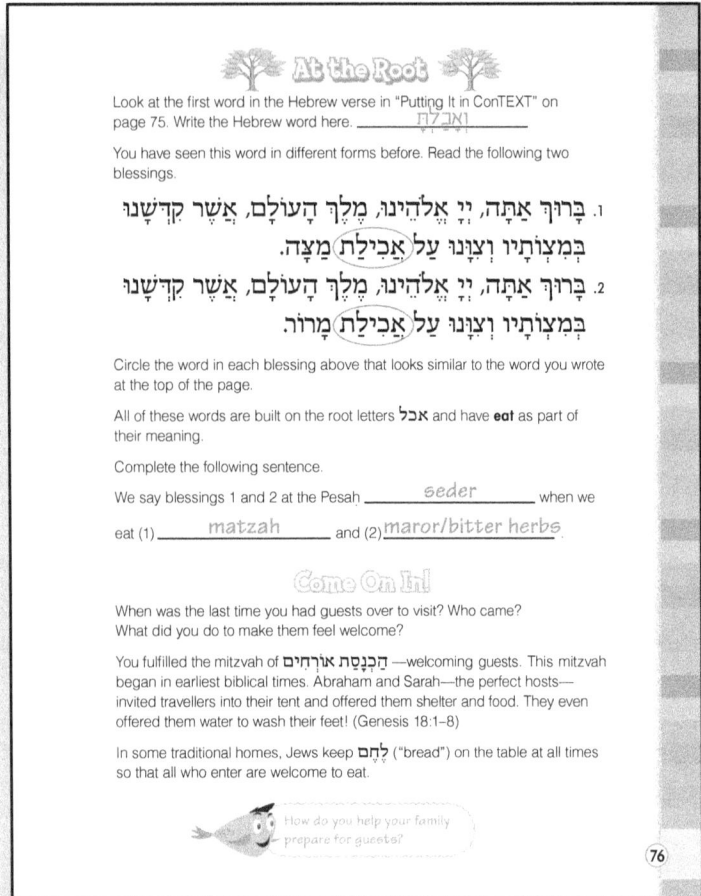

At the Root

Have students read and complete the activities with a partner. Call on a volunteer to read the answers and have all students check their own work.

Have the class chorally read the two blessings with you. Ask questions about these blessings, for example: What is the difference between these two blessings? (*the last word of each blessing*)

Which words show that these are בְּרָכוֹת שֶׁל מִצְוָה? (אֲשֶׁר קִדְּשָׁנוּ בְּמִצְוֹתָיו וְצִוָּנוּ) Which word means "the world"? (הָעוֹלָם)

Come On In!

Ask students the questions in the first paragraph of this section. Invite students to tell about their experiences as a host. Encourage students to share stories of when they have helped welcome guests into their homes, as well as stories of when they were welcomed into another family's home.

Have students read the remaining paragraphs with a partner. Ask: What is the Hebrew term for the mitzvah of welcoming guests? (הַכְנָסַת אוֹרְחִים) Which people from the bible are known as having been the perfect hosts? (*Abraham and Sarah*) Write the phrase הַכְנָסַת אוֹרְחִים on the board. Divide the class into groups of three students. Direct each group to brainstorm a list of reasons why הַכְנָסַת אוֹרְחִים is important. Have the groups share their lists and create one large class list on a poster entitled הַכְנָסַת אוֹרְחִים. You may choose to add a section to the poster listing the ideas about welcoming guests from the first part of the discussion.

In Abraham's Tent

Read your students the story of Abraham welcoming strangers to his tent (Genesis 18:1–8 or *The Explorer's Bible 1*, page 48). Ask: Why is הַכְנָסַת אוֹרְחִים such an important mitzvah? (*Suggestions may include: we help others by making them welcome in our homes; we strengthen friendships when we spend time*

together; *it is nice to be invited to others' homes.*)

For fun, invite a few students to act out the story. Ask: What are some of the ways that Abraham welcomes the strangers? (*He bows down to greet them; he offers them water, bread, and a full meal.*) What can we learn from Abraham about how to welcome guests? (*Responses may include: to be welcoming; to offer food and drinks; to be polite; to be generous*)

Doug the Fish

Invite a volunteer to hold the Doug puppet and ask Doug's question. Call on students to describe how they help their family prepare for guests. Have students share how helping prepare for guests can also help create and strengthen שְׁלוֹם בַּיִת. (*Responses may include: we help each other; we work together.*)

Bread, Bread, Bread

Have students read the first sentence silently. Remind students that according to our tradition bread has a special status and that the rabbis of the Talmud described how bread needed to be treated with respect (*B'rachot* 50b). See page 29 of this Teacher's Edition.

Have students read the מוֹצִיא then complete the activity. As a class, discuss the differences between the three kinds of bread and when each bread is used.

Inform students that there are different explanations for why we have a round ḥallah on Rosh Hashanah: The ḥallah is round, like the shape of a crown, reminding us that God is our Ruler; the round shape of the ḥallah reminds us of the cycle of life, the seasons, and the Jewish year.

Baking Bread

Arrange for your class to bake ḥallah. There are many wonderful ḥallah recipes in cookbooks and on the Internet. To save time, you may wish to use Rapid-Rise yeast. Consider preparing the dough during one class, and then allowing the dough to rise, covered and enclosed in a plastic bag in the refrigerator, for up to three days. The ḥallah can then be baked the next time your class meets. A local bakery may also be willing to supply dough.

Consider informing students that when baking ḥallah it is a mitzvah to break off a small piece of dough, about the size of an olive, and bake it separately. This piece reminds us of the portion of dough that was brought to the Holy Temple in Jerusalem and given to the Kohanim, the priests.

When we remove this portion of dough, we recite the following בְּרָכָה שֶׁל מִצְוָה:

בָּרוּךְ אַתָּה, יְיָ אֱלֹהֵינוּ, מֶלֶךְ הָעוֹלָם,
אֲשֶׁר קִדְּשָׁנוּ בְּמִצְוֹתָיו, וְצִוָּנוּ
לְהַפְרִישׁ חַלָּה.

Praised are You, Adonai our God, Ruler of the world, who makes us holy with commandments and commands us to separate the ḥallah.

Digital Application

Once in the kitchen, students can click on "Holiday Bread Match" to review when matzah, ḥallah, and round ḥallah are each eaten. (פֶּסַח, שַׁבָּת, *and* רֹאשׁ הַשָּׁנָה *respectively*) In the next class, review the blessing over bread (הַמּוֹצִיא לֶחֶם מִן הָאָרֶץ) and remind students that this blessing is recited over all types of holiday bread.

All or Nothing

Direct students to read and complete this activity with a partner. Call on volunteers to share ideas about why "all" and "everyone" appear so many times. (*Responses may include: to remind us that God provides for all creatures; to emphasize that everyone needs to be thankful for food; that we are thanking God not only for our food, but for everyone's food*)

Focus students on line 4 of the Hebrew on page 73. Chorally read this line with the class. Call on a volunteer to read the fourth word of the line (לְכָל). Have all students practice saying this word.

Remind students that they have seen other prayer words that

have a vowel ָ that is sounded as "oh." Challenge students to look back on page 42 and identify two words that have this same sounding vowel. (קָדְשׁוֹ, קָדְשְׁךָ)

Putting It in ConTEXT

Write the phrase הַכְנָסַת אוֹרְחִים on the board. Call on a volunteer to remind the class of its meaning. (*the mitzvah of welcoming guests*) Refer students to the poster you made earlier. Ask: What foods do you like to serve when guests come to your home? Call on several volunteers to respond.

Direct students to read this section aloud and complete the activity with a partner. Invite students to do dramatic readings of the quotes from Genesis and Exodus. Ask: What food do both Abraham and Jethro offer? (*bread*) What, according to Exodus, will God cause to rain down from heaven? (*bread*)

Challenge students to identify the word related to "eating" in the second verse. (וְיֹאכַל) Help them identify the root אכל. Focus students on the word for bread in this verse (לָחֶם). Inform students that sometimes in the bible the word לֶחֶם appears as לָחֶם. Even though one vowel sound has changed, the words have exactly the same meaning.

All Kinds of Bread

Ask students to name their favorite kinds of bread. Explain that in the bible we read about a special kind of bread, manna. The only time people ate manna was when God gave it to the Israelites in the desert. Read students descriptions of manna recorded in Exodus 16:31 and Numbers 11:7–8, or read the summary found in *The Explorer's Bible, Volume 2*, page 11.

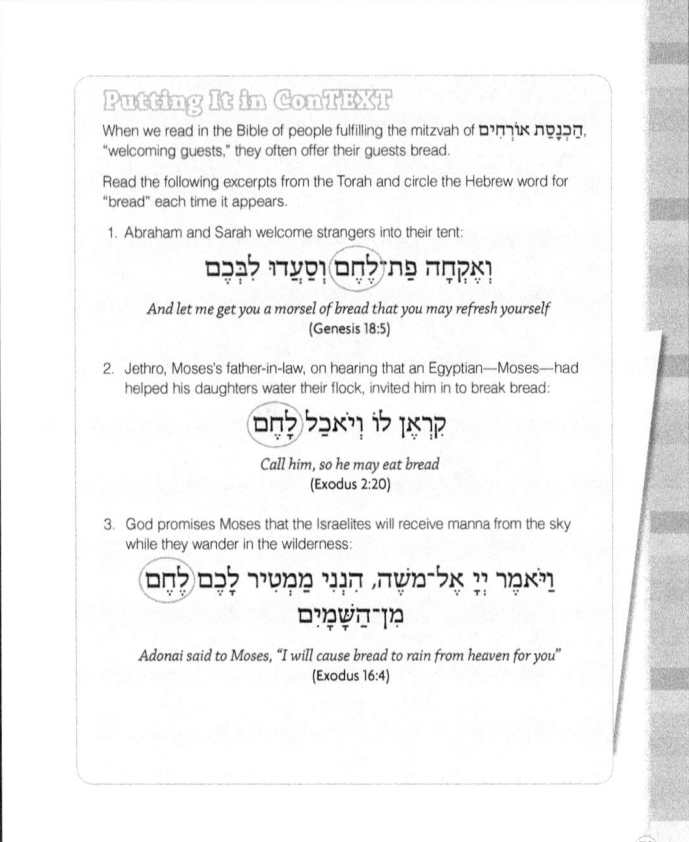

Clue to Cyberspace

Have students independently fill in the missing letters and discover the mystery words (בִּרְכַּת הַמָזוֹן). Walk around the room to assess students' familiarity with the phrases of בִּרְכַּת הַמָזוֹן.

Have students check their work with a classmate. Call on a volunteer to read the "Mystery Word." Direct students to read to a partner, taking turns reading alternate lines. Repeat so that both students have read all the lines.

Challenge students to read various lines. For example, ask a row of students to chorally read the line that has the word בְּטוּבוֹ. (4)

Digital Application

Once in the kitchen, students can click on the image of the ping pong ball to play the "Ping Pong" game and review vocabulary, which includes: בִּרְכַּת הַמָזוֹן (Grace After Meals), בִּרְכַּת הַמִצְוָה (blessing of mitzvah), (הַ)זָן (who feeds), (בְּ)חֶסֶד (with kindness), טוּבוֹ (God's goodness), and מָזוֹן (food). Remind students to use the mystery words to score bonus points. In the next class, ask students who scored the highest in this game. You might also wish to review the vocabulary from the game.

Review Game

Play one of the games described on pages 11–13 to review the words and concepts of this chapter. Questions might include: What is a Hebrew word for food? (מָזוֹן) When is בִּרְכַּת הַמָזוֹן recited?

My Own Siddur

If students are creating their own siddur, prepare a page by copying the opening paragraph of בִּרְכַּת הַמָזוֹן, leaving space for illustrations, onto a white sheet of paper. Give each student a copy of this page, and invite students to draw an illustration that represents בִּרְכַּת הַמָזוֹן or to write a few sentences that give בִּרְכַּת הַמָזוֹן personal meaning. Gather this page with all their other personal siddur pages.

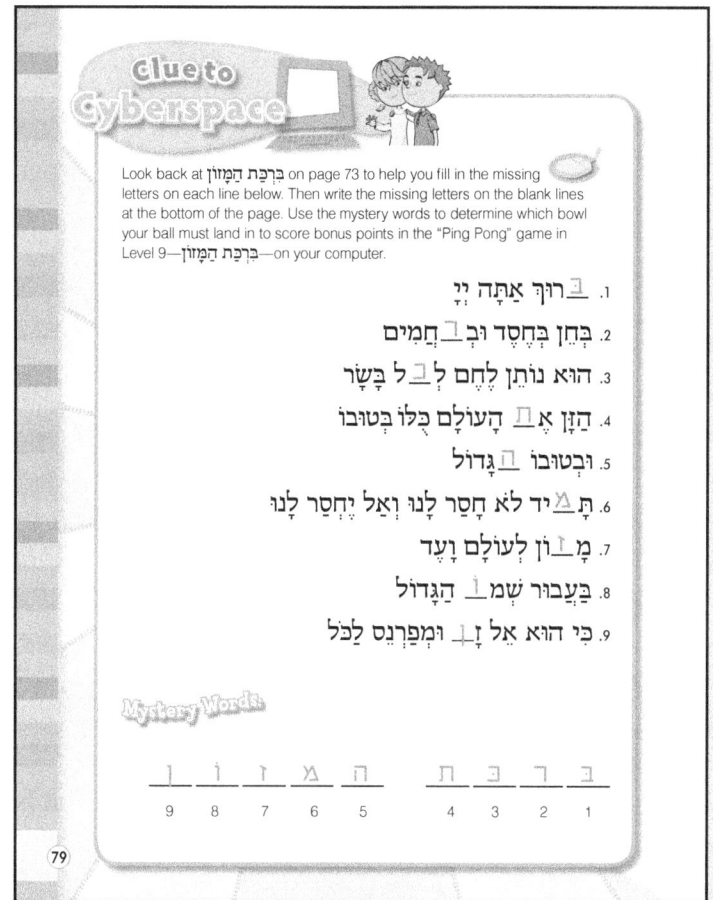

Assessment

As students are working on any of the above activities, meet individually with them to assess reading fluency and knowledge of prayer content. You can mark students' progress using the assessment chart and check their progress online at www.behrmanhouse.com.

What's Next?

Ask: At what time of day did our book begin? Allow students to look back to Chapter 1 and to recall that we began in the early morning. Tell them that we are about to close out the day with a prayer some people say at night before going to sleep—the שְׁמַע.

ABOUT THE PRAYER

The שְׁמַע comes directly from the Torah (Deuteronomy 6:4). The שְׁמַע is a statement of faith and allegiance to God. When we recite the words of the שְׁמַע, we affirm our belief in one God.

The second sentence of the שְׁמַע (בָּרוּךְ שֵׁם כְּבוֹד...) was first said in the ancient Temple in Jerusalem; it was the response given by the people after hearing the Divine Name pronounced by the High Priest. Later it became the response to the first line of the שְׁמַע. Traditionally, this line has been recited silently or in a soft voice, to distinguish it from the biblical passages of the שְׁמַע.

Its purpose is to affirm that, although Jews have lived under many monarchs, God is the only Supreme Ruler of Israel. When Jews say this line, they publicly declare the uniqueness of God.

LEARNING OBJECTIVES

Students will be able to:

- Identify various names that include the word יִשְׂרָאֵל.
- Recite the שְׁמַע fluently.
- Define key words found in and related to the שְׁמַע.
- Correctly use שְׁמִי, מַה שִּׁמְךָ?, מַה שְּׁמֵךְ?, and .

NEW WORDS AND PHRASES

Prayer Words:

hear	שְׁמַע
Israel	יִשְׂרָאֵל
one	אֶחָד

Related Words:

deep concentration	כַּוָּנָה
God	שַׁדַּי
Children of Israel	בְּנֵי יִשְׂרָאֵל
State of Israel	מְדִינַת יִשְׂרָאֵל
Nation (People) of Israel	עַם יִשְׂרָאֵל
Land of Israel	אֶרֶץ יִשְׂרָאֵל
God	אֵל
name	שֵׁם
What is your name? (m)	מַה שִּׁמְךָ?
What is your name? (f)	מַה שְּׁמֵךְ?
My name is…	שְׁמִי

INSTRUCTIONAL MATERIALS

Text Pages 80–87
Word Cards 76, 98–110

Digital Application: Lesson 10—Batya's room (see page 8 for a list of games and activities)

WHERE WE ARE

Batya and Ben are ready for bed. Before they go to sleep they recite the שְׁמַע.

INTRODUCING THE LESSON

Remind your students about the story of Rabbi Eliezer and Rabban Yohanan ben Zakkai (see page 105 of the Teacher's Edition). Ask: What were the first prayers that ben Zakkai taught to Rabbi Eliezer? (*the Sh'ma, the Amidah, and Birkat Hamazon*) Why do you think he chose to teach the שְׁמַע? (*Suggestions may include: the שְׁמַע is the most important prayer; the שְׁמַע is short and easy to learn; the שְׁמַע is said every day.*)

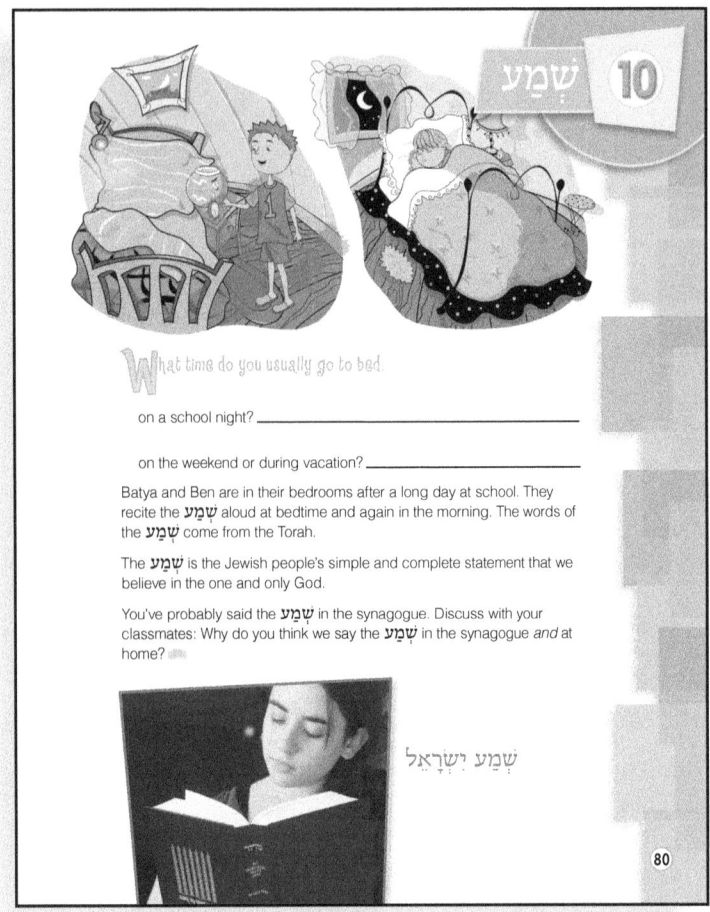

(*"Hear, Israel" is only asking the people to physically hear something; "Listen, Israel" is asking the people to hear, understand, and obey.*) Explain to students that *Hear* is often used in English translations of this verse but that we understand it to mean *Listen*.

INTO THE TEXT

Focus students on the illustrations of Batya and Ben. Call on volunteers to describe what they see in the illustrations. Explain that according to our tradition, the שְׁמַע is recited at bedtime.

Have students read page 80 silently and respond to the questions. Ask: When do Batya and Ben recite the שְׁמַע? (*bedtime and morning*) Where are the words of the שְׁמַע taken from? (*the Torah*) What does the שְׁמַע say we believe? (*that there is only one God*)

Invite students to suggest why the שְׁמַע is said both at home and in the synagogue. (*Responses may include: so we think about it in both places; it is a prayer that does not have to be said with a congregation [or minyan]; to remind us to say that we believe in one God wherever we are*)

Inform students that it is traditional to recite the שְׁמַע along with a prayer called the וְאָהַבְתָּ during the evening and morning prayers. Read aloud the words of Deuteronomy 6:7: "You shall teach them [words of Torah] to your children and speak of them when you are sitting in your house, when you are walking on the way, when you lie down and when you get up." Ask: Which part of this verse is the basis for saying the שְׁמַע during evening and morning prayers? (*when you lie down and when you get up*)

Photo Op

Focus students on the photo at the bottom of the page. Ask if anyone can read the Hebrew word on the spine of the book the girl is holding. Have a volunteer read the words next to the photograph. Tell students that in this phrase יִשְׂרָאֵל is referring to the people of Israel.

Write on the board: Listen—שְׁמַע—Hear. Explain that the root letters שמע are related to listening and hearing. Ask: What is the difference between hearing, as in "I don't hear you," and listening, as in "I won't listen to you"? (*Hearing is physical—you can hear a sound or words and not understand them; listening means hearing, understanding and obeying.*) What is the difference between "Hear, Israel" and "Listen, Israel"?

THE PRAYERS OF OUR PEOPLE I • כָּל יִשְׂרָאֵל   112

I Pledge Allegiance

As a class, chorally recite the words of the שְׁמַע. Direct students to respond to the questions. Call on students to chant the prayer.

Ask: How does saying the שְׁמַע show that you are a member of the Jewish people? (*because it says that we believe in one God*) What is a pledge of allegiance? (*a promise to be loyal to a person, group, or cause*) What promise do we make in the שְׁמַע? (*the promise to worship and believe in the one and only God, Adonai*) Encourage students to express why they do or do not consider the שְׁמַע to be like a pledge of allegiance to God.

Digital Application

Tell students that at home, before the next class, they should click on the שְׁמַע at the bottom of the screen to enter Batya's room. Once in Batya's room, students can click on "Practice Reading שְׁמַע." In the next class, ask students which word is repeated in the שְׁמַע. (*Adonai*)

Prayer Words

Display Word Cards # 76, 98, and 99, Hebrew side showing. Challenge students to identify and read the words that mean "Israel" and "hear." Write the numeral 1 on the board and say the word אֶחָד. Have students complete these sentences using the new Hebrew words:

- When we say the שְׁמַע, we are saying that God is _____ (אֶחָד).
- _____ (יִשְׂרָאֵל) is being told to listen.
- Israel is commanded: _____ (שְׁמַע).

Unscramble the Prayer

Direct students to complete this activity individually. Call on a volunteer to read the number order. Students should correct their own work. As a class, chorally read the words in the correct order.

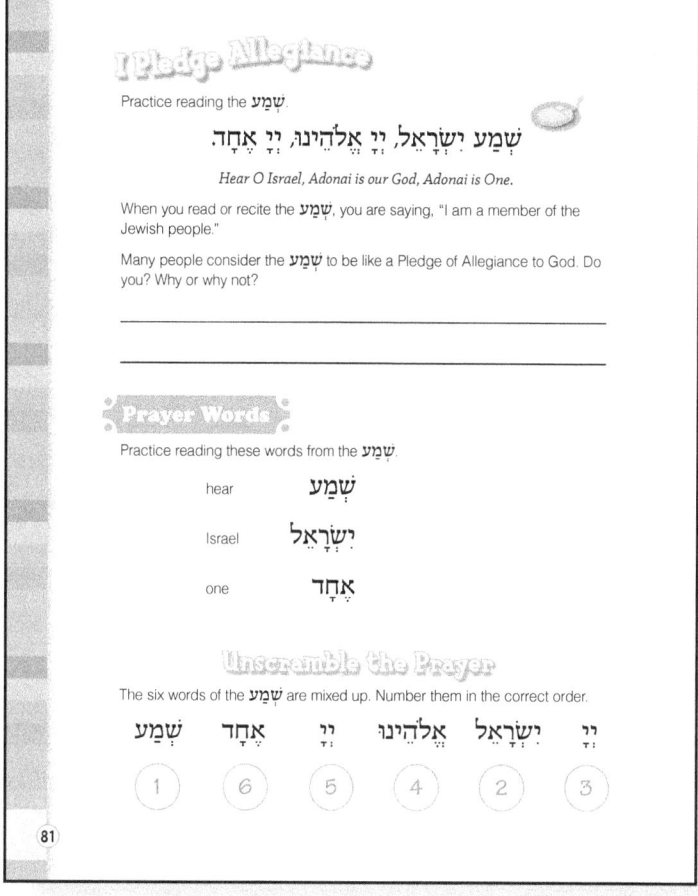

113 CHAPTER 10

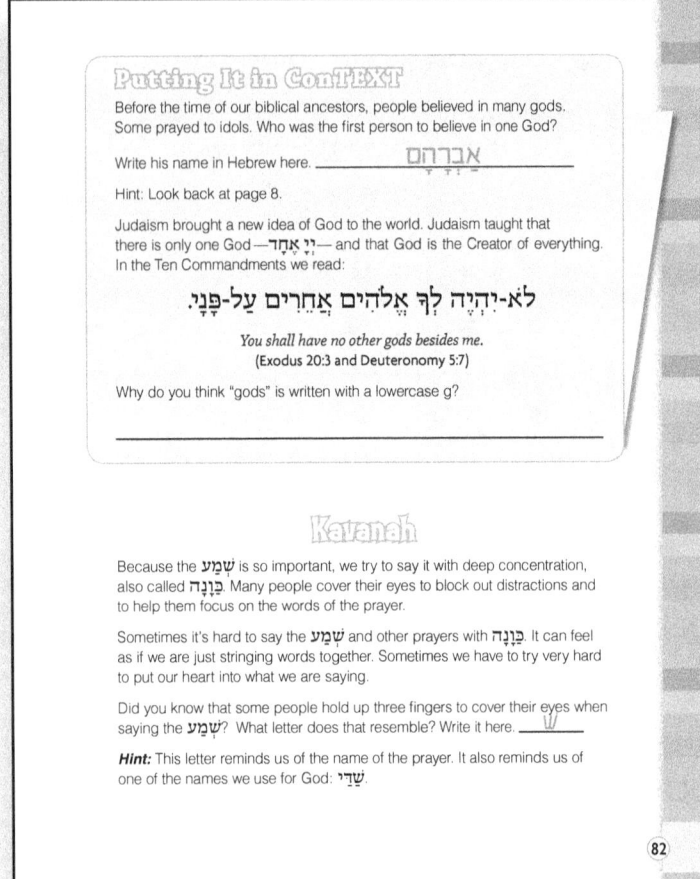

Kavanah

Direct students to silently read the paragraphs about כַּוָּנָה. After students have read the paragraphs, ask them to close or cover their eyes and to chorally recite the שְׁמַע. Ask: How can covering your eyes help you to have greater כַּוָּנָה? (*There are fewer distractions*) Does it work for you to close your eyes? Why or why not? Why is כַּוָּנָה important when we pray? (*Responses may include: it is easier to think about the meaning of the prayers; we can include more private, personal prayers.*) Acknowledge that it is often hard to pray with כַּוָּנָה.

 Putting It in ConTEXT

Direct students to read and complete "Putting It in ConTEXT" with a partner. Ask: Who was the first person to believe in one God. (*Abraham*) What new ideas did Judaism bring to the world? (*There is only one God; God is the Creator of everything.*)

Have the class chorally read the verse from the Ten Commandments in both Hebrew and English. Ask students to practice reading the Hebrew with a partner. Call on volunteers to suggest why "gods" is written with a lowercase g. (*When god is written with a capital G, God, it is referring to the one God. It is capitalized, like a name is capitalized. When it is written in lowercase, god, it refers to other gods people worshipped.*)

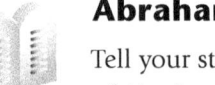 **Abraham and the Idols**

Tell your students the famous midrash of Abraham (his name was Abram at the time) and the idols. Remind students that a midrash is a story that helps to explain a biblical text.

Abraham's father, Terah, was an idolmaker, who sold carved images of stone. One day, Terah left Abram to take care of the shop. Abram saw the idols around him, and he picked up an ax.

When Terah returned, he found the shop littered with smashed pieces of stone. Only one large idol remained whole. "Who has done this?" cried Terah. "The big god took your ax and destroyed them all," replied Abram. Terah said, "Abram, you are mocking me! You know that idols can't move." Then Abram said, "Father, let your ears hear what your tongue speaks." (*B'reishit Rabbah 38:13*)

Ask: What was Abraham trying to show his father? (*That idols have no power*) What do we learn about Abraham from this story? (*Suggestions may include: that he was very brave; that he wasn't influenced by those around him; that he believed in God*)

THE PRAYERS OF OUR PEOPLE I • כָּל יִשְׂרָאֵל   114

What's in a Name?

As a class, chorally read the verse from Genesis in Hebrew and English. Have students underline the names יַעֲקֹב and יִשְׂרָאֵל. As a class, brainstorm and list what students know about יַעֲקֹב. (*Answers may include: he is the son of Isaac; he had twelve sons; he married Rachel and Leah.*)

Have students read the paragraph describing his name change. Ask: Does everyone call you by your birth name, or do some people call you by a different name? Ask for examples. Why do people sometimes go by more than one name? What are some examples of people changing their name or using an alternate name? Do you know your Hebrew name? What is it? When do people use their Hebrew names? (*Answers may include: on their Hebrew school notebooks; when they are called up to the Torah; when a prayer for their well-being is recited; when they are born; when they get married; on their tombstones*)

Write on the board the four names that include יִשְׂרָאֵל. Invite students to the board to identify and circle the word that is common to all the names. (יִשְׂרָאֵל) Invite the class to chorally read the four names.

Give each student a blank sheet of construction paper. Direct students to fold the sheet into four rectangles (each 4½" x 6") and to write the four names with Israel, a different one in each quadrant. Have students illustrate the meaning of each of these names. Ask: Which two names describe the Jewish people? (בְּנֵי יִשְׂרָאֵל, עַם יִשְׂרָאֵל) Which two names describe the Jewish homeland? (אֶרֶץ יִשְׂרָאֵל, מְדִינַת יִשְׂרָאֵל) You may wish to explain that מְדִינַת יִשְׂרָאֵל and אֶרֶץ יִשְׂרָאֵל are not exactly the same since מְדִינַת יִשְׂרָאֵל refers to the modern state of Israel and its present borders, while אֶרֶץ יִשְׂרָאֵל refers to the land during the days of the Bible.

Have students chorally join you in reading the phrase כָּל יִשְׂרָאֵל עֲרֵבִים זֶה בָּזֶה. Ask: What does it mean that all of Israel is responsible for one another? (*Responses may include: all Jews need to help other Jews; Jews need to respect each*

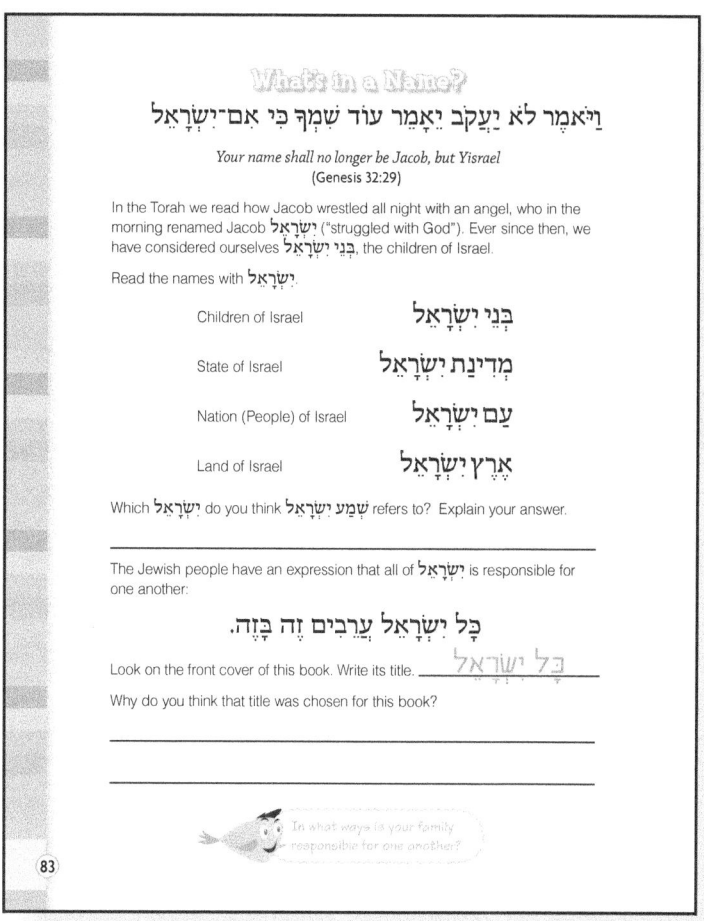

other; Jews need to help Jews all over the world.)
Refer students to the title of the book and ask if they see the connection.

Family Responsibilities

Invite a student to hold the Doug puppet and ask Doug's question. Call on volunteers to respond. (*Responses may include: My sister reminds me to bring my lunch; I help my grandmother cook dinner.*) Ask: How does being responsible for one another help to create שְׁלוֹם בַּיִת?

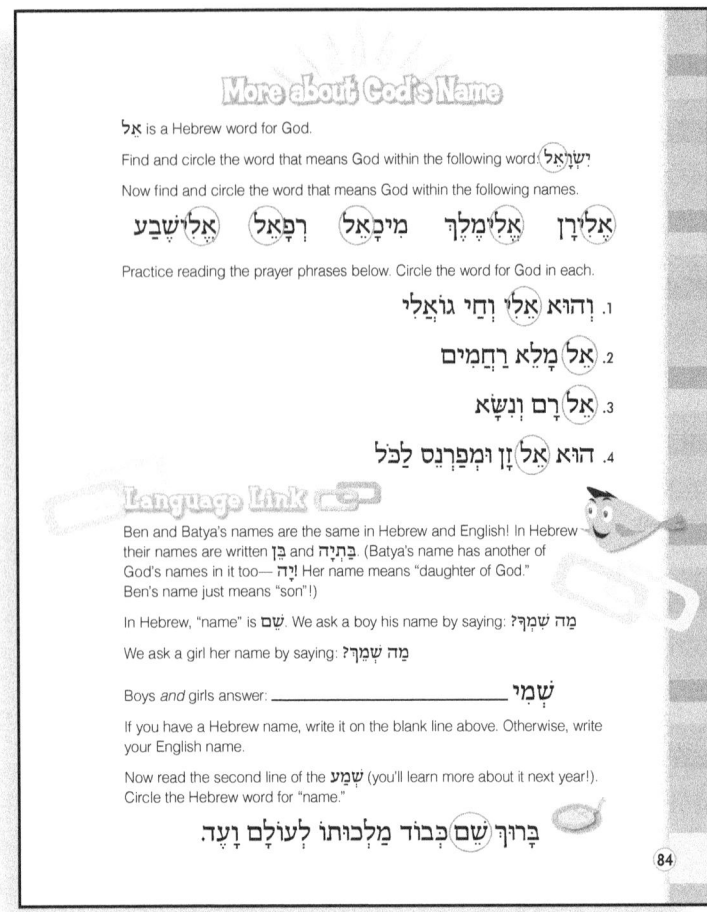

More about God's Name

Write the name יִשְׂרָאֵל on the board. Inform students that אֵל is the Hebrew word for God. Call on a volunteer to circle the word for God in יִשְׂרָאֵל.

Have students read and complete the activities about God's name with a partner. Have pairs check their answers with other classmates.

Call on pairs to read specific lines aloud. For example, ask students to read the line that has a word related to feeding (line 4) or to read the line that has a word beginning with the letter מ (line 2). Challenge students to identify the prayer from which phrase 4 is taken. (בִּרְכַּת הַמָּזוֹן)

Divide the class into groups of three. Give each student a siddur. Tell students that their group has three minutes to locate the name of God, אֵל, as many times as they can find it in the siddur. Inform students that they can list other forms of אֵל, such as אֱלֹהֵינוּ or אֱלֹהִים, but that the words אֶל and אַל do not mean God. Have each group write a list that includes the page number, the line number, and the word placement. For example, to indicate page 23, line 7, second word in the line, a group may write: 23, 7, 2.

After three minutes have groups count the number of times they have found God's name. Randomly select groups and review the words they found to be sure they are correct. The group with the longest list of correct words is the winning group.

Language Link

Read the first paragraph aloud to the class. Ask: What other names can you think of that are the same in English and Hebrew? (*Suggestions include: Talia, Avi, Aliza*)

Use two hand puppets (one masculine and one feminine), or sock puppets, to present a conversation in which two people are asking each other their names. The female puppet asks, "מַה שְּׁמֵךְ?"; the male puppet answers, "שְׁמִי דָּוִד" and then asks, "מַה שְּׁמֵךְ?" The female puppet then responds, "שְׁמִי דְּבוֹרָה."

Write the word שְׁמִי on the board. Point to yourself, and complete the phrase _____ שְׁמִי using your name. Point to a boy and ask "מַה שְּׁמְךָ?" Prompt the student to complete the phrase _____ שְׁמִי using his name. Point to a girl and ask "מַה שְּׁמֵךְ?" Prompt the student to complete the phrase _____ שְׁמִי using her name. Ask a few more students their names, encouraging them to respond in Hebrew. Direct students to turn to a partner and to have a Hebrew conversation in which they ask each other's names and tell their own names.

Have students complete the activity and read the second line of the שְׁמַע with a partner. Challenge students to identify and underline the word meaning: "blessed" or "praised" (בָּרוּךְ); related to "ruler" (מַלְכוּתוֹ).

Digital Application

Once in Batya's room, students should click on "Practice Reading שְׁמַע" to practice the second line of the שְׁמַע. They should also click on "Feed Your Fish" to review new vocabulary, which includes אֶחָד (one), שְׁמַע (hear), יִשְׂרָאֵל (Israel), and שֵׁם (name). In the next class, ask students: What is the שֵׁם of the orange fish? (*Doug*)

THE PRAYERS OF OUR PEOPLE I • כָּל יִשְׂרָאֵל   116

Word Search

Display Word Cards # 16, 26, 76, 98, 99, 100, 106, and 107. Have students close their eyes. Remove one of the cards. Invite students to look at the remaining words and to identify and translate the missing Word Card. The student who answers correctly replaces the Word Card and then removes another Word Card while classmates are not looking. Continue until all Word Cards have been identified and translated.

Have students complete the Word Search with a partner. Direct students to write the answer to each question below the word search.

If students have difficulty answering question 2, suggest that they refer back to page 25.

Challenge students to name the word from the שְׁמַע that is not included in the Word Search. (אֱלֹהֵינוּ).

Digital Application

Once in Batya's room, students can click on "Word Search" to review the new vocabulary, written without vowels, which includes כַּוָּנָה, יִשְׂרָאֵל, אֶחָד, מְזוּזָה, שְׁמַע, אֵל, שֵׁם, and יְיָ. In the next class, read this list of words aloud. Then, ask students which word in the שְׁמַע is missing from this list. (אֱלֹהֵינוּ—our God)

Personal Prayer Wrap-Up

In this book we have learned blessings and prayers that express our thanks to God for what we have and what we are able to do. Think back to a typical day this week. What did you learn? What did you accomplish? What were you grateful for? Reflect on that day and write a prayer that expresses your thoughts and feelings.

God, today/on _____ day, I _____
_____.

It made me feel _____ because _____
_____
_____.

So I wanted to say _____
_____
_____
_____.

I hope _____
_____.

_____
Your name here

What did you do to add shalom, peace, to your home?

Personal Prayer Wrap-Up

Read the introduction aloud as students follow along. Allow students to individually write their own personal prayer. Encourage students to use Hebrew prayer words in their own prayers.

Have students copy their prayers onto a separate sheet of paper. If your students have been creating their own prayer booklets, include this prayer in that booklet. Alternatively, you may wish to display the prayers, have students read them to the class, compile a booklet of class prayers, or have students share the prayers with their families at home.

Shalom at Home

As a class, create a list of ways students have added shalom to their homes. Create a second list of ways students can continue to add shalom. If time allows, have students draw illustrations of ways to create shalom at home.

THE PRAYERS OF OUR PEOPLE I • כָּל יִשְׂרָאֵל

Clue to Cyberspace

Have students read the first paragraph of "Clue to Cyberspace" with a partner. Ask: What is *gematria*? (*interpreting a Hebrew word by adding up the value of its letters*) Which word has the numerical value of 18? (חַי)

Have students work with a partner to discover the answer to the mystery question, "Which prayer do we put inside a מְזוּזָה? (שְׁמַע)

Digital Application

Once in Batya's room, students can click on the image of the skateboard to play "Batya's Vert Skate" game and review vocabulary, which includes בֵּן (son), בַּת (daughter), אַחַת (one), שְׁתַּיִם (two), מַה שִׁמְךָ (What's your name? [masculine]), מַה שְׁמֵךְ (What's your name? [feminine]), בֵּן (Ben), and בְּתִיָּה (Batya). Remind students to use the clue to do a bonus trick. (*one*) In the next class, ask students what the name Ben means. (*son*)

Ask students to complete Review 3 on their computer to assess what they have learned in Lessons 7 through 10. In the next class, divide students into two teams and challenge teams to write and ask their own review questions. (*Some questions and answers might include: How do we greet each other on holidays?* חַג שָׂמֵחַ; *What blessing do we recite after eating a meal?* בִּרְכַּת הַמָּזוֹן; *What do we shake on Sukkot? a* לוּלָב; *How do you say "good night" in Hebrew?* לַיְלָה טוֹב)

Number It

Invite a student to write on the board the numbers that correspond to a Hebrew word. Challenge classmates to decipher the Hebrew word. Call on a volunteer to read the Hebrew word and say its English meaning. Invite the student who correctly reads the word and says its meaning to write the numbers corresponding to a new Hebrew word.

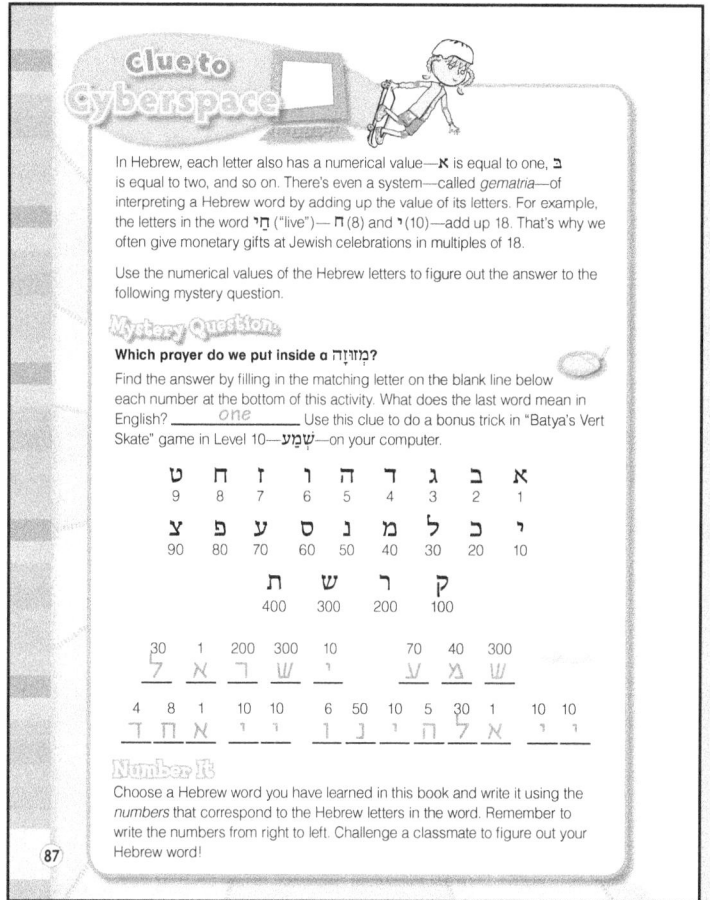

Siddur Squares

Review students' knowledge of בִּרְכַּת הַמָּזוֹן and שְׁמַע from chapters 9 and 10 by playing "Siddur Squares" as described on page 13. Sample questions:

- How are the words מָזוֹן and הַזָּן related to one another? (*they are both about eating or food*)
- What is the Hebrew word for "deep concentration"? (כַּוָּנָה)
- Which food is the symbol of food in Jewish life? (*bread*)

My Own Siddur

If students are creating their own siddur, prepare a page by copying the text of the Sh'ma, leaving space for illustrations, onto a white sheet of paper. Give each student a copy of this page, and instruct the students to draw an illustration that represents the Sh'ma or to write a few sentences that give the prayer personal meaning.

Assessment

As students are working on any of the above activities, meet individually with them to assess reading fluency and knowledge of prayer content. You can mark students' progress on the assessment chart and check their progress online at www.behrmanhouse.com.

What's Next?

As a class, brainstorm a list of all the prayers and blessings you have learned in *Kol Yisrael 1*. Congratulate your students on doing such a great job learning these prayers and blessings.

WRAP IT UP! FUN PRAYER ACTIVITIES

The closing activities on pages 88 through 94 allow students to review the prayers and blessings presented in *Kol Yisrael 1*. They also afford you an opportunity to assess how well students are able to read and understand these prayers and blessings.

Blessing Bee

Have students work with a partner to complete this activity. Direct students to take turns reading aloud the twelve blessings and naming the occasions on which they are recited.

After students have practiced reading and reviewing the blessings, you may use these pages in a number of ways.

- *As an individual assessment*:
1. Describe a blessing and have students write down the number of the blessing that was described. Say, for example, "The בְּרָכָה recited before eating a cookie." Students should write down the number 6. Other descriptions include: The בְּרָכָה recited when doing something for the first time that season (2); The בְּרָכָה recited before hearing the shofar (7); The בְּרָכָה recited after eating a meal (4).

2. For a greater challenge, read blessing descriptions, but instead of students writing the number of the blessing, they write the last two Hebrew words of the matching blessing.

- *As a review game*:

   Divide the class into two teams. Have teams take turns answering questions about the blessings. A team gains a point by fluently reading the correct blessing. For example, ask, "What do we say at the end of the first paragraph of בִּרְכַּת הַמָּזוֹן?" A team member would need to fluently read blessing 4. Play until you have asked questions about all twelve blessings. The team with the most points is the winning team.

- *To practice reading fluency*:
1. Have students read all the blessings to a

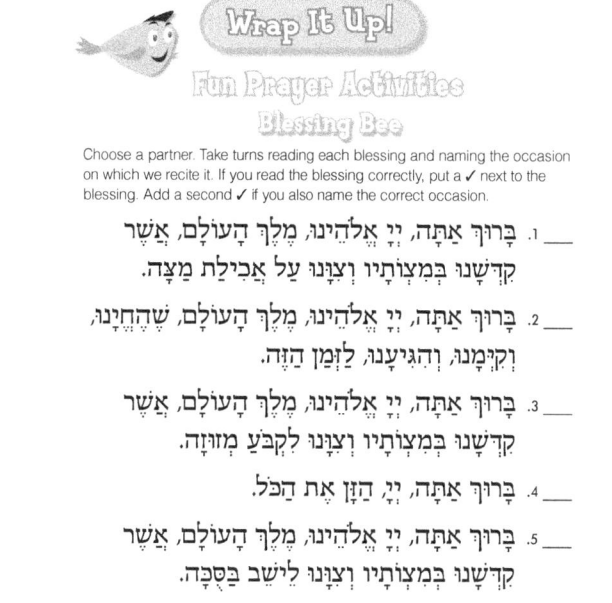

partner. Encourage students to time themselves as they practice reading so that they achieve a personal best, reading quickly, smoothly, and correctly.

2. Have students stand in a circle as they hold *Kol Yisrael 1* open to pages 88 and 89. Have students go around the circle taking turns saying the blessings. Student 1 recites blessing 1, student 2 recites blessing 2, and so on. Time the class. Work toward a class "best time." Remind students that the words need to be read correctly before the next student can continue.

- *To review key vocabulary*:

   Distribute Word Cards for words that appear in these blessings. Have each student come forward with their Word Card and do an activity to have the other students guess their word. Students might, for example, sing about it, draw it on the board, act out the word, or dramatize why it is useful. For example, the student who has the word מְזוּזָה might draw a picture of a מְזוּזָה on the board, point to a מְזוּזָה on the classroom doorpost, or recite the blessing for hanging a מְזוּזָה.

- *To review the context in which these blessings are recited*:

   Challenge students to recite other blessings said on the

8. ___ בָּרוּךְ אַתָּה, יְיָ, מְקַדֵּשׁ הַשַּׁבָּת.

9. ___ בָּרוּךְ אַתָּה, יְיָ אֱלֹהֵינוּ, מֶלֶךְ הָעוֹלָם, אֲשֶׁר קִדְּשָׁנוּ בְּמִצְוֹתָיו וְצִוָּנוּ לְהַדְלִיק נֵר שֶׁל שַׁבָּת.

10. ___ בָּרוּךְ אַתָּה, יְיָ אֱלֹהֵינוּ, מֶלֶךְ הָעוֹלָם, שֶׁעָשָׂה נִסִּים לַאֲבוֹתֵינוּ בַּיָּמִים הָהֵם בַּזְּמַן הַזֶּה.

11. ___ בָּרוּךְ אַתָּה, יְיָ אֱלֹהֵינוּ, מֶלֶךְ הָעוֹלָם, אֲשֶׁר קִדְּשָׁנוּ בְּמִצְוֹתָיו וְצִוָּנוּ לַעֲסוֹק בְּדִבְרֵי תוֹרָה.

12. ___ בָּרוּךְ אַתָּה, יְיָ אֱלֹהֵינוּ, מֶלֶךְ הָעוֹלָם, בּוֹרֵא מְאוֹרֵי הָאֵשׁ.

לַעֲסוֹק בְּדִבְרֵי תוֹרָה

---

same occasion as the listed blessing. For example, ask students to recite another blessing said on the same occasion as blessing 12. Students then recite another blessing recited during Havdalah—either בּוֹרֵא מִינֵי בְשָׂמִים or בּוֹרֵא פְּרִי הַגָּפֶן. This can be done as a game, having students respond as a team, or it can be a frontal review.

Photo Op

As a class, chorally read aloud the photo's caption. Ask: Which blessing on page 88 or 89 has these words? (*11*) What do the words mean? (*to engage in the words of Torah*) When would the girl in this photo have said this blessing? (*before studying Torah*) How might saying this blessing help the girl to have greater כַּוָּנָה? (*Responses may include: that the blessing might remind her that studying Torah is a mitzvah; that it is time to study; that what she is about to do is important and requires thinking*)

Rap-a-Rhythm

Invite volunteers to lead the class in beating a rhythm on their tables or desks as they say the sounds of these sound-alike letters. Encourage students to read these sound-alike letters to a variety of rhythms.

Sound-Alike Letters

Divide the class into two teams, א and ב. Display a selection of Word Cards, such as Word Cards 53, 65, 72, and 99 that include sound-alike letters. As a class, read the first set of sound-alike letters. Call on Team א to identify, read, and translate a Word Card on display containing one of these letters. The team receives one point for each task. If a team identifies, reads, and translates a word correctly, the team receives 3 points. If the team can only identify and read the word, but not translate the word, the team receives 2 points. Call on Team ב to look for an additional word with either of the sound-alike letters. Teams continue taking turns looking for words with a letter from the set of sound-alike letters. The team with the most points is the winning team.

Direct students to stand up and tap their feet as they join you in chorally reading these sound-alike letters. Begin by reading all the letters to a slow beat. Read the letters a second time to a slightly faster beat. Read them three more times, increasing the speed each time.

Thank You, God

Have students complete this activity individually. Call on a volunteer to read the correct answers as other students check their work. Ask: When do we recite בְּרָכוֹת שֶׁל יוֹם טוֹב? (*on holidays such as Rosh Hashanah, Sukkot, and Pesaḥ*) When do we recite בִּרְכַּת הַמָּזוֹן? (*after eating a meal with bread*) Does a boy say מוֹדָה or מוֹדֶה? (מוֹדֶה)

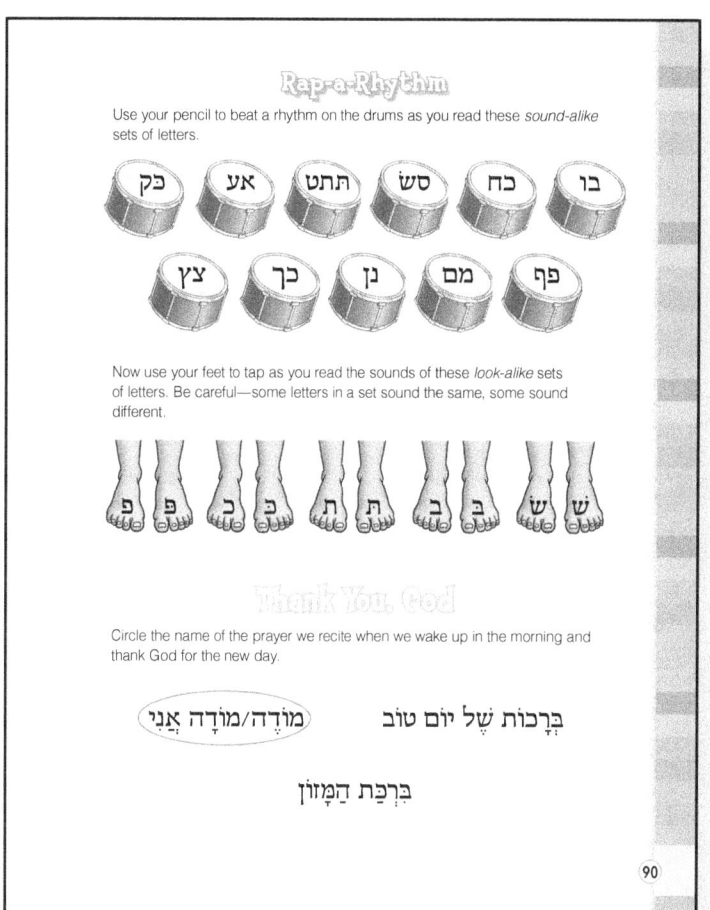

Holiday Blessing Review

Divide the class into groups of three. Challenge groups to list the endings of as many בְּרָכוֹת שֶׁל יוֹם טוֹב as they can recall in three minutes. (*Some endings of* בְּרָכוֹת שֶׁל יוֹם טוֹב *are:* לֵישֵׁב בַּסֻּכָּה, לִשְׁמֹעַ קוֹל שׁוֹפָר, בּוֹרֵא פְּרִי הָעֵץ, *and* לְהַדְלִיק נֵר שֶׁל חֲנֻכָּה.) At the end of three minutes, have each group read aloud its list. The group that has recalled the most בְּרָכוֹת שֶׁל יוֹם טוֹב is the winner.

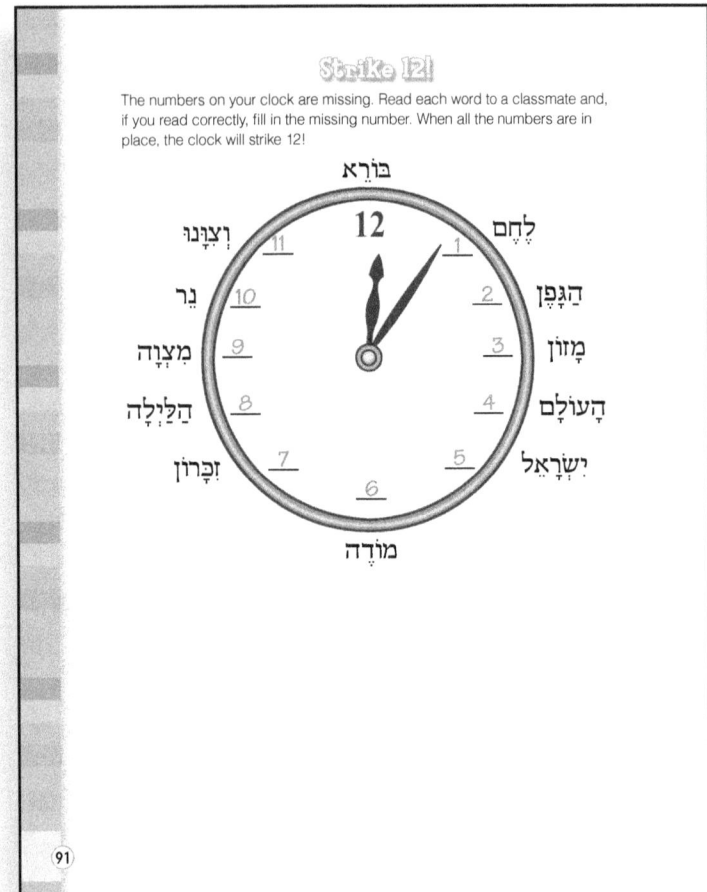

Strike 12!

Have students read and complete this activity with a partner. After all students have correctly read the words to a partner, challenge the pairs to write the English meaning of each word next to or below the Hebrew. Call on different pairs to read a word and say its English meaning. For example, ask a pair to read and translate the word at 4 o'clock. (הָעוֹלָם means the world.)

Divide the class into groups of three. Challenge the groups to list twelve blessings, prayers or phrases, one for each word on the clock. Award each group two points for each correct listing and an additional one point if they can tell something about the listing. (*Answers may include:*

לֶחֶם: הַמּוֹצִיא לֶחֶם מִן הָאָרֶץ—*said before eating bread;* הַגֶּפֶן: בּוֹרֵא פְּרִי הַגֶּפֶן—*said before drinking wine or grape juice;* מָזוֹן: בִּרְכַּת הַמָּזוֹן—*said after eating a meal with bread*)

Challenge students to locate in their book blessings and prayers that include the words from page 91. Call on volunteers to give the page number where they found a word. Have all students turn to the page and chorally read the word in its context. For example, word 1, לֶחֶם, can be found on page 77. Invite all students to turn to page 77 and read the blessing together. (*Examples of pages on which the clock words are used:*

הָעוֹלָם—*p. 13;* מָזוֹן—*p. 73;* הַגֶּפֶן—*p. 12;* יִשְׂרָאֵל—*p. 81;* מוֹדֶה—*p. 6;* זִכָּרוֹן—*p. 42;* מִצְוָה—*p. 20;* הַלַּיְלָה—*p. 66;* נֵר—*p. 29;* וְצִוָּנוּ—*p. 24;* בּוֹרֵא—*p. 47*)

THE PRAYERS OF OUR PEOPLE I • כָּל יִשְׂרָאֵל 124

Time It

- *As an assessment:*

  Have students complete the activity individually. Explain that students should refer to page 91 for the word bank, but that they should not refer to other pages in the text. After students have completed the page, collect all books and check students' answers. As you check the work, take note if students had difficulty with a particular phrase.

- *As a review:*

  Have students work with a partner to complete the activity. After pairs have completed the activity, call on volunteers to read the correct number and its complete phrase. Students check and correct their own work. Challenge students to name the source of each of the phrases. (1–blessing over fruit; 2–describes blessings recited before doing mitzvot; 3–beginning of מוֹדֶה אֲנִי prayer; 4–phrase meaning "All of Israel," begins phrase "All of Israel is responsible for one another"; 5–blessing over wine or grape juice; 6–part of every בְּרָכָה שֶׁל מִצְוָה; 7–beginning of the Four Questions; 8–blessing over bread; 9–phrase from Shabbat Kiddush; 10–phrase from בִּרְכַּת הַמָּזוֹן; 11–part of the blessing formula; 12–blessing over Ḥanukkah candles)

Photo Op

As a class, read the caption under the photograph. Ask: What might each of the people in the photograph be thinking? What makes you think that? With whom do you light Ḥanukkah candles? What was your favorite Ḥanukkah candle-lighting experience? What made that time special? How does lighting candles as a family help to create *sh'lom bayit*?

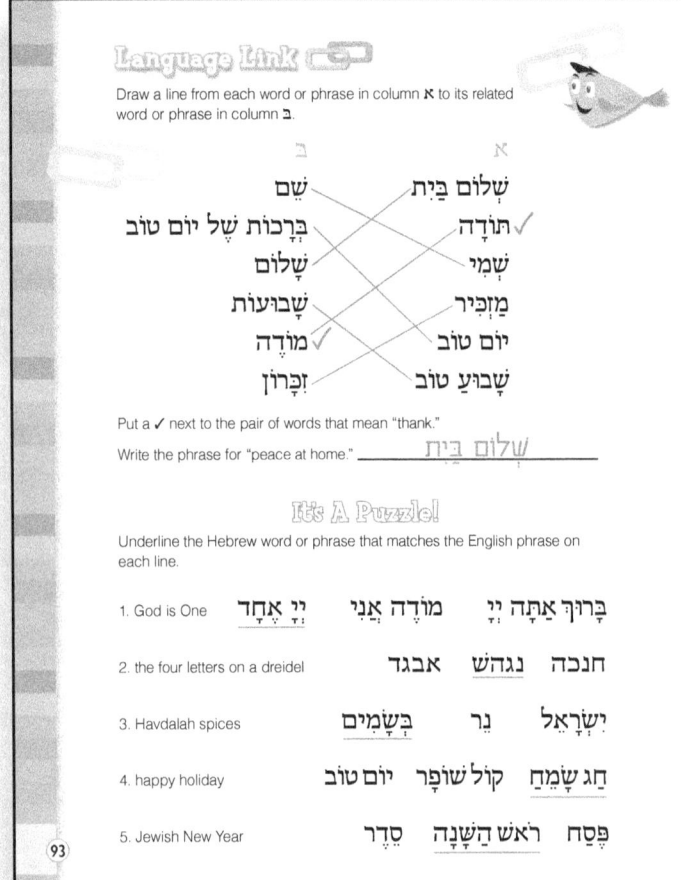

Language Link

Direct students to read the words and phrases to a partner as they connect them. Go around the room, having students read the matches as other students correct their work. Challenge students to explain the relationship between the related words and phrases. Students may note: שָׁלוֹם בַּיִת – שָׁלוֹם both include שָׁלוֹם, peace; מוֹדֶה – תּוֹדָה both have to do with thanking; שֵׁם – שְׁמִי both include שֵׁם, name; זִכָּרוֹן – מַזְכִּיר both have the root letters זכר and are related to remembering or memory; בְּרָכוֹת שֶׁל יוֹם טוֹב – יוֹם טוֹב both include יוֹם טוֹב, Jewish holiday; שָׁבוּעוֹת – שָׁבוּעַ טוֹב both include שָׁבוּעַ, week. Raise the challenge by asking students to explain each of the terms.

Have students place a check next to the words that mean "thank" and write the phrase for "peace at home."

It's A Puzzle!

- *As an assessment:*

  Have students complete this activity individually. You might ask more advanced students to write the English meanings of the words and phrases that are not "puzzle pieces." Walk around the room to assess how well students understand these Hebrew terms.

- *As a review:*

  Working in pairs, students take turns reading the Hebrew aloud with their partner as they determine which of the Hebrew terms matches the English. After students have completed the activity, call on volunteers to read an English phrase and its matching Hebrew. All students check and correct their own work.

  Challenge students to identify the remaining phrases and words. For example, ask: What is the Hebrew word for candle? (נֵר); Which Hebrew prayer words mean, "I give thanks"? (מוֹדֶה אֲנִי)

כָּל יִשְׂרָאֵל • THE PRAYERS OF OUR PEOPLE I

Batter Up

Direct all students to practice reading all four lines aloud to a partner. After students have had time to practice, call on a student to read line 1. If he or she reads the line correctly, the student draws a line to first base. After drawing the line, that student should now listen to a classmate read the line. At the same time, you will listen to a third student read line 1. Once those students have fluently read line 1, they in turn may check the reading of other classmates. Continue checking, and having other students check, students for reading accuracy and fluency. Repeat this with lines 2, 3, and 4 until all students have scored a home run.

Call on a volunteer to explain when these verses are recited. (*Havdalah*)

Divide the class into four groups. Have each group chorally read one of the blessings at the bottom of page 94. Ask: Over which foods are each of these blessings recited? (*parsley, bread/matzah, matzah, maror*) When are these blessings recited? (*during the Pesaḥ seder*)

Have students practice reading these blessings with a partner as they did with the first four lines on the page. Again, call on a student to read line 1. If that student has read the line fluently, that student may then check another student. Continue, as you did earlier, having students check one another's reading. The goal is for all students to score a home run.

After all (or the majority) of the students have scored a home run, chorally read all four blessings.

Personal Siddur

Have each student create a cover page for his or her personal siddur. Help students compile all the siddur pages and create a siddur by binding it or stapling. Consider inviting parents to view all the *siddurim*. Have students present their *siddurim* and describe some of their illustrations.

Plan a party and have students lead everyone in the blessings over various foods. If you include

bread in the menu, students can also chant בִּרְכַּת הַמָּזוֹן.

127   WRAP IT UP!

DOUG THE FISH PUPPET